Approaches to Teaching Shakespeare's *Othello*

Approaches to Teaching
World Literature

Joseph Gibaldi, series editor

For a complete listing of titles,
see the last pages of this book.

Approaches to Teaching Shakespeare's *Othello*

Edited by

Peter Erickson

and

Maurice Hunt

The Modern Language Association of America
New York   2005

© 2005 by The Modern Language Association of America
All rights reserved
Printed in the United States of America

For information about obtaining permission to reprint material from
MLA book publications, send your request by mail (see address below),
e-mail (permissions@mla.org), or fax (646 458-0030).

Library of Congress Cataloging-in-Publication Data

Approaches to teaching Shakespeare's Othello /
edited by Peter Erickson and Maurice Hunt.
p. cm. — (Approaches to teaching world literature ; 88)
Includes bibliographical references and index.
ISBN-13: 978-0-87352-990-7 (alk. paper)
ISBN-10: 0-87352-990-1 (alk. paper)
ISBN-13: 978-0-87352-991-4 (pbk. : alk. paper)
ISBN-10: 0-87352-991-X (pbk. : alk. paper)
1. Shakespeare, William, 1564–1616. Othello.   2. Shakespeare, William,
1564–1616—Study and teaching.   3. Interracial marriage in literature.   4.
Othello (Fictitious character)   5. Jealousy in literature.   6. Tragedy.   I.
Erickson, Peter.   II. Hunt, Maurice, 1942–   III. Series.
PR2829.A858 2005
822.3'3—dc22   2005020735
ISSN 1059-1133

Cover illustration of the paperback edition: *Paul Robeson as Othello*. Photograph by
Carl Van Vechten, 1944. From the Yale Collection of American Literature, Beinecke Rare
Book and Manuscript Library. Used with permission from the Van Vechten Trust.

Published by The Modern Language Association of America
26 Broadway, New York, New York 10004-1789
www.mla.org

In Memoriam
James R. Andreas

CONTENTS

PREFACE TO THE SERIES

In *The Art of Teaching* Gilbert Highet wrote, "Bad teaching wastes a great deal of effort, and spoils many lives which might have been full of energy and happiness." All too many teachers have failed in their work, Highet argued, simply "because they have not thought about it." We hope that the Approaches to Teaching World Literature series, sponsored by the Modern Language Association's Publications Committee, will not only improve the craft—as well as the art—of teaching but also encourage serious and continuing discussion of the aims and methods of teaching literature.

The principal objective of the series is to collect within each volume different points of view on teaching a specific literary work, a literary tradition, or a writer widely taught at the undergraduate level. The preparation of each volume begins with a wide-ranging survey of instructors, thus enabling us to include in the volume the philosophies and approaches, thoughts and methods of scores of experienced teachers. The result is a sourcebook of material, information, and ideas on teaching the subject of the volume to undergraduates. The series is intended to serve nonspecialists as well as specialists, inexperienced as well as experienced teachers, graduate students who wish to learn effective ways of teaching as well as senior professors who wish to compare their own approaches with the approaches of colleagues in other schools. Of course, no volume in the series can ever substitute for erudition, intelligence, creativity, and sensitivity in teaching. We hope merely that each book will point readers in useful directions; at most each will offer only a first step in the long journey to successful teaching.

Joseph Gibaldi
Series Editor

PREFACE TO THE VOLUME

The initial proposal for this volume originated with Jim Andreas and had been approved at the time of his death in February 2002. Having decided to proceed with the project as a memorial to Jim, the MLA asked the present editors to prepare a full prospectus.

In developing the volume, we have been guided by Jim's preliminary proposal; our starting point was his list of twenty-seven potential contributors, none of whom had actually been contacted. Of those twenty-seven on the original list, ten agreed to participate, thus ensuring continuity with Jim's vision. However, since Jim's suggested topics were hypothetical and generic, specific individual topics had to be negotiated and refined. We also selected an additional eleven contributors. The result is that the contents, including section headings and essay subgroups, were substantially revised and reorganized.

The memorial dimension that is crucial to the history of the volume is explicitly addressed in Peter Erickson's "*Othello* in the Work of James R. Andreas." In showing why *Othello* is at the center of Jim's work, the essay seeks not only to demonstrate that the conversation Jim started is ongoing but also to give his work the currency of a living memorial that must be included as an active part in the continuing conversation.

The editors would like to express particular gratitude to Jim's wife, Martha, and to Joseph Gibaldi, director of book acquisitions and development at the MLA, for unstinting support in the planning of this collection in Jim's honor. We also greatly appreciate the help of those—listed in the Survey Participants section at the end of the volume—who completed the MLA questionnaire on their teaching experiences with *Othello*.

We mourn the loss of one of our contributors, Cynthia Marshall, who died in August 2005 as this volume was in press.

Part One

MATERIALS

Editions

Complete Editions of Shakespeare

When teaching *Othello* from a complete edition, survey respondents chose Stephen Greenblatt's *Norton Shakespeare* by a two-to-one margin over G. Blakemore Evans's *Riverside Shakespeare* and David Bevington's *Complete Works of Shakespeare*. Only three respondents preferred Stephen Orgel and A. R. Braunmuller's *Complete Pelican Shakespeare*. Instructors who chose either the Evans or the Bevington edition are equally divided. Few respondents to our questionnaire used one of these texts in a graduate course including *Othello*. Complete editions of Shakespeare are used in sophomore Shakespeare courses and, more often, in upper-division undergraduate courses focusing on Shakespeare's plays.

For a comprehensive evaluation of the three major complete Shakespeare editions, see the review by Martha Tuck Rozett. The texts of the plays in the *Norton Shakespeare* are based on their much-debated counterparts in Stanley Wells and Gary Taylor's *William Shakespeare: The Complete Works*. The popularity of the *Norton Shakespeare* in our survey suggests that the initial reservations of some instructors toward those texts have been overcome. Walter Cohen's relatively short introduction to the text of *Othello* in the Norton edition is clearly written and useful for undergraduates. Among the general editors of Shakespeare volumes, Greenblatt in his general introduction best introduces undergraduates to the late-twentieth-century critical approaches to Shakespeare's plays. Students can easily find glosses of single words and phrases in *The Norton Shakespeare* because they appear in italics in the right margin of pages on the same line as the originals in the text. More extensive explanations appear at the bottom of pages. The notoriously gossamer-thin, onionskin pages found in Norton editions and anthologies make note taking difficult and uncreased pages a rarity. These drawbacks are exacerbated by the bulky size of the hard-to-handle 3420-page *Norton Shakespeare*.

Those teachers of *Othello* using *The Riverside Shakespeare* appreciate the play's introduction by Frank Kermode, who is especially insightful in all the introductions to the tragedies. Instructors also value the second, 1997 edition's updated bibliographies of commentary and criticism; Heather Dubrow's comprehensive review essay of twentieth-century criticism on the plays; and the account by William Liston of Shakespeare's plays in performance since 1970. Sometimes instructors complain that nothing in the texts of *The Riverside Shakespeare* signals a bottom-of-the-page gloss or explanation. Students consequently do not know when they should stop reading and look down to try to understand Shakespeare's language. Much of Shakespeare's bawdry, or off-color, punning is left unexplained. Finally, Evans has been criticized for modernizing the spelling of some words while leaving others in their original forms, as well as for the intrusiveness of the brackets in the text around variant readings.

Bevington's introductions and interpretive and explanatory notes in the fourth, updated edition of *The Complete Works of Shakespeare* have been praised for their capacity to be understood and thus used by undergraduate students. According to one respondent, "Bevington's introductions are clear, modest, and lacking in postmodern jargon, which seldom has anything to say about the plays as plays." (Interestingly, another respondent praises the introductions to the plays in *The Norton Shakespeare* for "reflect[ing] current trends in early modern cultural studies, but approach[ing] them in accessible language [for an upper-division or graduate audience, anyway].") *The Complete Works of Shakespeare* has just appeared in a fifth edition, with an introduction that includes a comprehensive review of types of Shakespeare criticism extending into the twenty-first century. In this respect, the fifth (as well as the fourth) edition deserves the accolade that has been reserved for *The Norton Shakespeare*. Bevington, unlike Evans, lightly punctuates Shakespeare's text, apparently to reflect a hypothesis about Shakespeare's practice. This editor unflinchingly includes glosses of Shakespearean obscenities. He chooses to signal bottom-of-the-page glossed words and phrases by printing the line number next to the line in which they appear, a decision that makes ascertaining beginning and ending line numbers of Shakespearean passages difficult when nothing is glossed in more than ten or twelve lines. The readability of the print and the durability of paper in this edition are superior. Like *The Riverside Shakespeare*, Bevington's *Complete Works* includes updated bibliographies of Shakespeare commentary and criticism on groups of plays and single plays reaching in the fifth edition to the year 2002. On the other hand, appendix 3, "Shakespeare in Performance," shows little evidence of updating beyond the 1970s and early 1980s.

The text of *Othello* in all three major complete editions is based on the text appearing in the First Folio (1623), which was revised repeatedly by variant readings introduced or substituted from the 1622 Quarto text of the play. The textual situation regarding *Othello* is famously obscure, as we explain in the following section, "Textual Studies and Sources." Because no editorial consensus exists on the readings to be introduced from the quarto text, the texts of *Othello* in complete works and single editions on occasion significantly differ. Not one of the complete-edition *Othellos* is superior, not one is inferior. All three are adequate.

Othello appears in several anthologies of literature, including a Penguin Academics volume titled *Drama: A Pocket Anthology*, edited by R. S. Gwynn. The notes are by Bevington. Richard Abcarian and Marvin Klotz include *Othello* in the eighth edition of their *Literature: The Human Experience*, in a section titled "Love and Hate," which also includes Susan Glaspell's *Trifles*. Finally, X. J. Kennedy and Dana Gioia combine *Othello* with *Hamlet* and *A Midsummer Night's Dream* in the eighth edition of their *Literature: An In-*

troduction to Fiction, Poetry, and Drama to form a section titled "Critical Casebook: Shakespeare." Here again explanatory notes are from Bevington's *Complete Works*. Among eleven critical interpretations appended to this section are "Iago as Triumphant Villain," by W. H. Auden; "Lucifer in Shakespeare's *Othello*," by Maud Bodkin; and "Black and White in *Othello*," by Virginia Mason Vaughan.

Single Editions

By a wide margin, the two most popular single editions of *Othello* are those in the Arden Shakespeare, third series (Arden 3), edited by E. A. J. Honigmann and the Shakespeare Signet Classic series, edited by Alvin Kernan. Instructors of graduate courses who teach *Othello* almost uniformly recommended the Arden 3 text, chiefly because the explanatory notes, glosses, and appendixes for the tragedy are more sophisticated and fuller than those in any other single edition of the play. (No one has recommended teaching *Othello* out of Furness's *New Variorum Edition of Shakespeare*). Near the end of his lengthy introduction, Honigmann inserts a brief performance history of the play. In three appendixes, he provisionally fixes the play's date, explains and illustrates the play's knotty textual problems, and describes the play's sources, reprinting the third decade, story 7 from Cinthio's *Hecatommithi* (1565) and keying lines, phrases, and words to their apparent counterparts in *Othello*. Because he is likely the most knowledgeable editor concerning the difficult details of the First Folio and 1622 Quarto texts of *Othello*, Honigmann's seventeen-page analysis in appendix 2 of *Othello*'s textual problem is especially valuable (351–67).

Instructors using Kernan's Signet Classic *Othello* praised it for its low cost, compact size, readability, and especially the commentaries following the text. While Kernan's introduction dates from 1963, the 1998 second edition updates the brief bibliographies at volume's end to the mid-1990s. (One defect of the Arden 3 Shakespeare is the absence of bibliographies.) Among the commentaries in this *Othello* is a performance-history essay by Marvin Carlson titled "Othello in Vienna, 1991." Madelon Gohlke Sprengnether's essay, " 'I Wooed Thee with My Sword': Shakespeare's Tragic Paradigms," dates from 1980. Sylvan Barnett's essay, "*Othello* on Stage and Screen," begins with Jacobean times but does not proceed beyond Jonathan Miller's 1982 BBC television *Othello*. The other two commentaries in this edition are those by Samuel Taylor Coleridge (titled "*Othello*") and by Maynard Mack (titled "The Jacobean Shakespeare: Some Observations on the Construction of the Tragedies").

Less-often-assigned paperback editions are the New Cambridge Shakespeare *Othello*, edited by Norman Sanders; the Pelican Shakespeare *Othello*, edited in a third edition by Russ McDonald; and the New Folger Library Shakespeare *The Tragedy of Othello*, edited by Barbara A. Mowat and Paul

Werstine. Some instructors use the New Cambridge *Othello*, updated in a second edition in 2003, because Sanders's introduction stresses the tragedy's performance history. Twenty-two drawings, paintings, and photographs bring to life Sanders's account of *Othello* on stage. McDonald's twenty-two page introduction to *Othello* is lively in the Pelican edition; instructors may want to consider using this text in conjunction with McDonald's popular, often recommended *Bedford Companion to Shakespeare: An Introduction with Documents*. Proponents of Mowat and Werstine's New Folger Library *Tragedy of Othello* cited the abundant, clear explanatory notes and glosses appearing on whole pages facing those of the text of the play. They also like the many woodcuts and other kinds of illustrations contemporary to Shakespeare. Taken from books and material in the Folger Shakespeare Library, these illustrations illuminate expressions and ideas in *Othello*. Werstine's pronouncements on the textual situation of plays in this series are authoritative. The New Folger Library *Othello* includes a short interpretive essay on the play by Susan Snyder titled "*Othello*: A Modern Perspective."

Appearing early in 2004, too late to have been mentioned by respondents in our survey, is the Norton Critical Edition of *Othello*, edited by Edward Pechter, a book whose comprehensiveness augurs well for its widespread adoption. Among the contents of this 407-page volume are John Edward Taylor's 1855 translation of the play's source in Cinthio, Pechter's fine essay on *Othello* in its own time, a textual commentary, and reprintings of seventeen pieces of criticism on *Othello*, ranging from those of Thomas Rymer and Charles Gildon to analyses written by, among others, Lynda Boose, G. K. Hunter, Mark Rose, James Siemon, Michael Neill, Patricia Parker, Michael Bristol, and Pechter. The often lengthy lists of works cited appended to individual criticisms of the play, added to the categorized selected bibliography at the end of Pechter's edition, make up a substantial catalog of readings on the play.

No survey participant mentioned the Bantam Classic *Othello*, edited by David Bevington, with a foreword by Joseph Papp. Mentioned only once is the Signet Classic *Four Great Tragedies*: Hamlet, Othello, King Lear, and Macbeth. (Kernan is listed as the editor of *Othello*.) *Four Great Tragedies* obviously allows an instructor to teach a unit on Shakespearean tragedy in an undergraduate drama or literature course focused, for example, on the genre of tragedy or on the application of literary theory to related works. Along these lines, *Othello* appears with Elizabeth Cary's *The Tragedy of Mariam, the Fair Queen of Jewry* (c. 1606–09) in a Longman Cultural Edition edited by Clare Carroll. Appended to the texts of these plays in this volume are their narrative sources and two sections of early modern readings titled "*Othello* in Context: Ethnography in the Literature of Travel and Colonization" and "*Othello* and *The Tragedy of Mariam* in Context: Tracts on Marriage." Finally, we must note that two single editions of *Othello* will soon be available. Kim Hall is editing *Othello* for the popular Bedford–St. Martin's Shakespeare Texts and Contexts series. Michael Neill's Oxford Shakespeare *Othello* will appear late in 2004 or early in 2005. A year or two later this edition will serve as the basis for the paperback Oxford World Classics *Othello*. An excellent companion volume for any textual edition of *Othello* is Lena Cowen Orlin's *Othello*, in the Palgrave Macmillan New Casebooks series. In this book, which is suitable for advanced undergraduates and graduate students, distinguished essayists provide readers with feminist, new historicist, cultural materialist, deconstructive, and postcolonial criticism on the play.

Several survey respondents have students choose their own edition of *Othello*:

> In fact I count on students bringing in and using various editions for class discussion so that they notice differences in lineation and word choice. . . . As Honigmann says in . . . Appendix 2 [of his Arden 3 *Othello*], "[a]lthough I have not checked every recorded edition of the play, I think it probable that no two editions are exactly alike and that no edition prints the play exactly as Shakespeare wrote it" (351). Especially in the advanced Shakespeare course, I find the students' discovery of these textual differences to be useful not only as an opportunity to discuss the varying implications of textual variants, especially variants in word choice, but also as an opportunity to discuss the collaborative work of the early modern theater, early modern print shop practices, and the vagaries of textual criticism—all three of which contribute something to the fluidity of Shakespeare editions.

For those instructors willing to spend the time necessary for such analysis, the benefits that result from classroom use of several editions of the same play are many.

Textual Studies and Sources

Two distinct texts of *Othello* exist—the 1622 Quarto (Q1) and the 1623 Folio, or First Folio (F1). A second quarto edition of *Othello* was published in 1630 (Q2), based on the earlier quarto but with additions and corrections from the F1 text. Editors generally disregard this text, using the initial two texts to construct their *Othello*. For construct they must: the Q1 and F1 *Othellos* differ in hundreds of readings (Evans claims, "more than a thousand" [Shakespeare, *Riverside* 1288]), "in single-word variants and in longer passages, in spelling, verse lineation and punctuation" (Honigmann, Arden 3 *Othello* 351). Since neither the Q1 nor the F1 texts of the play is adequate by itself, editors have always felt compelled to create a composite edition of the tragedy. (The theory that *Othello* resembles *King Lear* by existing in two separate Shakespeare texts has not gained many adherents.) Comprehensive accounts of the problematic relation between quarto and folio texts of the play appear in Honigmann's

Arden 3 edition, in Evans's *Riverside Shakespeare*, in Sanders's New Cambridge edition, and in Stanley Wells and Gary Taylor's *William Shakespeare: A Textual Companion*. Evans claims in *The Riverside Shakespeare* to have provided "a record of all significant variants, a few elided forms excepted, between F1 and Q1" (1288).

Teachers wishing to create classroom exercises comparing editions, along the lines suggested above, sometimes compare F1 of *Othello* in Charlton Hinman's *The First Folio of Shakespeare: The Norton Facsimile* with the Q1 *Othello*, which is reproduced in *Shakespeare's Plays in Quarto: A Facsimile Edition of Copies Primarily from the Henry E. Huntington Library*, edited by Michael J. B. Allen and Kenneth Muir. Allen and Muir conclude that "it is a mystery why [the 1622 *Othello*] should appear, clearly based on an inferior manuscript, when the Folio version was already in press based on a superior manuscript (The Folio was printed from April 1621 to December 1623)" (xviii). Scott McMillin also prints the Q1 text in *The First Quarto of* Othello: accompanying the text is analysis intended to demonstrate that the 1622 Quarto's myriad differences from F1 can be accounted for by assuming that "the Quarto was printed from a theatre script reflecting cuts and actors' interpolations made in the playhouse. . . . [and that] the playhouse script was apparently taken from dictation by a scribe listening to the actors themselves, and thus reveals how *Othello* was spoken in seventeenth-century performance" (i). A classroom lesson designed to focus on such pronunciation could be enlightening. McMillin's theory offers a plausible explanation for the existence of the 1622 Quarto *Othello*: Thomas Walker, its publisher, or someone close to him became aware of the F1's imminent publication and beat it to the streets in the "unauthorized" version, created as described above. Honigmann's *The Texts of* Othello *and Shakespearian Revision* amounts to a bibliographic analysis of the texts of Q1, F1, and Q2 intended to illuminate Honigmann's editorial decisions in creating the Arden 3 *Othello*. Honigmann suggests that Shakespeare "wrote a first draft or 'foul papers' [of *Othello*] and also a fair copy, and that these two authorial versions were both copied by professional scribes, the scribal transcripts serving as printers copy for Q [1] and F. So the 'texts' of [Honigmann's] title refer not to two but . . . to six versions of the play" (1). "Unfortunately textual relationships can turn out to be almost as complicated as human relationships," Honigmann concludes; "[a]s will appear, Q and F are not entirely independent strains, since F shows signs of 'contamination' directly from Q, a cross-fertilisation as unwelcome . . . as are other kinds of incest" (1).

Classroom instruction or exercises based on such textual complexity are best reserved for graduate Shakespeare courses or for graduate courses in bibliographic method. Teachers wishing to show students differences in meaning created by choosing selected Q1 over F1 readings (and vice versa) in local passages might consider using the New Folger Library *Tragedy of Othello*. Upper-division undergraduates easily grasp Mowat and Werstine's introduction to the textual issues surrounding the play, mainly because the editors explain that, having chosen the F1 text, they have added Q1 words when "their omission would seem to leave a gap in our text" (xlvi) and substituted Q1 readings for F1 words "when a word in the Folio is unintelligible . . . or is incorrect according to the standards of that time for acceptable grammar, rhetoric, idiom, or usage. . . . or when a word in the Folio seems to be the result of censorship or 'damping down' of an oath or solemn declaration" (xlvi–xlvii). These editorial decisions facilitate easy classroom discussion and analysis because Mowat and Werstine enclose "[a]ll the words in this edition printed in the Quarto version but not in the Folio . . . in pointed brackets," "[a]ll full lines that are found in the Folio and not in the Quarto . . . in square brackets," and all the words "different from what is offered by either" Q1 or F1 "in half brackets" (xlvii–xlviii). Consequently, "a reader can use this edition to read the play as it was printed in the Folio, or as it was printed in the [1622] Quarto, or as it has been presented in the editorial tradition, which has combined Folio and Quarto" (xlviii).

A basic understanding of the text of a Shakespeare play can be attained by reading Evans's essay "Shakespeare's Text," which appears in the first edition of *The Riverside Shakespeare*, as well as Stephen Greenblatt's "The Dream of the Master Text" in *The Norton Shakespeare*, an essay that essentially amounts to a defense of Wells and Taylor's Oxford texts of the plays appearing in the *Complete Works of Shakespeare*. More advanced treatments of the subject of Shakespeare's text appear in W. W. Greg's *The Editorial Problem in Shakespeare: A Survey of the Foundations of the Text* and in Wells and Taylor's *William Shakespeare: A Textual Companion*. Also useful is Hinman's two-volume *Printing and Proofreading of the First Folio of Shakespeare*.

Shakespeare's play derives from Cinthio's *Hecatommithi* (third decade, story 7), a collection of a hundred tales printed in Italy in 1565. No English translation of this work dated during Shakespeare's lifetime has survived (although one may have existed). In 1584, Gabriel Chappuys's French version appeared. It is possible that Shakespeare read Italian or French or both languages, but it is also possible that someone acquainted with English playhouses specially translated this story for him. Bevington claims that "[t]he verbal echoes in Shakespeare's play are closer to the Italian original than to Gabriel Chappuys's French version" (*Othello* [Bantam ed.] 133).

Translations of Cinthio's tragic story, with bottom-of-the-page cross-references to Shakespeare's play, are found in the Arden 3 *Othello* and in Carroll's Longman Cultural Edition of Othello *and* The Tragedy of Mariam. Kernan in the Signet Classic *Othello* and Bevington in the Bantam Classic *Othello* include an English version of Cinthio's story, but without cross-references to the play. Bevington, however, introduces Cinthio's story and compares details of *Othello* with their counterparts in the Italian narrative. In the section on single editons of *Othello* above, we mention an abridged 1855 translation of Cinthio included in the *Norton Critical Editon* of the play.

Almost without exception, the English translation of Cinthio's story that current editors of *Othello* prefer is Geoffrey Bullough's, as it appears, cross-referenced to the play, in volume 7 of his *Narrative and Dramatic Sources of Shakespeare*. Bullough prefaces his translation of *Hecatommithi* with a fine analysis of the relation of Cinthio's tale to Shakespeare's tragedy (193–238). As a possible source, he prints selections from discourse 4 of *Certaine Tragical Discourses* of Matteo Bandello, translated by Geoffrey Fenton (1567). As a probable source, he reproduces an excerpt from *The Generall Historie of the Turkes*, by Richard Knolles (1603). Bullough's comparative analysis is complemented by that of Kenneth Muir in *The Sources of Shakespeare's Plays*.

Teaching Resources

Critical and Pedagogical Studies

Since a comprehensive bibliography is not possible within the scope of this book, our aim—guided in part by the survey respondents listed at the end of the volume—is to select specific critical perspectives that can be used as suggestive points of departure. Readers should also consult the individual essays in part 2 for additional references not included here.

We begin with bibliographic surveys of two topics—gender and race—that correspond to the first two sections of part 2. The division between gender and race stems partly from the sequential and to some extent separate development of these two components in recent criticism; gender was brought into sharp focus by feminist criticism of the late 1970s and early 1980s, and race received major attention in the late 1980s and 1990s. Especially evident in the criticism on *Othello* is that some tension is inevitably generated over the question of whether gender or race should be given interpretive priority. However, after we acknowledge the distinctive relevance of each category, the ultimate challenge remains not to choose between gender and race but to combine the two terms in a single multifaceted approach, as exemplified by Kim Hall's title *Things of Darkness: Economies of Race and Gender in Early Modern England*.

New historicism had an immediate impact on the interpretation of *Othello* through Stephen Greenblatt's chapter, "The Improvisation of Power," in his 1980 pathbreaking *Renaissance Self-Fashioning*. However, no critical approach gave more attention to the play than did the feminist criticism that emerged during the same period. The initial wave of feminist work in the second half of the 1970s included Lynda Boose's "Othello's Handkerchief," Shirley Garner's "Shakespeare's Desdemona," Carol Neely's "Women and Men in *Othello*," and Gayle Greene's " 'This That You Call Love.' " Feminist analysis of the play strongly continued with new voices in the 1980s, in chronological order: Edward Snow's "Sexual Anxiety and the Male Order of Things," Coppélia Kahn's *Man's Estate*, Madelon Sprengnether's " 'All That Is Spoke Is Marred,' " Marianne Novy's *Love's Argument*, Peter Erickson's *Patriarchal Structures*, Richard Wheeler's " 'And My Loud Crying Still,' " and Peter Stallybrass's "Patriarchal Territories." Work from the 1990s includes Janet Adelman's *Suffocating Mothers*, the subgroup of essays entitled "Implicating Othello" in Shirley Nelson Garner and Madelon Sprengnether's *Shakespearean Tragedy and Gender*, and Peter Erickson's overview in "On the Origins of American Feminist Shakespeare Criticism."

This body of work presents educational opportunities both for teacher preparation and for direct student involvement. The rich bibliographic lode with its density of cross-references provides material for an extensive case study in criticism. At the same time, the analyses are varied in their approaches to gender issues. Contrasting points of view thus can be selected to stimulate student thinking. Moreover, the ongoing capacity of feminist analysis to generate new directions for critical inquiry is demonstrated by two recent threads. First, a pair of essays on *Othello*—Susan Frye's "Staging Women's Relations to Textiles" and Dympna Callaghan's "Looking Well to Linens"—concentrate on the highly specific details of women's material and cultural production of various kinds of textiles. Second, the cluster by Harry Berger—"Impertinent Trifling," "Acts of Silence," and "Three's a Company"—greatly extends the possibilities for intensive close reading of the play's language as manifested in the Othello-Desdemona relationship. As such, Berger's work has an affinity with what Emily Bartels, in this volume, calls "the volatile insides of domesticity and desire."

The decade of the 1990s marked a renewed, concerted focus on race in early modern studies. As Michael Neill notes in this volume, there was a twenty-year gap, amounting to a suspension, between G. K. Hunter's "Othello and Colour Prejudice" in 1967 and the sharp reemergence of the topic at the end of the 1980s. Both Karen Newman's " 'And Wash the Ethiop White' " and Ania Loomba's *Gender, Race, Renaissance Drama* strongly address, and redefine, race as a crucial topic. The ongoing momentum that definitively established race as a growing Renaissance field in the mid-1990s was provided especially by Margo Hendricks and Patricia Parker's *Women, "Race," and Writing*, which contained Parker's "Fantasies of 'Race' and 'Gender': Africa, Othello, and Bringing to Light," and by Kim Hall's *Things of Darkness*. The impact powerfully continues in the new century in the monographic sequence of Arthur Little's *Shakespeare Jungle Fever*, Joyce Green MacDonald's *Women and Race in Early Modern Texts*, Ania Loomba's *Shakespeare, Race, and Colonialism*, and Mary Floyd-Wilson's *English Ethnicity and Race in Early Modern Drama*. Capsule summaries of this rapidly developing field are available in Hendricks's "Forum: Race and the Study of Shakespeare."

In the field of early modern race studies, two important subgroups deserve mention. First, racial whiteness has been introduced as a distinct topic by Callaghan's " 'Othello Was a White Man.' " Just as there were no women on Shakespeare's stage and the female roles were played by boy actors, so there were no blacks and black roles were played by white actors in blackface. Callaghan's crucial point has a clear link to Virginia Mason Vaughan's "Teaching Richard Burbage's Othello" in this volume. Related work on whiteness includes Kim Hall's " 'These Bastard Signs of Fair,' " Erickson's " 'God for Harry, England, and Saint George' " and "Images of White Identity in *Othello*," Floyd-Wilson's *English Ethnicity and Race*, and Gary Taylor's *Buying Whiteness*. Second, the literary study of race in the Renaissance has included a significant cross-disciplinary connection to art history. Numerous visual examples can be found in the final chapter of Kim Hall's *Things of Darkness*; Erickson's essays "Representations of Blacks and Blackness" and "Representations of Race"; and *Black Africans in Renaissance Europe*, edited by Thomas F. Earle and K. J. P. Lowe. This visual base will be greatly increased by the completion of volume 3 of *The Image of the Black in Western Art*. Now in preparation, volume 3 consists of three parts covering the sixteenth through eighteenth centuries. This publication is produced by the research project and photo archive created by the Menil Foundation and located since 1994 at Harvard University, under the auspices of the W. E. B. Du Bois Institute.

The question of historical validity for the Renaissance looms far larger in relation to race than to gender, and the tendency to deny the relevance of race is correspondingly greater. Yet the parallel "do and do not" phrasing in the formulations from two respondents suggests that the real scholarly challenge is to avoid all-or-nothing, yes-or-no extremes in favor of a balanced contrast:

> In recent years, students have approached the question of Othello's identity with more and more sophistication. It is no longer enough to treat him as a racial "other" and be done with it. Now students are eager to talk about the history of racial concepts and to understand the particular ways in which Early Modern and contemporary understandings both do and do not overlap.

> I am often able to help students define more precisely what exactly "race" does and does not mean in the seventeenth century.

In this connection, Stuart Hall provides a comprehensive, four-phase historical framework from the Renaissance to the present against which changing concepts of race might be differentiated and calibrated. Hall's large-scale model, in a passage compact enough for use in the classroom (193–95), has two advantages. First, it offers a vision of history that decisively begins in the Renaissance period: "I date globalization from the moment when Western Europe breaks out of its confinement, at the end of the 15th century, and the era of exploration and conquest of the non-European world begins" (193). Second, without implying a smooth, automatic continuum, it offers a broader historical perspective. It thus provides a counterbalance to overemphasis or magnification of isolated bits of specificity in narrowly focused microhistories by asking us to take equal account of "a longer historical *durée*" (194).

A particularly exciting means of focusing on the use of *Othello* as a cross-historical reference point—an approach that correlates with this volume's final section of essays on comparative contexts—is the consideration of specific allusions to Shakespeare's play in the work of later writers. Approaches to allusion divide into two very different paths: influence studies and appropriation studies. A passage from Berger's *Fictions of the Pose* (427–29), which can be excerpted for class discussion, graphically highlights the difference as a question about which direction the "lines of force" (428) move between the original artist, in this case Shakespeare, and the new artist.

In influence studies, the transmission is from Shakespeare to the successor, with the emphasis on the former's authority and control and the latter's homage and indebtedness. In appropriation studies, the stress falls on the successor's agency in reshaping the Shakespearean legacy to create new critical perspectives that go beyond Shakespeare. According to this appropriation approach, what might have been construed as signs of indebtedness are treated instead as indicators of reinterpretation. Berger's formulation is especially helpful because, in offering an alternative to Harold Bloom's well-known *Anxiety of Influence*, it provides the basis for in-class debate about the methodological implications, and the advantages and disadvantages, of each position.

In Shakespeare studies in the 1990s, the development of a line of criticism has given Berger's concept of "conspicuous revisionary allusion" (429) a stronger contemporary political inflection. This criticism is inspired by Adrienne Rich's articulation, in "When We Dead Awaken," of re-vision as intervention in the service of change: "Re-vision—the act of looking back, of seeing with fresh eyes, of entering an old text from a new critical direction—is for women more than a chapter in cultural history: it is an act of survival" (35). The leader in this field of appropriation studies has been the three pioneering volumes edited by Novy all bearing, in Rich's sense, the title phrase "women's re-visions" of Shakespeare.

From 1990 to 1999, the focus of Novy's books has expanded from an initial, nearly exclusive emphasis on gender to a wider inquiry that encompasses questions about racial difference. This expanded scope includes *Othello*-specific essays such as Margaret Ferguson's on Aphra Behn's *Oroonoko* ("Transmuting") and Novy's on Ann-Marie MacDonald and Paula Vogel ("Saving Desdemona"). The attention to women authors in Novy's edited collections can be supplemented through the addition of related work on male writers' revisionary responses to Shakespeare. Examples of the male authors considered include Richard Wright's *Native Son*, Ralph Ellison's *Invisible Man*, and Amiri Baraka's *Dutchman* in Jim Andreas's "Othello's African American Progeny";

Murray Carlin's *Not Now, Sweet Desdemona* and Tayeb Salih's *Season of Migration to the North* in Jyotsna Singh's "Othello's Identity"; Ishmael Reed's *Japanese by Spring* and Caryl Phillips's *The Nature of Blood* in Peter Erickson's "Contextualizing *Othello*"; Salman Rushdie's *The Moor's Last Sigh* in Ania Loomba's " 'Local-Manufacture Made-in-India Othello Fellows' "; and Tayeb Salih's *Season of Migration* in Thomas Cartelli's *Repositioning Shakespeare*.

For many, the comparison of Shakespeare with himself is the most immediate. Survey respondents reported a wide array of comparative possibilities among Shakespeare's plays. *Othello* is taught in the sequence of major tragedies from *Hamlet* through *Macbeth*, *Coriolanus*, and *Antony and Cleopatra*; one respondent saw the Othello-Desdemona relationship as one in a series of "self-destructive pairs." Others highlighted *Othello*'s evocation (as well as disappointment) of comic expectations through structural associations with Shakespeare's comedy. Starting from *A Midsummer Night's Dream*, one respondent spreads a wide net:

> We discuss the blocking father, the forbidden marriage, the assertive daughter, the parodic charivari in 3.1, and the circumscribed festivity authorized by Othello's proclamation in 2.2. I situate *Othello* within generic categories as a transitional play written around the time of the problem comedies (*Troilus*, *All's Well*, and *Measure*). I make a connection to *Romeo and Juliet*, another tragedy with comic elements (or New Comedy gone wrong).

Another set of cross-generic connections links *Much Ado about Nothing*, *Othello*, and *The Winter's Tale* in a study of the effect of male jealousy on the relations between Claudio and Hero, Othello and Desdemona, and Leontes and Hermione.

Examination of Othello's racial status leads to comparative links back to *Titus Andronicus* and *The Merchant of Venice* and forward to *Antony and Cleopatra* and *The Tempest*. In an interesting expansion of the motif of ethnicity, one respondent develops a differentiated category of foreigner by placing *Othello* "in the context of *Henry IV* and *Henry V* and *The Merry Wives of Windsor* to talk about how being Welsh, Irish, or Scottish can be a form of difference in the Early Modern period, a form of difference both linked to and separate from the difference represented by Moors, Egyptians, and Turks."

As many respondents noted, an understanding of Shakespeare is enhanced if his works are taught in comparison with works by his contemporaries. One example must suffice: "In my graduate course on Mediterranean plays, I do *Othello* in the context of *The Jew of Malta*, *The Knight of Malta*, *The Battle of Alcazar*, *The Raging Turk*, *Tamburlaine*, *A Christian Turned Turk*, *The Re-*

negado, The Virgin Martyr, The Fair Maid of the West (Parts I and II), and
The Island Princess."

At the practical pedagogical level, a number of respondents addressed the
potential difficulty of speaking about race in the classroom context. The best
way to convey this concern is through a sampling of direct quotations:

> My own scholarly bent virtually requires me to lead students' attention
> to the topic of race in the play, but I'm never sure what I'm going to
> get back from my students in return. I've had everything from genuine
> curiosity and surprise to indifference and even hostility (this latter, rel-
> atively rare, stemming primarily from students' belief that the sanctity
> of Shakespeare should be preserved from the intrusion of such a divisive
> topic and, less frequently, from the belief that people didn't think in
> racial terms "back then").

> I was embarrassed and ill at ease, particularly with Iago's horrifying racist
> imagery in act one, scene one. But I quickly learned that to treat the
> play gingerly was to empower it in the wrong ways, and that to do so
> would undermine my central contention, which is that this play is about
> racism, but it does not promote a racist ideology.

> Students are both obsessed with and terrified of any discussion of race.
> They are most comfortable talking about Iago, and most uncomfortable
> talking about Othello himself (I often read them T. S. Eliot's comments
> on Othello's final speech—they are so horrified at what they see as
> Eliot's snobbery and lack of compassion that they then finally feel able
> to make their own criticisms of the representation of Othello).

> One of the best classes I ever had was a discussion of the racially charged
> language of *Othello*. I had them read out the opening scene. First, I
> made it clear that it was permissible in my classroom to express offense,
> even with Shakespeare and Shakespearean characters, and asked them
> to pick out particular words or phrases that they found offensive. . . .
> The discussion of literary tropes allowed us to get past their fear, de-
> fensiveness, and disgust without pretending it did not exist.

> My students are very conservative. They enjoy most the romance ele-
> ment of the play. They are primarily attracted to a liberal humanist
> notion that love can play across racial boundaries. I try to resist this by
> providing them with readings that highlight racial or ethnic and sexual
> and gender concerns. I try to make them very aware of the problem
> *Othello* presents for a racial politics and to dissuade them from seeing
> the play as a solution to racial issues.

Valuable pedagogical essays based on actual courses and classroom situations include Kim Hall's "Beauty and the Beast," Leila Christenbury's "Problems with *Othello*," and Sharon O'Dair's "Teaching *Othello*." Another resource to consult is the *Teaching Shakespeare* Web site created by the education department at the Folger Shakespeare Library. A particularly innovative model is suggested when Francesca Royster's project, described in "Everyday Use" and "Everyday Shakespeares," is linked with her contribution to this volume, "Rememorializing *Othello*." In an approach to revision that combines the roles of scholar and artist, Royster pursues her scholarly exploration by taking on the activist stance of the artist. Through her own performance art and collage, she literally produces an alternative creation that stands in critical contrast to *Othello*. From a pedagogical standpoint, the crucial move is Royster's next step in transferring this creative freedom from teacher to student in the form of a class assignment described in the present volume.

Suggested Student Reading

Survey respondents indicated that they refer students to, and occasionally assign, specific essays already mentioned in the preceding section. One respondent comments, "One of my favorite assignments requires students to read a critical article on *Othello*, to summarize it, to critique it, and to generate an arguable thesis statement in response to the article or book they have read." Another describes an essay topic "that invites students to find, read, summarize, and compare four articles on race in *Othello*." However, rather than repeat individual titles, this section notes more general introductory resources.

The respondents as a group draw introductory material from the full range of Shakespeare editions—Arden, Bevington (*Complete Works*), Folger, Norton, Pelican, Riverside, and Signet. The most frequently cited independent comprehensive guide is Russ McDonald's *Bedford Companion to Shakespeare: An Introduction with Documents*, now in a second edition. The specific guide to *Othello* most often mentioned is Vaughan's Othello: *A Contextual History*. Kim Hall's Bedford edition, Othello: *Texts and Contexts*, will contain significant ancillary materials for student use.

Performance and Theater Studies

Evidence of the first recorded performance of *Othello* surfaces in Edmund Tilney's Revels accounts for the 1604–05 season: " '*Hallowmas Day Being the First of November a Play in the Banqueting House at Whitehall Called the Moor of Venice* [Othello]' " (qtd. in Shakespeare, *Norton* 3385). In 1610, the tragedy was performed in April at the Globe and in September in Oxford. That the play was acted at Oxford in 1610 we know from a letter of Henry Jackson's, in which he praised several tragedies. "Among these," he writes, "a few aroused tears, not only through their words, but even their gestures. . . . But truly Desdemona, having been killed by her husband before our eyes, although she pleaded her cause superbly throughout, nevertheless she moved [us] more after she had been murdered, when, lying upon her bed, her face itself implored pity from the onlookers" (qtd. in Shakespeare, *Norton* 3336). Only a few references to additional performances of *Othello* before the 1642 closing of the London theaters have survived, but many pre-1660 references to or borrowings from the play in English literature and written documents of the time suggest it was popular.

During the Restoration and throughout the eighteenth century, *Othello* was one of Shakespeare's most frequently performed plays, apparently because it— minus the clown—seemed to conform to the so-called classical unities more than most Shakespeare plays did (Vaughan 93). Until the nineteenth century, Othello was often played in blackface; beginning with the Romantic age, actors and audiences insisted that the Moor be a white man, dark skinned perhaps but not black. In this respect, a teacher might present to a class versions of the ideas and illustrations in Paul H. D. Kaplan's "The Earliest Images of *Othello*," a particularly useful essay, one respondent claims, for "helping students develop a sense of how ideas about race show up in [the tragedy]." The American-born actor Ira Aldridge (1807–67) was apparently the first black man to play Othello, not, however, in the United States but in London, Paris, Moscow, and a host of other European cities. A black man would not memorably play the Moor again until Paul Robeson did so in 1930 in London and, finally, for the first time, in America on Broadway in 1943. Racist resistance to a black Othello can be seen in the popularity during the 1800s of olive-skinned Tommaso Salvini's delivery of the protagonist's speeches exclusively in Italian in an otherwise English version of the play. Since Robeson's revolutionary performances, many gifted black actors have played Othello. In fact, several respondents to our questionnaire persuasively claimed the role no longer should fall to a white actor in or out of blackface. A listing of the most important post-Robeson performances of *Othello* (until 1999), each complete with date and the names of theater, director, designer, and principal cast members, appears in an appendix to Lois Potter's *Othello* in the Shakespeare in Performance series. Among the best of these were the productions of Tyrone Guthrie in 1938 at the Old Vic Theatre, of Tony Richardson in 1959 at the Memorial Theatre in Stratford-upon-Avon, of John Barton in 1971-72 at the Royal Shakespeare Theatre in Stratford-upon-Avon, of Terry Hands in 1985 at the Royal Shakespeare Theatre in Stratford-upon-Avon, and (especially) of Trevor Nunn in 1989 at The Other Place in Stratford-upon-Avon.

The most classroom-friendly accounts of the stage history of *Othello* include, in addition to Potter's aforementioned book, Marvin Rosenberg's *The Masks of Othello: The Search for the Identity of Othello, Iago, and Desdemona by Three Centuries of Actors and Critics*; J. L. Styan's *The Shakespeare Revolution: Criticism and Performance in the Twentieth Century*; Richard David's

Shakespeare in the Theatre; Martin L. Wine's *Othello*; Virginia Mason Vaughan's Othello: *A Contextual History* (part 2); Jonathan Bate and Russell Jackson's *Shakespeare: An Illustrated Stage History*; and Andrew Hadfield's *A Routledge Literary Sourcebook on William Shakespeare's* Othello (94–110). Wine's book is particularly useful because, after a helpful description of varieties of theatrical interpretation of *Othello* from 1943 to 1982, it provides, in separate chapters on the roles of Othello, Iago, and Desdemona, synopses of how these characters were played in different productions of this time period.

Harley Granville-Barker's reading of *Othello* in volume 2 of his *Prefaces to Shakespeare* remains one of the best performance-based interpretations of the tragedy. Teachers desiring a general introduction to the playing conventions and practices of Shakespeare's age as well as an overview of the physical design of early modern theaters, their companies, players, and the makeup of their audiences should consult the following studies: Styan's *Shakespeare's Stagecraft*; Alan C. Dessen's *Elizabethan Stage Conventions and Modern Interpreters* and *Recovering Shakespeare's Theatrical Vocabulary*; Andrew Gurr and Mariko Ichikawa's *Staging in Shakespeare's Theatres*; Gurr's *The Shakespearean Stage 1575–1642* and *Playgoing in Shakespeare's London*; Ann Jennalie Cook's *The Privileged Playgoers of Shakespeare's London, 1576–1642*; Bernard Beckerman's *Shakespeare at the Globe 1599–1609*; Herbert Berry's *Shakespeare's Playhouses*; and Gurr and John Orrell's *Rebuilding Shakespeare's Globe*. This last volume (published in 1989) and Gurr and Ichikawa's *Staging in Shakespeare's Theatres* (2000; see esp. ch. 2) include findings about the dimensions and nature of the original Globe Theatre that were discovered in its celebrated reconstruction and that modify or correct certain claims of Berry, Beckerman, and others.

Visual Materials and Other Artistic Media

Although the first known cinema versions of *Othello* date from 1906 and 1908 and although several other international films of an abbreviated tragedy were released just before and during World War I (Brode 152–53), critics usually cite Dimitri Buchowetzki's 1922 Teutonic film of the play as introducing Shakespeare's masterpiece in this twentieth-century medium. Unfortunately, "a likely classic instead emerged as a disaster" (Brode 153). This means that Orson Welles's 1952 production, with Michael MacLiammoir as Iago and Suzanne Cloutier as Desdemona, along with Sergei Yutkevich's 1960 Russian version, with Sergei Bondarchuk as Othello, Andrei Popov as Iago, and Irina Skobtseva as Desdemona, mark at mid-century the usable beginning of twentieth-century film *Othellos*. Welles's *Othello* has been praised as one of the greatest film renditions of a Shakespeare play, partly because of the brilliance of its pacing, its black-and-white cinematography, and the nervous intimacy of the Moor and Iago. But it has recently been criticized for the tyranny of its representation of a male gaze and its entailed diminishment of Desdemona's role (Vaughan 199–216).

Five memorable film *Othello*s followed: Stuart Burge's 1965 production (a film of the 1964 National Theatre production), starring Laurence Olivier as Othello, Frank Finlay as Iago, and Maggie Smith as Desdemona; Liz White's remarkable 1980 *Othello*, with Yaphet Kotto as Othello and all other roles played by black men and women enrolled in Howard University;[1] Jonathan Miller's 1982 BBC Time-Life film, featuring Anthony Hopkins as Othello, Bob Hoskins as Iago, and Penelope Wilson as Desdemona;[2] Janet Suzman's 1988 *Othello* (the production at the Market Theatre, Johannesburg), with John Kani as Othello, Richard Haddon Haines as Iago, and Joanna Weinberg as Desdemona;[3] and Trevor Nunn's widely praised 1990 production, starring Willard White as Othello, Ian McKellen as Iago, and Imogen Stubbs as Desdemona.[4] The 115-minute White *Othello* exists in limited availability through Howard University's cultural committee, a regrettable fact since Yaphet Kotto's is the first film Othello played by a black man. Hopkins's Othello and especially Olivier's blackface "Caribbean" Moor have in the last several decades been criticized for using a white actor to play a black man as artificial or forced impersonations. (Olivier was accused of reducing Othello to Al Jolson or Uncle Tom.) The last chapter of Vaughan's *A Contextual History* analyzes the merits of Nunn's *Othello*, considering especially the brilliance of McKellen's Iago and the play's setting, variously described by critics as the American Civil War, the Franco-Prussian War, or the Austro-Hungarian War (also see Potter, *Othello* 188–92).

In 1995 Oliver Parker's film *Othello* was made, starring the African American Laurence Fishburne as Othello, the popular British Shakespeare director and actor Kenneth Branagh as Iago, and the Swiss actress Irène Jacob as Desdemona.[5] Fishburne enjoys a reputation as the most widely known black filmic Othello. Nonetheless, critics have lamented that Parker cut fifty percent of the play to provide plenty of visual excitement; that Branagh's depiction of Iago's evil is never fully convincing; and that Desdemona's and her father's (Pierre Vaneck's) Germanic-sounding accents make them, along with Othello, seem like outsiders in Venice (Potter, *Othello* 193). A later transformation of Shakespeare's *Othello* is Tim Blake Nelson's American film *O* (2001); in a high-school setting, a teenage Iago fatally sets a star black basketball player against his innocent white girl friend. Another film in which the performance of *Othello* is key is *Stage Beauty* (2004), starring Billy Crudup and Claire Danes.

An obvious pedagogical goal in showing parts or all of more than one cinematic *Othello* is to encourage a classroom discussion of not only the aesthetic but also the cultural differences involved in casting a white or black man as Othello, notably against a white or black Desdemona. Evaluations of and commentaries on film and television *Othello*s published between 1971 and

2002 are included in Roger Manvell, *Shakespeare and the Film*; Jack J. Jorgens, *Shakespeare on Film*; Peter S. Donaldson, *Shakespearean Films / Shakespearean Directors*; Samuel Crowl, *Shakespeare Observed: Studies in Performance on Stage and Screen*; Herbert R. Coursen, *Watching Shakespeare on Television*; Davies and Wells, *Shakespeare and the Moving Image*; Vaughan, *Othello: A Contextual History*; Russell Jackson, *The Cambridge Companion to Shakespeare on Film*; Douglas Brode, *Shakespeare in the Movies: From the Silent Era to* Shakespeare in Love; Deborah Cartmell, *Interpreting Shakespeare on Screen*; and Potter, *Othello* (Shakespeare in Performance series). Especially useful is James C. Bulman and Coursen, *Shakespeare on Television: An Anthology of Essays and Reviews*. For other recent studies in this vein, see the works cited by Kathy Howlett in her essay in this volume.

Barry M. Parker, in *The Folger Shakespeare Filmography: Directory of Feature Films Based on the Works of Shakespeare*, records essential details, including those pertaining to personnel, production, and distribution, for feature-length film adaptations or derivatives of *Othello*. These include the director George Cukor's *A Double Life* (1947), in which Ronald Coleman plays "an emotionally disturbed actor who can no longer distinguish between the stage role of Othello and his own self" (30); *Anna's Sin* (1953; dir. Mastrocinque), in which "a black American actor . . . falls in love with a white woman playing Desdemona to his Othello" (31); and *All Night Long* (1962), in which the director, Basil Dearden, "takes the Othello theme to a London East End jazz club, where an evil-minded musician . . . seeks to ruin the interracial marriage of his bandleader . . . by spreading vicious rumors about the bandleader's wife" (31). Teachers of *Othello* have profitably compared *A Double Life* with the similar scenario of the celebrated 1945 French film *Les enfants du paradis* (T. Howard 305). For extended accounts of these and other offshoots of *Othello* (*Men Are Not Gods* [1937], *Jubal* [1955]), instructors should read the section on *Othello* in Tony Howard's "Shakespeare's Cinematic Offshoots."

The highly acclaimed opera based on Shakespeare's tragedy is Giuseppe Verdi's *Otello* (1887), produced as a film by Franco Zeffirelli (1986). Jane Hawes's *An Examination of Verdi's* Otello *and Its Faithfulness to Shakespeare* is a resource for teachers wishing to show Zeffirelli's film in conjunction with classes devoted to *Othello*. In this respect, chapter 22 in Gary Schmidgall's *Shakespeare and Opera* is useful. Also of interest is Patrick McGoohan's 1974 film version of Jack Good's rock opera *Othello* retitled *Catch My Soul*. Starring Richie Havens as the Othello figure, a modern evangelist trying to build a new church, the musical is set in a hippie commune near Santa Fe, New Mexico, with Iago a redneck satanist and Desdemona a hippie who dies "by the altar before being welcomed into Heaven by a half-black, half-white Christ" (T. Howard 304).

A dramatic offshoot of *Othello* is Paula Vogel's *Desdemona: A Play about a Handkerchief*. In this short drama, Desdemona, secretly working in a brothel with Bianca, is guilty as charged. One respondent "find[s] that classic African American literature—Cleaver's *Soul on Ice*, Ellison's *Invisible Man*, Malcolm X's *Autobiography*, and John Howard Griffin's *Black like Me*—is particularly helpful in illuminating the racial issues of the play." Teachers interested in these juxtapositions should read a section of Coursen's *Watching Shakespeare on Television* (138–47). Other teachers have linked their presentation of *Othello* to explication and discussion of one or more of the following works: Tayeb Salih's *Season of Migration to the North*, Michelle Cliff's *No Telephone to Heaven*, Djanet Sears's *Harlem Duet* or *Afrika Solo*, and Ann-Marie Mac-Donald's *Goodnight Desdemona (Good Morning Juliet)*.

NOTES

[1]This item may be available by special order from the Howard University Cultural Committee, Howard University, Washington, DC, 20059.

[2]Available from www.ambrosevideo.com.

[3]Available from www.films.com or from Films for the Humanities and Sciences, PO Box 2053, Princeton, NJ 08543-2035.

[4]Available from www.libraryvideo.com or from Films for the Humanities and Sciences.

[5]Available from www.libraryvideo.com.

Part Two

APPROACHES

Introduction

Peter Erickson

The twenty-one essays that compose the main body of part 2 begin with a prologue that focuses on the role of *Othello* in the work of Jim Andreas. The goal is not only to recognize the memorial circumstances at the inception of this volume but also, at the moment of transition from part 1 to part 2, to place Jim's work at the center of our conversation. In terms of overall organization, Jim's contribution can be seen to have especially strong connections with the first and last sections, "Histories of Race" and "Comparative Contexts," his concept of "African plays" (see "Rewriting Race") serving as a point of entry for the former and his readings of Richard Wright, Ralph Ellison, and Amiri Baraka in "Othello's African American Progeny" providing a model for the latter.

Michael Neill's "*Othello* and Race" builds on his three earlier essays on the play collected in the section "Race, Nation, Empire" in *Putting History to the Question*. Race is an unavoidably primary question for *Othello* and *Othello* criticism, and placing Neill's essay at the beginning has the effect of squarely facing the issue of race at the outset. For Neill, "[w]hat makes this tragedy so remarkable . . . is that, far from capitulating to the emergent popular chauvinism that it documents so well, it exploits the continuing fluidity of contemporary ideas to hold the question of color up to scrutiny." Neill's rich, complex, and comprehensive treatment opens up, for both teachers and students, many avenues for further investigation and development.

In discussions of race as a historical category, it is important to distinguish between two uses of the term *anachronism*. In one use, the anachronism card is played as a conversation stopper to rule race out of bounds as inapplicable (or completely benign) before the massive English involvement in the Atlantic slave trade. The other use draws a more nuanced line between early and full modernism by treating the early modern period in England as a time of transition. In this view, an initial concept of race is present as one element in a mixture. Race is thus neither triumphantly monolithic nor totally absent, neither the only issue nor a nonissue; the salient point is that conceptual instability does not exclude race.

As his substantial recourse to Mary Floyd-Wilson's *English Ethnicity and Race* in the conclusion of his essay indicates, Neill defines *anachronism* primarily in this second sense when, quoting Floyd-Wilson, he finds *Othello* positioned at a rhetorically charged "crossroads in the history of ethnological ideas." For Floyd-Wilson, the play becomes a discursive conflict pitting older humoral conventions against a new vocabulary of race and tipping the balance toward race. As noted in my review of *English Ethnicity and Race*, Raymond Williams's three-part model set forth in "Dominant, Residual, and Emergent" may be used to articulate the relative strength of the two sides in tension: the emergent force of race challenges the older humoralism, which is dislodged from its dominant linguistic position and moves toward residual, though still powerful, status. *Othello* thus marks a moment when this shift begins to happen.

The interpretive value of Neill's insistence on fluidity, inconsistency, and ambiguity is shown in his understanding of Othello as a "stranger" from an imagined "everywhere" (1.1.137–38) that includes locations in Islamic Mediterranean and sub-Saharan Africa but does not see as mutually exclusive these counterpointing identities. Since Othello is a "composite figure," as Ania Loomba comments, "it is impossible, but also unnecessary, to decide whether Othello is *more* or *less* 'African'/'black' than 'Turkish'/Muslim" (*Shakespeare, Race* 92).

In keeping with the deliberately plural "Histories of Race" section heading, the next contributor, Francesca Royster, employs a two-directional model of history that moves back and forth between past and present. Adding to Neill's brief art-historical comment, the strong visual emphasis of Royster's essay further expands the artistic line of inquiry through four interrelated components: "*Othello*'s afterlife in visual culture," "the larger traditions of depicting the black body in Western art," "film versions of *Othello*," and contemporary African American art that displays "new possibilities for challenging past images of blackness." Having established this visual base, Royster describes an innovative class project in which students directly engage in hands-on visual work by constructing collages that "rememorialize Othello." This memorial suggests a twofold action: achieving a revision through literal revisualization and putting Othello to rest by giving him a proper burial, thereby freeing oneself. In Royster's words, the goal is to "[put] students in the role of re-creating and shaping public memory." Students interested in Royster's use of popular visual culture can be directed to her book *Becoming Cleopatra*.

The section heading "Genealogies of Gender and Sexuality" responds to Valerie Traub's argument in *Desire and Anxiety* and *The Renaissance of Lesbianism* that *gender* and *sexuality* be treated as distinct terms designating "two inextricably related yet independent systems" (*Desire* 95). Nicholas Radel in this volume, like Traub, draws on and contributes to the growing field of early modern queer studies. Rejecting modern conceptions of homosexuality as historically inappropriate for Shakespeare, Radel's insightfully intricate analysis reveals two distinct forms of male homosocial bonds in *Othello*—a normative and a socially disruptive version. In Radel's view, both versions are capable of expressing male same-sex erotic desire and misogynist attitudes toward women. Given these elements in common, the key differential is the second version's transgression of social hierarchy, which is the defining feature of Iago's commitment to his own self-advancement: "Iago destabilizes homosocial bonding by exposing it as a location not only for negotiating social hierarchies but also for transgressing their boundaries."

In "Improvisation and *Othello*: The Play of Race and Gender," Emily Bartels recalibrates the dynamic interplay between race and gender by presenting gender as the site with greater room for improvisational maneuver: "If Othello's status as Moor marks him as an isolated subject whom we might read through the established outsides of history and prejudice . . . , his status as husband requires that we view him in relation to his wife, through the volatile insides of domesticity and desire." Both through intensive close reading and a remarkably versatile performance exercise, Bartels shows how male and female gendered positions in the persons of Othello and Desdemona, when placed under the pressure and flux of "domestic dis-ease," produce outcomes that are unpredictable. Above all, Bartels wants to recover for the play the dramatic energy of unpredictability that opens a gap "between what we know and what we've yet to know."

Returning to the terrain of Carol Thomas Neely's early feminist account of the three women characters in *Othello* ("Women and Men"), Cynthia Marshall in the next essay applies a Lacanian-based psychoanalytic approach. For Marshall, *Othello* dramatizes competing male and female "orders of fantasy"; in the female subject, "fantasy functions as an empowering means to resist the established norms and to imagine alternative possibilities." Though women's independent agency is ultimately defeated, its existence nevertheless enables Marshall to reverse the tendency to treat female characters as merely objects of male fantasy. Further discussion of Marshall's psychoanalytic critical method can be found in her essay "Psychoanalyzing the Prepsychoanalytic Subject."

"Generic Frameworks" turns to the forces that shape *Othello*'s form. In an essay that has links to the two previous sections on race and gender, Jean Howard sees *Othello* as an innovative reconfiguration of the standard conventions in the newly created genre of English adventure plays. This observation enables her to formulate the play's cross-cultural dimension with poignant precision: "the handkerchief is at times a symbol of hope—the hope that a foreigner and a native can bridge the cultural and racial gap that makes their marriage seem an impossibility to members of the Venetian community such as Brabanzio. But it also becomes a symbol of seemingly unbridgeable cultural difference." Douglas Bruster's essay surveys the changing history of tragedy as well as the impact of cross-generic mixing of comedy with tragedy. In particular, the comic effects help "explain many things in the play that . . . are nonconventionally tragic." By focusing on the revenge play, Cynthia Lewis forges a powerful link between *Othello* and the immediately preceding tragedy *Hamlet*. Locating both in the established genre of revenge drama, Lewis shows that Shakespeare's two tragedies work against type by activating "antirevenge sentiment." Genre is crucial to an assessment of *Othello*: this cluster demonstrates that the play can be placed in different generic contexts, each of which leads in a different interpretive direction. The overall result of this section is to challenge students to test and to encompass multiple, shifting definitions of the play's genre.

The purpose of the section "Classroom Strategies" is to gather different interpretive gambits that can be used as takeoff points for initiating class discussion. As a major participant in current textual criticism through his work on versions of *King Lear*, Michael Warren here addresses the problem of how to deal with variant texts of *Othello*. After a general introduction to the nature of the quarto and folio *Othellos*, he describes three significant instances of variation and their implications for interpretation. This material makes it possible to raise the issue of the status of the text, a topic that will be new to many students. Maurice Hunt explores the conundrum, endlessly provocative for students, of Iago's opacity, so triumphantly registered in his final cryptic taunt, "What you know, you know" (5.2.309). Hunt sees Iago's elusive, scattershot account of his motivation as a strategic ploy that Iago uses to hide himself the better to confuse others. The analysis concentrates on religious imagery, finding that allusions to Iago as devil are ultimately misleading in the face of his undeniably human status.

While Hunt's essay suggests how a single-character approach can be used to open up class discussion, Geraldo de Sousa makes a similar move with the single image of the house. Drawing on anthropological and philosophical perspectives, Sousa encourages students to elaborate on the meanings of house and their reverberations with Othello's term "unhoused" (1.2.26). Tracing the surprisingly frequent references to the word *house* in *Othello* builds a linguistic and metaphoric network of such depth that it illuminates the play as a whole. Martha Tuck Rozett's account of teaching the play with students who are themselves teachers gives special prominence to the role of pedagogical strategy. Through the lens of Rozett's essay, we see teachers in the act of consciously working out ways to engage students in the classroom. Further background for the four essays in this section is available in Warren's *Complete King Lear, 1608–1623*, Hunt's *Shakespeare's Religious Allusiveness*, Sousa's *Shakespeare's Cross-Cultural Encounters*, and Rozett's *Talking Back to Shakespeare*.

Covering theater, film, and television, "Approaches to Performance" begins with a wide-ranging introduction by Virginia Mason Vaughan, author of *Othello: A Contextual History*, the entire second half of which is devoted to performance history. Vaughan's historical approach here stresses that, as "a 'blackface' role, a part made for a skilled white impersonator," Othello "was not the essential black hero but the product of a white imagination represented by English actors to a light-complexioned audience." Performativity is thus built in to Othello's character at the most basic level because his racial identity is literally performed. Focusing principally on contemporary stage productions, Miranda Johnson-Haddad shows how "performance choices" can either reinforce "the potential for racist and stereotypical portrayal" or move in the opposite direction to open up "performance opportunities." Particularly valuable in this regard are the specific examples of in-class performance exercises, which incidentally fit well with the exercise described in Emily

Bartels's essay. Also compelling is Johnson-Haddad's explanation of the difference between nontraditional and color-blind/gender-blind casting practices.

The next two authors have helped develop the field of Shakespeare film studies, for which core bibliographic sources include Samuel Crowl's *Shakespeare at the Cineplex* and Kathy Howlett's *Framing Shakespeare on Film*. In Crowl's essay in this volume, the "idea of choice" is illustrated through a highly detailed comparison of two productions—Trevor Nunn's television version and Oliver Parker's film. Tracking the camera-eye view, Crowl pays particular attention to the way visual meaning is created by the location and action of the camera at each moment.

A different way of highlighting choice is exemplified by Howlett's discussion of the wide variations in the way five productions present a single visual image, the arrangement of bodies in the tragic loading of the bed. Howlett's specific focus on the disposition of Emilia, in view of her request to "lay me by my mistress' side" (5.2.244), is especially telling and moving. Questions about who gets to be on the bed and, once there, what position one's body occupies in relation to the others have special complexity in the ending of Parker's film, which, in Howlett's words, is "the first (and only) film version of the play to honor Emilia's request." Moreover, Howlett's emphasis on the final status of the Desdemona-Emilia alliance resonates with the issue of female empowerment evoked in earlier essays by Bartels and Marshall. It is noteworthy that, in addition to all four authors in the performance section, five other contributors mention Parker's film, making it the most frequently cited version and, from various points of view, a touchstone for the volume.

Taken as a group, the four essays in the final section, "Comparative Contexts," link *Othello* to a remarkably wide range of individual works: Cinthio's *Hecatommithi* (1565), the play's source; Elizabeth Cary's closet drama *The Tragedy of Mariam* (1613) and Aphra Behn's novella *Oroonoko* (1688); Giuseppe Verdi's opera *Otello* (1887); Isak Dinesen's short story "The Blank Page" from her *Last Tales* (1957); and two contemporary plays, Paula Vogel's *Desdemona: A Play about a Handkerchief*, given its "first staged reading" in 1987 (Fischlin and Fortier 234), and Djanet Sears's *Harlem Duet* (1997). However, the overall purpose of this section is not only to offer a variety of specific examples but also to suggest larger possibilities for different ways of formulating and deploying such juxtapositions.

Drawing on the proliferation of new studies on women writers in the period, Lisa Gim transfers the question of gender from the level of character to the level of author. She develops the concept of gendered authorship by probing differences in the way male and female writers portray men and women and their relationships. Sheila Cavanagh's essay situates Shakespeare in a network of authorial relations in which Shakespeare is both successor and precursor—the former with respect to Cinthio, the latter with regard to Verdi and Vogel. Applying this mosaic of comparative perspectives, Cavanagh shows that Shakespeare "appears to have deliberately countered reader expectations and narrative desires at key moments." In a related contribution on reader response, Janelle Jenstad uses the ambiguity of Dinesen's blank page to highlight and examine conflicting interpretations of the linked symbolic sites of handkerchief, wedding sheets, and Desdemona herself. As Jenstad indicates, the Dinesen story has the additional advantage of allowing the teacher to introduce "without critical fanfare" key deconstructive concepts such as "slippage." The interpretive reach of Jenstad's essay can be further expanded by linking it to Susan Gubar's " 'The Blank Page' and the Issues of Female Creativity," which discusses Dinesen's story in a wider literary context, with a brief reference to *Othello* (75).

In the final essay, Joyce Green MacDonald shows how Sears's *Harlem Duet* affords a strategic contrast that

> forcibly dislocates a strictly patriarchal reading of Shakespeare's play by telling its story from the perspective of the black women who are her own main characters and who, I have argued elsewhere, haunt the memory of *Othello*: Othello's absent mother, the Egyptian "charmer" who enchanted the strawberry-embroidered handkerchief, Desdemona's maid "Barbary."

When MacDonald's essay here on Sears is combined with her analysis of the displacement of black women in her book *Women and Race in Early Modern Texts*, the result is a sweeping, nuanced historical perspective that encompasses the full spectrum from early modern culture to contemporary revisions of Shakespeare. Because of this historical breadth, MacDonald's extended project provides a fitting conclusion both to this section and to the volume as a whole. In its discussion of *The Tragedy of Mariam* (60-64) and *Oroonoko* (100–12), *Women and Race in Early Modern Texts* brings us back full circle to texts discussed by Gim at the beginning of this section. The essay on Sears returns us to the issue of race in the volume's first essay by Neill, with the citation of MacDonald as its opening epigraph.

NOTE

Contributors cite the following editions of *Othello*: Radel, Bruster, Lewis, Rozett, Crowl, MacDonald (Evans ed.); Neill, Warren, Hunt, Vaughan (Honigmann ed.); Erickson, Royster, Howard, Jenstad (Greenblatt ed.); Bartels, Marshall (Sanders ed.); Howlett (Bevington ed.); Sousa (Orgel and Braunmuller ed.); Gim, Cavanagh (Carroll ed.).

Othello in the Work of James R. Andreas

Peter Erickson

The evocative title of Jim Andreas's most important essay—"Rewriting Race through Literature: Teaching Shakespeare's African Plays"—makes a powerful double claim. I return to the main title later; I begin here by noting how the subtitle signals Andreas's key critical move: to place *Othello* in the larger context of a five-play sequence designated by the novel category of African plays.

The significance of this cluster is that it produces a solid core for addressing the issue of race that goes beyond a single-play approach and hence provides an antidote to the superficial perception that *Othello* is the only Shakespeare play that really focuses on racial questions. Andreas's group of five—*Titus Andronicus, The Merchant of Venice, Othello, Antony and Cleopatra*, and *The Tempest*—offers a different kind of cross-section that, by cutting across standard generic and chronological divisions, spans Shakespeare's entire career. This comprehensive coverage shows that, far from being alone, *Othello* is part of a larger strand that runs through Shakespeare's work as a whole.[1]

The generative richness of Andreas's core group is indicated by its resonance with some of the most advanced scholarship on conceptions of race in the early modern period. First, Ania Loomba's trenchant summary account in *Shakespeare, Race, and Colonialism* adopts an organizational model that highlights the same five plays as Andreas. Second, work done at the level of individual plays correlates with, and strengthens, Andreas's overall interpretive framework. This intensive attention given to each of the five plays is exemplified by Francesca Royster's essay "White-Limed Walls" on *Titus Andronicus*; Janet Adelman's "Her Father's Blood" on *The Merchant of Venice*;[2] Celia Daileader's *Racism, Misogyny, and the* Othello *Myth*; Arthur L. Little's chapters on *Antony and Cleopatra* in *Shakespeare Jungle Fever*; and Jonathan Gold-berg's "The Print of Goodness" on *The Tempest*.

If in one direction Jim Andreas's work points to the most sophisticated scholarly explorations of the discourse of race in Shakespeare, in another di-rection it points to public education in the broadest sense. Jim's career was characterized by an unusual degree of engagement with a wide spectrum of different audiences, an engagement that placed him in a pivotal position to serve as an intermediary capable of negotiating the divide between the acad-emy and the outside world.

Academics know the value of disseminating scholarly debates to a general public. We are painfully aware that failure to do so results in a sharp split between specialist and generalist realms of discussion in which the vacuum in the generalist realm is filled by traditionalist commentators such as William J. Bennett, Allan Bloom, Lynne V. Cheney, Roger Kimball, and Arthur M. Schlesinger, Jr.[3] The outcome is that widely publicized accounts of new critical developments in the field of literary studies are distorted, alarmist, and hostile. Few academics attempt to counter this misleading version by actually entering the public arena as Jim did.

Jim's practical investment in this area is epitomized by his creation and ten-year directorship (1991–2000) of the Clemson Shakespeare Festival, an event comprising a whole series of activities, including theater and film productions as well as scholarly presentations and panel discussions. Particularly relevant is the weeklong program for the seventh festival in 1998, Shakespeare and the Black Experience (see the Web site *Shakespeare and the Black Experience*). I witnessed firsthand Jim's special talent for designing and managing larger forums to make scholarly issues accessible to a wider audience. Central to the success of the festival as an institutional network were Jim's administrative and organizational ability and his boundless personal energy.

The festival is only the most visible instance of Jim's commitment to large-scale public education. Another major manifestation of this educational out-reach is his interest in high school teaching. In his most comprehensive con-tribution, "Silencing the Vulgar and Voicing the Other Shakespeare," Andreas proposes that the conventional secondary school lineup of *Romeo and Juliet*, *Julius Caesar*, *Macbeth*, and *Hamlet* be replaced by an "alternative curricu-lum" that displays "the other Shakespeare" (75). The purpose of this "new curriculum," consisting of *A Midsummer Night's Dream*, *The Merchant of Venice*, *Othello*, and *The Tempest*, would "not be the *avoidance* but the *pursuit* of controversy" (76), including, in the case of *Othello*, the issues of "misceg-enation" and "racial hatred" (85). The link between Andreas's scholarly over-view in "Rewriting Race through Literature" and his pedagogical recommen-dations in "Silencing the Vulgar" is immediately apparent: three of the four plays in the revised curriculum are familiar from his list of five African plays.[4]

Andreas's principal point of entry into secondary school education is through his critical deployment of the concept of censorship, which takes two distinctly different forms. The first and more obvious is the literal editing of Shakespeare's text through expurgation in a misguided attempt to sanitize. In Andreas's view, pursued in systematic detail in "The Neutering of *Romeo and Juliet*," this sanitizing editorial procedure is unacceptable because it screens out the full complexity of Shakespeare's language and hence the full impact of his meaning. In particular, to protect students from sexual humor is to deprive them of the plays' vital resources for creating multiple perspectives and possibilities—what in "Writing Down, Speaking Up" he calls "existential alternatives to the tragic paradigm" (26) and "faith in comic *belief*, not simply comic *relief*" (28). So emphatic is Andreas's desire to prevent suppression of the text and to celebrate the counterbalancing value of festive release that at times he verges on overemphasis and romanticization of the efficacy of comic potential, as though it were possible to mitigate or even offset the tragic action in *Romeo and Juliet*, *Hamlet*, and *Macbeth*.

A shift of focus from sexuality to race, however, quickly makes clear that, in the context of race, censorship can take a different form, whereby humor is a destructive force rather than a saving grace. Andreas begins his essay on the African plays by acknowledging the anxiety surrounding the issue of race: "We understand that race is a sensitive topic, one that most of our students, and even more of their parents, would like us to ignore. Discussion of racial topics invites embarrassment for the teacher, uneasy silence from our classes, and occasional sniggers from the uninformed" ("Rewriting Race" 215). No amount of textual bowdlerizing can conceal or remove the issue of race. In this context, humor becomes an obstacle to be confronted instead of an asset to be celebrated. *Othello*, in particular, represents the limit case where humor, located in Iago's sardonic wit, takes on a negative tonality and turns into a vehicle for aggression. Race is too serious to be a joking matter in *Othello*, and humor will not get us through. A different kind of engagement is needed, and Andreas does not shrink from this more difficult task.

In this connection, I now return to the main title of the essay "Rewriting Race through Literature" as a statement of Jim's philosophy of education. The phrase announces an inspiring and ambitious goal, and in the essay's final paragraph Jim explains the theoretical basis for his belief in education as a vehicle for racial change:

> Racism cannot long survive without the verbal and symbolic apparatus that generates and sustains it: the names, the jokes, the plays, the speeches, the casual exchanges, the novels. In short, racism is a cultural virus that is verbally transmitted and its antidote must therefore be verbally transmitted as well. Shakespeare adapted his source for *Othello*, Giraldi Cinthio's *novella* of Othello, Iago, and Desdemona in his *Hecatommithi*, by adding the compelling motif of race reflected in the rise of the morally questionable slave trade in sixteenth-century Europe. Shakespeare in turn offers *Othello* and its companion plays about

Africans, as opportunities for his audience and our students to consider the behaviors and consequences of the new form of xenophobia that continues to plague Europe and America up to our own day.   (233)

I want to consider two questions—one minor, one major—in relation to this passage. First, what is the status of the adjective "quiet" in Andreas's subsequent reference to "a quiet, legitimate opportunity to discuss the controversial subject of racism" (234)? Does "quiet" convey too low a profile, imply a stance that is too soft or timid? My answer is that we should not underestimate the force Andreas puts behind the unassuming word "quiet." As evidence, I cite the strength of his outspoken critique of Harold Bloom in "Shakespeare and the Invention of Humanism." In this finely honed, effective polemic, Andreas appears at his most passionate. There is no holding back in this defense of "racial readings" of the five plays with "African characters" (182).

But fundamental questions concerning Andreas's larger vision of antiracism education are harder to answer. Are there a rhetorical excess and an overreaching in his claim that "racism cannot long survive" linguistic exposure? How much can be accomplished in the classroom setting and what are the limits? The power of racism does not rest on linguistic authority alone; Andreas's picture of the classroom seems overoptimistic because it leaves out the recalcitrant, intractable social structures with built-in patterns of differential power relations that may be impervious to "rewriting race through literature." This is not to say that classroom work is futile and worthless, but its capacity to offer a solution to the problem of race is limited and tensions among skepticism, hope, and humility are a necessary accompaniment to our literary critical efforts.

A second component of Andreas's work expands the historical and cultural scope for the strategy of rewriting. His major contributions, "Othello's African American Progeny" and "Signifyin' on *The Tempest* in Gloria Naylor's *Mama Day*," examine twentieth-century African American writers' responses to Shakespeare. These essays move beyond the strict limits of Shakespeare's work and open up more room for maneuver and revisionary play. When revision is confined to the terms and dynamics of *Othello* proper, it is hard in the end to avoid a sense of limited options, even of racial entrapment from which there can be no escape, only repetition. But the creation of an implied critical dialogue between Shakespeare and later black writers suggests a way forward, if not automatically a way out. Jim's prospectus for "Signifyin' on Shakespeare: African American Appropriations of *Othello* and *The Tempest*," the book for which he had an advance contract from University Press of Florida, sets a general course for this revisionary project:

Signifying as a literary methodology holds real hope for the desperate canonical reconfiguration of race and class that any truly "new world" will demand in the twenty-first century. Signifying is all about words,

about rearranging words and verbal patterns to configure new meanings
and identities.   (Andreas, "Signifyin' on Shakespeare")

As one starting point for further exploration, I cite the work of the African
American installation artist Fred Wilson, who represented the United States
at the 2003 Venice Biennale. Paul Kaplan's contribution to the exhibition catalog, which provides a survey of black figures in Venetian Renaissance visual
art, discusses the Othello-Venice connection (Wilson 15–16), a motif elabo-
rated in Kaplan's "Earliest Images of Othello" (179) and "Contraband Guides"
(192–94). More specifically, Salah Hassan describes Wilson's invocation of
Othello in *September Dream* as follows:

> Four monitors show videos from four different opera and film produc-
> tions of *Othello*, in which the role of the Moor is played by white actors.
> Wilson plays murder and suicide scenes from the productions back-
> wards, evoking a "September 12th" dream, where the violence and dis-
> asters of history are open to reversal.   (qtd. in Wilson 40)

The overall effect of this literal reversal is to enact an escape from the inev-
itability of Othello's fate.

The quotation from Othello's final speech (5.2.351) in the title of Wilson's
exhibition—*Speak of Me as I Am*—suggests a paradoxical double resonance.
In its reversal of Iago's malevolent "I am not what I am" in the play's opening
scene (1.1.65), Othello's insistent "as I am" signals his reassertion of linguistic
control and his regaining of the power of self-definition that he had ceded to
Iago. Wilson's choice of this statement implies his affirmation of Othello. Yet,
at the same time, Wilson is also taking over these words and speaking them
in his own voice. "Speak of me as I am" signifies very differently depending
on whether we hear it as voiced by Othello or by Wilson. Although echoing
Othello's emphasis on speaking, Wilson's inflection makes this difference felt:
"How can I be anything but an individual and speak with my own voice?"
(Madoff 35). The closure Othello faces in the final moment of Shakespeare's
play is reopened through Wilson's artistic revisiting of Venice four centuries
later, and this reopening makes it possible to imagine the "new meanings and
identities" to which Jim Andreas looked forward.

NOTES

[1]This is not to argue, however, that analysis of race should be limited to these five
plays. Rather, the ultimate goal is to extend the analysis to all Shakespeare's work, as
eloquently stated by Jonathan Crewe: "For Shakespeare, I would suggest, this racializing potentiality of the matrix, actualized as historical pressure and occasion dictate in
such figures as Aaron, Tamora, Shylock, Jessica, Othello, Cleopatra, and Caliban, is not

exhausted by the production of these characters and situations. The fact that the racializing potentiality is not localized, and cannot *be* bounded within a set of racial characters, means that it is indeterminable, always exorbitant" (21).

²Andreas's most detailed essay on *Othello*, "The Curse of Cush," overlaps with Adelman's work in its emphasis on black-Jewish connections in *The Merchant of Venice* and on links between *Merchant* and *Othello*.

³I present a detailed examination of this problem in my *Rewriting Shakespeare, Rewriting Ourselves* (ch. 6), "The Two Renaissances and Shakespeare's Canonical Position," and "Multiculturalism and the Problem of Liberalism."

⁴*A Midsummer Night's Dream*, the one apparent exception in Andreas's curricular reform, is actually consistent with the overall motif of ethnicity. Though Andreas's own brief account of the play does not mention this element (83–84), Loomba's "The Great Indian Vanishing Trick" makes its relevance a convincing focal point.

Othello and Race

Michael Neill

> *Othello* has retained its power to reach audiences
> precisely because it uncannily seems to play out what
> they think they already know . . . about race and sex.
> —Joyce Green MacDonald

> If [*Othello*] did not begin as a play about race, then its
> history has made it one.
> —Ben Okri

When Iago, in the course of the tirade with which he opens *Othello*, slightingly refers to the protagonist as "his Moorship" (1.1.32), he immediately highlights the ethnic tensions that are implicit in the play's oxymoronic subtitle, *The Moor of Venice*.[1] Not once in the scene that ensues do he or his interlocutors refer to Othello by name; instead he is simply "the Moor" (lines 39, 115, 124, 145, 162, 175), "the thicklips" (65), "an extravagant and wheeling stranger" (134)—a man defined by his alien condition, his estrangement from the people among whom he lives. Iago resents all foreigners, as his dismissal of Cassio as "a Florentine" reveals (19), but the imagery of monstrous bestiality with which he daubs the lovemaking of Othello and Desdemona makes it apparent that a quite particular disgust is excited by the Moor's color: "an old black ram / Is tupping your white ewe. . . . you'll have your daughter covered with a Barbary horse. . . . your daughter and the Moor are now making the beast with two backs" (1.1.87–88, 109–10, 114–15). Brabantio similarly believes that his daughter's liaison with a Moor is "Against all rules of nature" (1.3.102);

and although the Duke seeks to gloss over the old man's insults by insisting that in the spectrum of virtue "Your son-in-law is far more fair than black" (1.3.291), it is plain that the bigotry that Iago stirs up is widely disseminated through the society of the play. Indeed Othello himself will come to fear that aversion to his blackness may account for Desdemona's supposed infidelity (3.3.267–72); and he will internalize Venetian prejudice to the point where he imagines her reputation as "begrimed and black / As mine own face" (390–91), as though blackness were indeed the mark of damnation. Most painfully of all, the ending of the tragedy can even seem to confirm this reading of color; for in the last scene Othello's murder of his wife is framed by his "Put out the light" soliloquy (5.2.1–22), with its baffled emphasis on the unsullied whiteness of Desdemona's body, and by Emilia's fierce denunciations, with their repeated stress on Othello's black skin as a sign of inward filth and diabolic wickedness (5.2.129, 153, 160)—a mark of the reprobate destiny to which he despairingly consigns himself (5.2.269–78).

From the perspective established in the play's first scene, then, what we nowadays call "race" would appear absolutely central to the tragedy of Othello; and if it is true, as Edward Pechter has claimed, that *Othello* has replaced both *Hamlet* and *Lear* as "the tragedy of choice for the present generation" (2), that undoubtedly has a great deal to do with the color of its protagonist. Race has been among the most fiercely debated social issues of our times, and as a result the significance of Othello's blackness has come to dominate interpretation of the play, whether on the stage or in the study, to an extraordinary degree. *Othello* now appears to be exactly what the hero's namesake in Murray Carlin's *Not Now, Sweet Desdemona* called it thirty years ago, a play "about colour, and nothing but colour" (32). But Ben Okri's comment is a useful reminder of how time-bound and local such seemingly unavoidable responses can be. The *Othello* that John Barton directed for the Royal Shakespeare Company in 1971, for example, was clearly a very different play from the one that Carlin had evoked for East African audiences only three years earlier; for, to the evident relief of several reviewers, Barton's production satisfied them that "Shakespeare's tragedy isn't really about race" and that "Othello's 'blackness' is not a large issue in the play" (Bryden, "Moor"; Lloyd Evans 22). Yet many of the same critics had rhapsodized over Laurence Olivier's Moor a decade earlier, claiming that, with his studious impersonation of African speech patterns and body language, he "embodie[d] blackness" and indeed "*was* the African continent" (Kretzmer; Bryden, "Olivier's Moor").

While the play's treatment of race has become intensely controversial at certain times, the extended critical and performance histories of *Othello* show that at others it has been treated as a matter of relative insignificance. It is moreover a striking fact that the only surviving account of a performance of *Othello* in the dramatist's lifetime fails to mention the play's racial dimension. Henry Jackson, who saw the tragedy performed at Oxford in 1610, remembered the extraordinary effect of the murder scene when "the celebrated

Desdemona, slain in our presence by her husband . . . entreated the pity of
the spectators by her very countenance," but he did not even trouble to note
that the murderer was a Moor (qtd. in *Othello* [ed. Hankey] 18). We cannot
now know whether that fact appeared insignificant to Jackson or whether he
simply felt it too obvious to be worth mentioning. But it seems telling that
comments by the mid-century clergyman Abraham Wright, a great reader of
plays, while praising the characterization of "Iago for a rogue and Othello for
a jealous husband," is equally silent about the hero's color (qtd. in Roberts
121).[2] By the end of the seventeenth century, however, indignation and disgust
at the union of Othello and Desdemona were clearly among the driving motives of Thomas Rymer's derisive attack on the tragedy: he returns repeatedly
to the impropriety of the match between a senator's daughter and a "black-
amoor" in terms that recall the racial slurs of Iago. Citing Horace on the
unnatural commingling of species, "non ut Serpentes avibus geminentur, ti-
gribus agni" ("snakes do not mate with birds, or lambs with tigers"; my trans.),
Rymer implies a consonance between the "monstrous" nature of the match
and the monstrousness of the play's mixed design as a "bloody farce" ([1693]
88, 146).[3] There is clearly a connection between Rymer's contemptuous attitude toward Africans and the rapid acceleration of British involvement in the
slave trade at the end of seventeenth century; yet oddly enough the eighteenth
century seemed, for the most part, to find the idea of a black hero relatively
unproblematic. However, concern with Othello's color reemerged strongly
during the years of political turmoil that followed the French Revolution, as
abolitionism gathered strength.[4] In France, Ducis's translation, with its "sans-
culotte Othello," was hailed as an artistic expression of the republican spirit,
reflecting its disdain for "the aristocracy of colour" (*Othello* [ed. Hankey] 76).
Later in the nineteenth century, liberal Russians would interpret the performance of Ira Aldridge, the great African American actor, as giving voice to
"the far-off groans of his own people, oppressed by unbelievable slavery"
(*Othello* [ed. Hankey] 81).[5]

   In such a context it is easy to see how Samuel Taylor Coleridge's notorious
repudiation of "a veritable negro" Othello as "something monstrous" was entirely in accord with the reactionary anti-Jacobinism of his later years (1: 42).
Much grosser expressions of the sentiments voiced by Coleridge are to be
found in the burlesque parodies of *Othello* that flourished in Britain in the
period between the abolition of the slave trade and that of slavery itself (1807–
33) and that surfaced again in the United States in the wake of emancipation
(1865). These burlesques use increasingly crude parody to neutralize the racial
anxieties stirred up by Shakespeare's play, translating its sublime word-music
into absurd jingles and compressing the plot to suggest, once again, its kinship
with farce. It was no doubt partly as a reaction to this destructive tradition
that actors such as Edmund Kean and his Victorian successors consciously
turned their back on the convention (which probably went back to the first
Othello, Richard Burbage) of playing Othello as a black African, producing

instead the light-skinned North African Moor described by the great Edwardian actor Beerbohm Tree as "a stately Arab of the best caste" (*Othello* [ed. Hankey] 67). This orientalized version of the hero, although allowing the actor to display the emotional extravagance thought to be characteristic of Mediterranean peoples, soothed the extreme racial sensitivities that could be aroused by a black Othello—especially when played by a black performer like Aldridge (*Othello* [ed. Hankey] 81).[6] In this new dispensation it was ostensibly culture rather than color that lay at the heart of *Othello*, which became the tragedy of an acculturated barbarian whose thin veneer of civilization cracks under the strain of unbearable jealousy.

This reading of the play achieved its most sophisticated form in F. R. Leavis's 1937 essay "Diabolic Intellect and the Noble Hero" and continued to influence criticism as recently as the 1980s, when Norman Sanders's New Cambridge edition could describe Othello as "a primitive man, at odds with the sophisticated society into which he has forced himself, relapsing into barbarism" (47). However, such attempts to bypass awkward questions about the significance of color in the tragedy are often just as revealing about the anxieties it can excite as readings more explicitly preoccupied with race are; and it is telling that Leavis's essay provided much of the inspiration for John Dexter's interpretation of the play in the 1964 Olivier version, which presented Othello as a "pompous, word-spinning, arrogant black general" of a type already becoming familiar in newly independent African countries (Tynan 4). In retrospect, especially when Olivier's performance is exposed to the merciless eye of the camera in Stuart Burge's filmed version, it is easy to see how this production capitulated to racial stereotype. Nevertheless, to the extent that Olivier's studiously African version of the Moor was also influenced by Paul Robeson's groundbreaking Othello, it may be seen as helping to prepare the way for the black actors who have increasingly dominated the role since the mid-1980s.

For Robeson, the first black actor to play the role since Aldridge, the productions in which he starred in London (1930) and New York (1943) were (despite the ambiguous intentions of his two directors, Nellie Van Volkenburg and Margaret Webster) both a contribution to his lifelong struggle for black civil rights and a personally liberating experience. Seeing the play as a mirror for the "position [of the] coloured man in America today" (Robeson, qtd. in Vaughan 187),[7] the actor declared that "Othello has taken away from me all kinds of fears, all sense of limitation, and all racial prejudice. Othello has opened to me new and wider fields; in a word, *Othello has made me free*" (qtd. in Vaughan 192; emphasis added).[8]

The power of Robeson's conviction was enough to persuade one American reviewer that "no white man should ever dare play the part again" (Potter, " 'Unhaply' " 19); but in fact—with the exception of the aging Robeson's return to the part at Stratford-upon-Avon in 1959—Othello would continue to be the virtual monopoly of white actors for a long time to come. Although Dexter's theatrical reinvestigation of Othello's blackness was matched by the work of a small group of critics—G. M. Matthews, Eldred Durosimi Jones, and G. K. Hunter—who took the first steps toward a systematic and fully historicized exploration of Shakespeare's treatment of race, it would be another two decades before the directions charted in the mid-1960s were pursued by a new generation of critics and theater practitioners. More than anything, perhaps, it was the prominence given to racial issues by the gathering crisis of apartheid in South Africa that prompted a renewed focus on the significance of Othello's blackness, and it was the deliberate political appropriation of the play by two South Africans, one a Shakespearean scholar, the other an actor and director, that marked the decisive turning point: the 1987 publication of Martin Orkin's essay "*Othello* and the 'Plain Face' of Racism" (whose activist agenda was announced by the title of the book in which it was reprinted, *Shakespeare against Apartheid*)[9] coincided with Janet Suzman's defiantly multiracial production of the play at the Market Theatre in Johannesburg, with the prominent Xhosa actor John Kani in the title role. For his performance Kani was adorned with a heavy necklet, a piece of barbaric jewelry that disconcertingly resembled a slave collar and from which hung the small knife with which Othello would ultimately kill himself. The importance of *Othello*, for the makers of this production as much as for Orkin, lay in its transhistorical immediacy: "in its rejection of human pigmentation as a means of identifying worth," Orkin insisted, "the play, *as it always has done*, continues to oppose racism" ("'Plain Face'" 168). Thus there was no more appropriate work, Suzman and Kani believed, "to describe the utter tragedy of our country. . . . The play addresses the notion of apartheid four hundred years before the epithet was coined—and rejects it."[10]

Suzman's *Othello* achieved a wide international currency through television and videotape and contributed to the growing politicization of the play outside South Africa—especially in Britain, where the emergence of a cadre of classically trained black actors had begun to make the propriety of continuing to cast white actors in the role of Othello a matter of controversy. Significantly, when the British actor Patrick Stewart was offered the lead by the Washington Shakespeare Company in 1997, he would agree to take it only in a so-called photo-negative production, in which a white Othello faced an entirely black world. And when in the same year the play returned to London, the National's choice of the youthful David Harewood provoked a flurry of complaint about "political correctness" (see Macaulay 25; Lister 13). Harewood responded angrily to such criticisms, insisting that "[i]t is now ridiculous to see a white person blacked up," and arguing (like Robeson) that the play had given him "a grounding in . . . black consciousness. . . . That's where Othello has helped me, I'm not playing—I'm being" (14). As Harewood's comments imply, the politics of black casting had a number of strands: it was a reaction to the perceived offensiveness of "blacking up," a convention that was seen as inextricably compromised by "nigger-minstrel" racism; it answered to the belief, apparent from Aldridge's time onward, that a black actor's "natural" sympathy with the part must lend his performance an authenticity transcending mere art; and it was an obvious corollary of the desire to make the play speak to contemporary racial issues. Thus the critic Richard Wilson supplied a program note for David Thacker's 1984 Young Vic production in which he promoted *Othello* as "Shakespeare's most topical tragedy . . . his most prophetic analysis of the psychology of colonialism and power." The key to understanding the play, Wilson argued, lies in the fact that

> Othello is a freed slave. He prides himself on his "free condition" and his "free and open nature." Liberated from the chain-gang, he imagines that "All slaves are free." . . . Othello's "free and noble nature" is as oppressed in this "free" society as when he was a galley slave . . . bound by the invisible chain of words and images. . . . *Othello* is a tragedy based on the crudest race myth, the legend of the negro's sexual danger.

Wilson's insistence on the play's "prophetic" character, reinforced by his anachronistic reference to the chain gangs of segregationist America and to a Fanonian "psychology of colonialism" with its attendant sexual fantasies, firmly relocated the play in the context of twentieth-century racial politics. One danger with productions that seek such political immediacy is that through their choice of familiarizing detail they can sometimes reinforce the very stereotypes they seek to combat. This seems to have happened in Michael Boyd's 1984 *Othello* at the Lyric Studio in Hammersmith: invoking the late-Victorian essentialism of Joseph Conrad, Christopher Edwards described Joseph Marcell's Sandhurst-educated African as "retreat[ing] to the *heart of darkness*" when, succumbing to Iago's temptations, he heard "bongo drums and jungle rhythms" and then reentered "with chicken feathers in his hair" as if coming from "a voodoo sacrifice" (Edwards 34; emphasis added).

It was partly to counter the persistent "view that Othello behaves as he does because of his race" that the 1989 Greenwich production, codirected by Sue Dunderdale and Hugh Quarshie, matched its black Othello with a black Iago: as Quarshie's program note explains, Cyprus with its "olive-skinned natives" was to be seen as a "colonial" society governed by a deeply internalized hierarchy of color in which Iago's influence over the hero was determined partly by the relative lightness of his skin. By 1998, however, Quarshie had come to question whether the play was really amenable to the kind of reading that he and Dunderdale had attempted: whereas in 1989 he had insisted that an authentic performance required that Othello be "a black man, and not someone impersonating a black man," a decade later, in a lecture entitled "Hesitations on *Othello*,"[11] he argued that "being a black actor gives . . . no greater insight into . . . the play than being Danish would into *Hamlet*" (Quarshie, *Second Thoughts* 3). Going further, Quarshie even speculated that since this was "a role written for a white actor in black make-up and for a . . . white audience . . . [o]f all the parts in the canon, perhaps Othello is the one which should most definitely not be played by a black actor"; after all, "if a black actor plays a role written for a white actor does he not risk making racial stereotypes seem legitimate and even true. . . . does he not encourage the white way, or rather the wrong way, of looking at black men, namely that [they] are over-emotional, excitable and unstable" (Quarshie, *Second Thoughts* 5).[12] With some reluctance, Quarshie conceded that to challenge "the racist conventions that have persisted for so long" black actors should continue to play the part—especially since, by combining "a radical re-reading of key passages" with "some judicious cutting and textual emendation," it might yet be possible to produce "a non-racist interpretation" of what he had come to think of as a fundamentally racist play (*Second Thoughts* 20, 21, 3, 7).[13]

Quarshie's reservations about the play, his deep suspicion that it cannot in the end be liberated from the prejudice of the culture that created it, have been mirrored in some recent criticism—the best of it often written by black critics who remain skeptical that a part written for performance by a white actor in blackface can ever fully escape the conditions of its production. Thus Jack D'Amico's study *The Moor in English Renaissance Drama* supports Orkin in arguing that Shakespeare invoked the negative stereotypes of the passion-driven, bestial, diabolic black man only to confound them by appealing to the contrary stereotype of the noble tawny Moor. But D'Amico nevertheless sees Othello as ultimately debasing himself by submitting to the role that Iago foists onto him:

> To those in the audience who would await a return to his barbarous self, the altered behaviour merely confirms what the black visage promised, as the seemingly noble Moor becomes . . . the incoherent savage. . . . The final paradox is that Othello is like everyone (particularly the European spectators) in his readiness to accept the negative, oversimplified stereotype of himself.   (177, 195–96)

In the view of Anthony Barthelemy this "tragic relapse to the stereotypical Moor" is tantamount to surrender on the play's part, ensuring that the audience's sympathy for Othello is only "sympathy for his struggle to escape his fate, not sympathy for what he is fated [by his colour] to be" ("Ethiops" 100, 102).[14] In an influential essay Karen Newman discovers a similar ambivalence in a work that presents Othello as "both monster and hero" (" 'Wash' " 152), whereas Arthur Little, although he finds the play sometimes "daring in its social critique," nevertheless identifies in it the outlines of an all too familiar story, since Othello "becomes in effect the first black rapist [violating] white womanhood" (92).

Little's essay is a reminder of how dangerously charged Shakespeare's tragedy can become when read from a particular position or performed for a particular audience. Most teachers of *Othello* will be well aware of how contentious its treatment of racial matters can prove in the classroom too—but in the classroom also context can be decisive. When I was first asked to lecture on the play in the early 1980s, M. R. Ridley's 1958 Arden edition was still the only widely available scholarly edition. With its interpretation of the Moor as a creature of instinct who thinks like a "not . . . very intelligent child" and its bizarre attempt (by distinguishing "color" from "contour") to demonstrate that Othello need not "look sub-human" simply because he is black (liv, li), Ridley's introduction has since become notorious as a document of unconscious racism. At the time, however, a member of the Arden editorial team responded with surprise to the suggestion that the edition had become an embarrassment and should be replaced. Insisting that the tenor of the introduction had never created difficulties with his London students, he conceded that "working where you do, you are no doubt more sensitive to such matters than I" (personal communication).

In fact, however, my teaching in New Zealand did not necessarily guarantee any particular sensitivity to the play's racial dimension. Indeed, more than a decade later, when the entrance examination for the country's universities invited candidates to "discuss some of the ways in which race contributes to the tragedy of *Othello*," it provoked a small storm of protest from high school teachers, one of whom complained to the chief examiner that although "race is an issue [in the play] . . . it is not a vital enough issue to allow students to write essays of depth in content, thought, and argument" (Silverstone 79). It might seem strange that so innocent a view of the tragedy could be asserted in a country whose politics over the previous two decades had been increasingly troubled by the racial legacy of nineteenth-century colonialism and where a controversial reworking of *Othello* by the experimental Theatre at Large troupe had recently used it as a vehicle for debating precisely these issues.[15] But it was, of course, in the territories of the former empire, where the education system successfully promoted Shakespeare as the simultaneous vehicle of British civilization and of universal human values, that the idea of a bard who stood loftily above mere politics proved most stubbornly long-lived.

By contrast, in the United States, whose independence predated the installation of Shakespeare as the patron bard of empire, *Othello* has always been liable to more explosively local interpretation. Thus the French novelist Stendhal recorded an extraordinary event during a Baltimore performance in 1822, when "a soldier who was on guard duty inside the . . . theatre, seeing Othello . . . was about to kill Desdemona," intervened to protect her: "It will never be said that in my presence a confounded Negro has killed a white woman!" he shouted, and then fired his gun . . . breaking the arm of the actor who was playing Othello (222).[16] A century and a half later, similar (though less violent) outrage greeted the first black actor to perform the role in the southern United States (Iyengar 112). The continuing immediacy of the play for American audiences was made apparent by the nationwide reaction to the O. J. Simpson scandal in 1994: when the African American football star and sports broadcaster was arrested for the murder of his white wife, journalists across the country immediately drew comparisons with Othello. By providing an explanatory template for Simpson's crime, Shakespeare's tragedy even seemed to confirm the accused's guilt, some observers claiming to recognize in him the symptoms of a particular jealous psychosis known as "Othello syndrome"—a disorder in which racial anxiety was supposedly a key component (Todd and Dewhurst). The extent of the resulting popular fascination with *Othello* as a mirror for contemporary racial controversy is indicated by the fact that in 2004 the *Google* search engine lists no fewer than eighty-eight pages of Web sites exploring the parallels between the Simpson case and Shakespeare's play.

At the same time, in an inevitable feedback, the Simpson case began to inflect reactions to the play itself, to the point where, in a somewhat hyperbolic comparison, Barbara Hodgdon was able to argue that "[m]uch as the Holocaust . . . altered forever the meanings of Shakespeare's *Merchant of Venice*, the Simpson trial . . . made *Othello* the timeliest of Shakespeare's plays" ("Race-ing" 72). Thus a number of reviewers responded to Parker's 1995 film of *Othello* as though it were a self-conscious metacommentary on the scandal—a reading reinforced by the casting of Laurence Fishburne (previously cast as the wife-beating Ike Turner in *What's Love Got to Do with It*) as Othello (Potter, *Othello* 193; J. MacDonald, "Black Ram" 189). In Britain, the Barbadian novelist Austin Clark contributed an essay entitled "Orenthal and Othello" to the program for the 1997 Talawa Theatre Company production: in it he pursued the parallels between Simpson and Othello as black men whose success in mastering the white world (epitomized by their acquisition of white wives) exposed them to racial backlash. According to Clark, the parallels between the two cases, each of which exposed white society's "psychosexual obsession with black men who lie in bed with white women," demonstrated the unchanging character of racism:

> Nothing has changed. Nothing can. [OJ's] invisibility . . . is now stripped away; the flesh of racism is added, to make him into a savage, brutish man, a black who hid his oppositeness beneath a façade of whiteness. He achieved his white destiny, but he still retained that aspect of his character. The General on the other hand is defined, even in the heyday of his municipal success, also in terms of the beast.

For Clark "racism has an enduring nature, and is perennially fixed in our consciousness and in our blood"; yet recent scholarship has shown us that in fact a great deal has changed since the seventeenth century and that Renaissance ideas of human difference were so "fluid, multiform and complex" as to make any simple equation with contemporary racist thought unsustainable (K. Hall, "*Othello*" 364). In the minds of Shakespeare and his contemporaries the very term *race* had more to do with lineage than with biology,[17] and their lexicon had no consistent vocabulary for describing or explaining the pheno-typical and cultural differences that would later be subsumed under that term. At the very least, knowledge that the play's earliest commentators appear to have been unmoved by the racial conflict in the tragedy teaches us a valuable lesson about perspective: what appears central in *Othello* (or any other literary text) is to some degree dependent on the position from which it is seen or read.

Might current readings, then, with their emphasis on race, be significantly anachronistic? Was the schoolteacher's refusal to accept Othello's color as a key to the understanding of his tragedy less perverse than at first appears? Would Shakespeare's contemporaries have responded to his story of interracial marriage, jealousy, and murder in an entirely different way from modern au-diences? Is it even conceivable, as I have argued elsewhere, that for seven-teenth-century audiences it might have seemed to be a play more centrally concerned with the corruption of master-servant relationships than with issues of race as we have come to understand that slippery term (see Neill, " 'His Master's Ass' "; " 'Servile Ministers' ")?

To answer such questions it may be helpful to reflect on the context out of which the play grew. *Othello* was written at the end of a century of unprec-edented expansion that had transformed European understanding of the globe: voyages of exploration and trade, driven by a mushrooming demand for luxury goods on the one hand and fueled by dreams of imperial glory on the other, had not only remade the world but also filled it with hitherto unknown peoples, whose appearance, customs, and beliefs seemed almost as strange as those of the mythical monsters with which the classical and medieval imagi-nation had populated the regions beyond the boundaries of acknowledged civilization. Under the pressure of alien encounter, the physical and cultural differences that would later be explained by the pseudobiology of race had necessarily become a focus of intense curiosity and anxiety. But notions of alterity, shaped as they were by a whole variety of competing biblical, theo-logical, quasibiological, climatological, and humoral theories, remained re-markably fluid. Othello's identity as a Moor would have been capable of many different constructions. The dark skin that sets Othello apart from his fellow Venetians might be identified as the badge of inherited sin, a proof of sub-human animality, a marker of inherited temperament, the purely accidental consequence of the sun's burning rays—or some combination of these. The term *Moor* was itself a remarkably flexible one in this period. Although it could be used with a certain ethnographic precision to specify the Arab Berber population of North Africa, it was often more promiscuously employed as a religious category, referring to Muslims in general, or as a vaguely racial de-scriptor, embracing all dark-skinned peoples, including even natives of the New World (Neill, " 'Mulattos' "). Within this last group, gradations might sometimes be acknowledged among *white*, *tawny*, and *black* Moors. Thus a

Moor might be a Muslim infidel or an idolatrous pagan, a tawny Arab or an African negro. From an English perspective, a Moor might be barely distinguishable from his Turkish fellow Muslims; he might be regarded as an enemy of all Christendom or (as Queen Elizabeth's diplomacy sometimes assumed) seen as a potential ally against the antichrist of papal Rome and its most dangerous instrument, Catholic Spain.

Clearly, then, if we are to understand the significance of what would nowadays be called the race of Shakespeare's protagonist, we need to take the instability of Renaissance terminology into account. To some extent, of course, Othello's Moorishness will have been defined by the imagined geography of the play: it is set, after all, in a relatively familiar Mediterranean world, where the wonders of discovery were of less moment than the clash of civilizations between Christendom and Islam that had continued since the Crusades. The first act of the play, in which the state of Venice prepares to resist a Turkish attack on Cyprus, reminds us that the sixteenth century had seen this conflict move into a critical phase: following the fall of Constantinople in 1453, the burgeoning empire of the Ottoman Turks had pushed rapidly westward, overwhelming the Christian strongholds of Rhodes (1530) and Cyprus (1573), besieging Malta (1565), and twice invading Hungary before the century was over. Othello is conceived as a Venetian condottiere, a mercenary general employed to combat the Turks in the Cyprus wars, but as a "moor" he is ambiguously linked to a previous wave of Islamic expansion that had once conquered most of Spain. The last of the Moorish rulers had been expelled from Granada in 1492. However, the North African Moors remained a force to be reckoned with, and corsairs from the Barbary Coast presented a threat to European shipping for much of the sixteenth and seventeenth centuries, their slave raids reaching as far as Britain (Matar, *Turks* and Introduction; Vitkus, *Turning Turk* 78–79). Like the man on whom he was partially modeled, John Leo Africanus, author of the ethnographic compendium *A Geographical Historie of Africa*, Othello is a Christian convert.[18] The place that he occupies in the Venetian military hierarchy means that he is now defined by the parameters of Mediterranean conflict and by his vaunted "service" to the state (1.2.18; 5.2.337). Yet it can hardly be an accident that his nemesis is given a Spanish name that recalls the patron saint of the reconquista, Sant' Iago Matamoros (Saint James, the Moor Slayer). Shakespeare's Iago, however, is no warrior-saint but (as Othello calls him) a "demi-devil" (5.2.298), whose evil seductions compel the Christianized Moor, in symbolic terms at least, to "turn Turk" and to become the "circumcised dog" (5.2.253) whom only suicide can destroy (5.2.350–54).

In the context of contemporary politics, then, it is possible to see how the treatment of the hero was simultaneously inflected by fear of the Islamic other and by a compensating hatred of Catholic Spain. However, the imaginative boundaries of the tragedy are not confined to its Mediterranean setting; for in the person of Othello, sneered at by Roderigo as "the thicklips," "an extravagant and wheeling stranger / Of here and everywhere" (1.1.65, 134–35), and caricatured by Iago as "an old black ram" (1.1.65, 87), Shakespeare seems to have envisaged a sub-Saharan African, who derives from regions as remote and exotic as those of the New World itself. As we learn from the romantic tales with which he wooed Desdemona, the Moor's origins lie in the strange borderlands of the new cartography, twilight zones where such bizarre wonders as "men whose heads do grow beneath their shoulders," creatures straight from the medieval fantasy world of Sir John Mandeville's *Travels*, could coexist with the "cannibals" whom Columbus had discovered in the Antilles (1.3.143–46).

Like his Moorishness, Othello's remote and mysterious origins present him in an ambiguous light. Black Africa, sometimes called Ethiopia, was the home of legendary figures like Balthazar, third among the Magi at Christ's birth, whom painters had identified as a Negro king; the black warrior-saint Maurice; and the fabled Christian monarch Prester John, whom medievals had hoped to enlist in the struggle against the Muslim enemy. Like the dark-skinned daughters of Niger, played by Queen Anne and her ladies, who traveled to pay tribute to King James in Ben Jonson's masque *Blackness* (1605), Othello, who claims to "fetch my life and being / From men of royal siege" (1.2.21–22), is invested with some of the glamour and mystery of this fantastical world. But Africa was also the original realm of monsters, the fearful hybrids first described by the Roman geographer Pliny, and the images of monstrosity that Iago projects on the Moor derive a terrifying subliminal power from that association. Thus when Othello threatens to "chop [Desdemona] into messes" (4.1.197), it is as if Iago's metaphor for jealousy as "the green-eyed monster, which doth mock / The meat it feeds on" (3.3.168–69) has become literal, so that the Moor stands disclosed as one of the monstrous denizens of the wilderness he once roamed, "the cannibals that each other eat, / The Anthropophagi" (1.3.144–45).

Moreover, if Othello conjures up his homeland as a place of mystery where an Egyptian sybil could weave magic into a handkerchief made from "hallowed" silk and "dyed in mummy . . . [c]onserved of maidens' hearts" (3.4.75, 77), his traveler's tales also hint at a more brutally historical geography, for his Africa is a place where a man can be "sold to slavery" (1.3.139). Thus, although the Moor's enslavement may reflect the common fate of prisoners in Mediterranean wars, it also acts as a reminder of the new trade in human beings that had opened up along the West African littoral in the sixteenth century. It is true that the English were latecomers to this trade, and although Othello's color seems to associate him in Brabantio's mind with "[b]ond-slaves and pagans" (1.2.99), it would not be until the late seventeenth century that an English writer could declare "the two words Negro and Slave . . . Homogeneous and Convertible" (qtd. in Orr 21).[19] Nevertheless it was partly in response to the dehumanizing pressures of slavery that the negative connotations of blackness—shaped by biblical symbolism and by the primitive fears that associated darkness with evil and death—began to develop their ascendancy over the European imagination.

The association of blackness with both innate evil and natural servitude is exemplified in Aaron, the demonic Moor of Shakespeare's earliest tragedy, *Titus Andronicus*. Early in the play, the ambitious Aaron seeks to cast off his "slavish weeds and servile thoughts" (2.1.18), yet when he calls the child of his adulterous liaison with the Empress a "thick-lipp'd slave" (4.2.175), it is as though he instinctively recognized the baby as marked for servitude by its appearance. At the same time, wishing only to "have his soul black like his face" (3.1.205), Aaron celebrates his own color as the badge of a wickedness he shares with almost all the other black characters of early modern drama. In *Othello*, although Desdemona may claim to see her husband's noble "visage in his mind" (1.3.253), Emilia makes the same equation of inner and outer blackness when the Moor confesses to Desdemona's murder: "O, the more angel she, / And you the blacker devil!" (5.2.128–29). There was scriptural authority for this equation, of course: "Can the black Moor change his skin? or the leopard his spots?" demanded the prophet Jeremiah, "Then may ye also do good, that are accustomed to do evil" (Jer. 13.23 [Geneva Bible]). In the biblical tradition blackness was not just an analogical metaphor for ingrained sinfulness but the visible demonstration of its presence. It was, moreover, strongly associated with sexual transgression, since its origins were supposed to lie in God's curse on the wickedness of Ham. The travel writer George Best explained the color of "all these black Moors which are in Africa" as evidence of a "natural infection" visited upon Noah's son when he flouted his father's prohibition against copulation in the ark: "God would a son should be born [to Ham] whose name was Chus, who, not only [him]self, but all his posterity after him, should be so black and loathsome, that it might remain a spectacle of disobedience to all the world" (qtd. in Hakluyt 263–64).[20] In Jeremiah, the black sins that cannot be hidden from God are of the same character: "Therefore will I discover thy skirts upon thy face, that thy shame may appear. I have seen thy adulteries, thy neighings, the lewdness of thy whoredom, and thine abominations" (Jer. 13.26–27 [Geneva Bible]). Somewhere behind Iago's obscene characterization of Othello as a rutting "barbary horse," Shakespeare's audience members will have heard these bestial "neighings" (1.1.110), prompting them to recognize something grossly improper in the act of miscegenation ("[f]oul disproportion, thoughts unnatural" [3.3.237]).

The powerful strain of biblical imagery on which Iago draws was often reinforced by a habit of climatological and humoral theorizing that ascribed hot, passionate temperaments to the denizens of sweltering southern regions, which helped color the frequent pseudoethnographic caricatures of black Africans as anarchic, passion-driven, lustful and dangerously jealous people, closer to beasts than to human beings. Thus, for example, in Francis Bacon's *New Atlantis*, the Spirit of Fornication is said to take the form of "a little foul ugly Ethiope."[21] Iago exploits stereotypes of this kind, not just in his images of bestial appetite but in his stigmatization of Othello as a "lusty" adulterer (2.1.293), an "erring Barbarian" whose promiscuous desires can only confirm the irrational nature of a people notoriously "changeable in their wills [i.e., sexual appetites]" (1.3.356, 347). But his assumptions hardly go unchallenged, for the oldest and most authoritative geohumoral theories would actually have supported Desdemona's belief that the torrid southern climate would burn up the hot and moist humors liable to cause jealousy, leaving the African temperament cool, dry, and melancholy: "I think the sun where he was born / Drew all such humours from him" (3.4.30–31). Africans, according to this belief, were naturally wiser, more constant, and more restrained than northerners whose cold environment left them prey to the passionate influence of hot, moist humors (Floyd-Wilson, esp. introd. and ch. 6).

This, then, is the context in which we must read *Othello* if we are to assess the true significance of color in the Moor's unfolding tragedy: while there can be no doubt that early modern culture offered plenty of purchase for the bigotry that Iago successfully awakens among the Venetians, there was no single explanatory template to which audiences could automatically refer in their response to a black Moor. If there is something disconcertingly familiar about Iago's language of hate, that is because the play, in Mary Floyd-Wilson's words, "stands at a crossroads in the history of ethnological ideas" (140). *Othello*, we have come to recognize, is a key text in the emergence of modern European racial thought—a work that trades in constructions of human difference that, although they are by no means identical to those that have stained the history of our own time, are recognizably ancestral to them. What makes this tragedy so remarkable, however, is that, far from capitulating to the emergent popular chauvinism that it documents so well, it exploits the continuing fluidity of contemporary ideas to hold the question of color up to scrutiny, rendering the meaning of the protagonist's blackness intensely problematic. Thus, while Iago's opening slurs capitalize on the vulgar stereotypes of unbridled black sensuality, they are immediately reversed when Othello and Desdemona are arraigned before the senate: here it is the white woman who speaks the language of sexual passion, boasting of the "downright violence" of her feelings and openly asserting her entitlement to "[t]he rites for which I love him" (1.3.250, 258); the black man, by contrast, is at pains to deny that "appetite," "heat," or the "light-winged toys / Of feathered Cupid" have any part in determining his behavior (261–75). To the end Othello will insist on his fundamentally dispassionate nature as one "not easily jealous" (5.2.343). Far from being an example of the self-deception of which Leavis and others have accused the Moor, this claim is not only consonant with mainstream geohumoral theory but also supported by other characters: Lodovico, astonished by Othello's violence in 4.1, recalls the "solid virtue" and sufficiency of a "nature / Whom passion could not shake" (4.1.265–66); Iago himself acknowledges the Moor's "constant, loving, noble nature" (2.1.287); while Desdemona, even after she has been subjected to his first angry outbursts against her, continues to believe that jealousy is alien to her husband's nature. If anything, as Floyd-Wilson demonstrates, Iago's brooding interiority and habitual suspiciousness identify him with the naturally jealous temperament that the English were as likely to attribute to Italians as to Moors (142–46).

Shakespeare's ability to draw on a whole range of competing ideas about color partly underlies the shifting, ambiguous responses that the play had produced toward its hero; and it is this deep-laid ambivalence that in turn explains the strikingly contradictory accounts that have been offered of the play's role in the history of racial discourse. At one extreme, activist critics and directors, like the white South Africans Suzman and Orkin, can salute the play for its "transhistorical opposition to racism" (Orkin, " 'Plain Face' " 188). At the other extreme, black theater professionals like Quarshie (*Second Thoughts*), Onyekachi Wambu, and Sheila Rose Bland have seen it as deeply implicated in the history of racist thought, or denounced it as a "grotesque fantasy" (Wambu, unpub. comment) calculated to promulgate the most offensive ethnic stereotypes. No wonder that Vaughan, in the course of her wide-ranging and deeply meditated "contextual history" of the play and its reception, should find herself oscillating helplessly between the two positions: "I think this play is racist, and I think it is not." But Vaughan goes on to warn against the impossibility of escaping this conundrum, since "Othello's example shows me that if I insist on resolving the contradiction, I will forge only lies and distortions. . . . the discourse of racial difference is inescapably embedded in this play just as it was embedded in Shakespeare's culture and our own" (70). Like *Othello* itself, we may resist this discourse, but (as the play's reception and performance histories demonstrate) learning to think outside its parameters is a much more difficult matter.

NOTES

[1]Citations to *Othello* are from the Arden 3 edition; those from other plays by Shakespeare are from *The Riverside Shakespeare*.

[2]Roberts takes this quotation from British Library Add MS 22608, fol. 84v.

[3]On critical denunciations of the play's monstrosity, which are related to anxieties of miscegenation, see Neill, "Unproper Beds" ([Neill, *History*] 260–62).

[4]On the effect of abolitionism on responses to *Othello*, see Cowhig.

[5]The emotive power of Aldridge's Russian performances was apparently enhanced by his deliberate play on the parallels between black slavery and Russian serfdom (Iyengar 110; Potter, *Othello* 116).

[6]See also Marshall and Stock 265–66.

[7]See also Rosenberg 151–52.

[8]See also Duberman 138.

[9]The only important essay to engage with the play's racial dimension in the years between Hunter's British Academy Lecture and Orkin's essay—Doris Adler's "The Rhetoric of *Black* and *White* in *Othello*," published in the year of the Soweto uprising

in South Africa—grew out of the author's experience as a white teacher of black students at Howard University in 1969 at the height of the Black Power movement (Adler 248).

[10]Suzman, introducing her *Othello* on television in 1988.

[11]Quarshie's lecture was first delivered as the Shakespeare Birthday Lecture in Stratford-upon-Avon in 1998, then (in a substantially revised form) as the first of the 1998–99 Hudson Strode Lectures at the University of Alabama. It was this later version that formed the basis of *Second Thoughts about* Othello.

[12]Compare Marks's suggestion that "the tricky combination of 'strangeness' and 'kinship' [needed for the part] is best achieved not by a black actor, someone who is likely to imagine for Othello a subjectivity formed of the particular experiences of a black man, but an actor in what could usefully be called 'racial drag.' . . . A real black actor . . . has too much independent selfhood getting in the way" (116–17).

[13]Some of Quarshie's arguments had been anticipated in an important essay by Dympna Callaghan, " 'Othello Was a White Man': Properties of Race on Shakespeare's Stage," which explores in a sophisticated fashion the implications of the role's having been written for a white actor.

[14]A comparable position had been argued, albeit a little less forthrightly, in Lloyd Evans. Vitkus, though he is interested in the Moor as an Islamic rather than a black African figure, reaches a similar conclusion: "A baptized Moor turned Turk, Othello is 'doubly damned' for his backsliding. . . . He has 'traduced' the state of Venice and converted to the black Muslim Other. . . . His identity as 'the noble Moor of Venice' dissolves as he reverts to the identity of the black devil, and exhibits the worst features of the stereotypical Moor or Turk—jealousy, violence, cruelty, frustrated lust, faithlessness, lawlessness, joylessness" (" 'Turning Turk' in *Othello*" 176).

[15]*Manawa Taua / Savage Hearts* was performed by Theatre at Large in 1994. Disputes within the company over the politics of this play subsequently resulted in an embargo on publication. See Silverstone 84–90 and Neill, "Post-colonial Shakespeare" 181–84.

[16]Only slightly less extravagant was the interjection of an audience member responding to Edwin Forrest's Iago in 1825: "You damn'd lying scoundrel, I would like to get hold of you after the show is over and wring your infernal neck" (*Othello* [ed. Hankey] 1).

[17]See, e.g., K. Hall, *Things*; Hendricks, "Civility"; and Boose, " 'Getting' " 35–54.

[18]For evidence that Shakespeare made use of this work, in the translation by John Pory (1600), see Whitney; Bullough 208–11.

[19]Orr quotes from Morgan Godwyn, *The Negro's and Indians Advocate* (1680) 3.

[20]See also Neill, "Mulattos" 364 and "Opening the Moor" (esp. 145–48). On the motif of "washing the Ethiop white," see Newman " 'Wash' " and also Massing.

[21]By contrast the Spirit of Chastity is said to have "the likeness of a fair beautiful Cherubim" (Bacon sig. D2v).

Rememorializing Othello:
Teaching *Othello* and
the Cultural Memory of Racism

Francesca T. Royster

More than any other of Shakespeare's plays, *Othello* demands a method of teaching that bridges the past with the present. Many students know about *Othello* even if they haven't read it. Perhaps this is because in our culture, the story of *Othello* is often retold as a story of the black experience in white culture. It is a story told to warn us about the dangers of miscegenation, of multiracial living, of trust and alliances between the races, and especially of the inherent guilt of the black male predator, from nineteenth-century American minstrel shows like Maurice Dowling's *Othello Travestie*, to O. J. Simpson to the recent film *O*. We might consider as well its echoes in a description of a "routine" police stop involving a black man and a white woman. In the essay "Police Brutality: Portent of Disaster and Discomforting Divergence," the critical race theorist and lawyer Derrick Bell gives the following narrative from one of his white female students, a top student at the Harvard Law School who was also getting her medical degree. The speaker and her lover, John, a black man, are pulled over by the police in Westport, Connecticut, a very affluent and very white suburban enclave:

> A police car came up behind us, seemingly out of nowhere. Its flashers and siren were on. It was June 1985. Fear, disgust, anger, and then that learned pervasive calm affected each of us in sequence. We did not need any words. We both knew the routine far better than we wished we did. But there was a twist this time. Neither of us was surprised when the cop approached the car. Neither of us was surprised when, instead of saying, "May I see your license and registration, sir," the cop reached in the window, unlocked the door and pulled John from the car. Neither of us was surprised when he threw John against the car and ordered him to spread his legs, sprinkling the sentence with various and assorted profanities and comments about "niggers" and "nigger lovin' White sluts." Neither of us was surprised by the body search. We were not even surprised when the cop removed his gun from his holster, having uncovered no weapon from John's person. We knew better than to speak or ask questions. As far as we were concerned, these were not fellow human beings.
>
> But we were surprised when the cop placed the gun not by his side, or against John's back or abdomen, but against his right temple. Now all the cop wanted was an excuse, any excuse, to pull the trigger. Neither

John nor I dared even move our eyes. I sat stone still. He did not flinch. I knew that if I sneezed or burped, they would blow my man away.

Now that they had a gun to John's head, they wanted to talk. Where were we from, where were we going, whose car was it, did I have any identification, did I know this man, for how long, why were we in Westport, etc., etc.? The gun never moved. When they asked me for my license (they had already discovered John's during the body search) I asked if I could reach down to get it or if they would prefer to get it themselves. I told them I was afraid to reach down. "Why is that, ma'am?" the "officer" responded. The other cop came around and retrieved my purse. He pulled out the wallet. He did not search the bag. The partner returned to the patrol car. The other cop's gun remained ready to fire into John's right temple. And the boy in blue just smiled on. Clearly, we had made his day.

About five minutes later, the partner returned. "They do own the car," he mumbled. The gun was placed back in the holster. Then, I received the requisite apology. After all, I was the White woman with the registration and had a medical school ID. The trespass had not been the gun at John's temple, but the ten-minute delay I suffered as a result of "a police computer error." Clearly, John was still a "nigger," but I was apparently no longer a "nigger lovin' slut."   (92)

The scripted quality of the police search—"We both knew the routine far better than we wished we did"—speaks of the ways that we find public life influenced by cultural narratives of racial mixing like *Othello*. As in *Othello*, both members of the couple are under heightened moral scrutiny by the people around them because of their interracial coupledom. In the play, Iago believes that Moors are "changeable in their wills" (1.3.339–40) and that Desdemona is only driven by lust and youth: "When she is sated with his body, she will find the error of her choice" (1.3.342–43).[1] Iago tells Roderigo that "[i]t cannot be long that Desdemona should continue her love to the Moor— put money in thy purse—nor he his to her" (1.3.335–37). But other characters in the play participate in the scrutiny of the lovers as well. The fascination with their love (and lovemaking) that we see reflected in Cassio's phallic wordplay in 2.1—"Great Jove, Othello guard, / And swell his sail with thine own powerful breath, / That he may bless this bay with his tall ship, / Make love's quick pants in Desdemona's arms, / Give renewed fire to our extincted spirits, / And bring all Cyprus comfort" (2.1.78–83)—eventually turns to disgust. By play's end, Graziano concludes that Desdemona and Othello's marriage killed Brabantio, and this interpretation gets no correction from the other people on stage: "Thy match was mortal to him, and pure grief / Shore his old thread in twain" (5.2.212–13).

We see how easily idealized white womanhood can fall from its pedestal when associated with blackness. This guilt by association reveals anxieties about the potential monstrosity of female desire, white or otherwise. Desdemona's desire, like the woman's in the police search, is viewed by those in control as treasonous and unnatural—at least for the moment.[2] Brabantio calls Desdemona's marriage to Othello a "treason of the blood" (1.1.170), and later warns Othello to "[l]ook to her" (1.3.291). Yet in Bell's narrative, we also see how the white woman's social power as owner of property and as medical student still trumps the black man's in this case, even if identified as a "nigger lover." That the white woman owns the vehicle the couple has been driving restores the natural order of things. In the same way, in *Othello*, Emilia, by presenting Desdemona as the martyr to her black demon lover, vocally redeems Desdemona's reputation. She says, when learning of the murder, "O, the more angel she, and you the blacker devil" (5.2.140). In the police-search narrative, the couple's fear and intimidation are staged, choreographed, and manipulated during the search for the entertainment of the officers. This theater seems to have a cathartic effect for the officers, who are then able to continue with ordinary police business. And *Othello* too has been produced as a means to work out larger cultural anxieties about blackness, treasonous daughters, and failed marriages. The play was one of several plays performed as part of the celebration at Princess Elizabeth's wedding to Prince Frederick of Heidelberg in 1612-13 (Potter, *Othello* 12). Whether *Othello* was chosen because of its past popular and commercial success, its shock value, or its wedding theme, the play's tragic suicide and murder of a black man and his highborn wife is nonetheless an eerie choice for a celebration. This performance featured Richard Burbage in blackface (Vaughan 94). The play has since been linked in the media to the marriage of O. J. Simpson and Nicole Simpson and to Clarence Thomas's "high-tech lynching" (*Thomas Hearings*; Garber; Starks).

The presumption of black violence and also black gullibility, vulnerability, and tragedy that is played out to its logical conclusion in *Othello* haunts people of color in our own neighborhoods, still choreographs our steps, motivates full body searches by the police when they stop a car for a missing left headlight, and moves passengers to lock their car doors as we jaywalk across the street in front of them. Teachers can use the lessons of *Othello* to talk about how people of color navigate our public and private landscapes. How do all of us in this society live authentic lives despite the scripts of racism? How do we face our fears and self-doubt? What happens when we confront institutional forms of racism? One of the biggest conditions of impossibility that people of color face every day is the isolation and self-destruction felt by Othello. In many ways, the maneuvering of these myths requires creative solutions.

In this essay, I discuss my strategies for teaching the play as well as some exercises that ask students to think of the construction of Othello as a cultural icon and the significance of that construction for the ways that they negotiate public space, especially students who are working class and students of color. I teach at DePaul University, an urban institution, located in the middle of

Chicago's Lincoln Park neighborhood. In the 1950s and 1960s, when DePaul's student body was primarily first-generation, working-class students, the nickname of the university was "The Little University under the El," because the student union and classrooms were located alongside the El train, Chicago's primary means of public transportation (Suchar 120–21). The location of DePaul fit in with its original Vincentian mission of social justice, which was to serve the poor. DePaul still serves this mission, but now the neighborhood on which the central campus of DePaul sits, Lincoln Park, is among the most valuable pieces of real estate in the city. This formerly Puerto Rican neighborhood has been undergoing a twenty-year process of gentrification. As students negotiate the campus, they are negotiating class and racial tensions that typify a city neighborhood undergoing gentrification and particularly affect students of color and working-class students, many of whom commute to school from their home neighborhoods. In this essay, I propose some ways that students can connect the issues of surveillance and racial tension that accompany Othello's presence in Venice to their own experiences on campus and off.

To understand the connection between the public spaces of the university and Othello's Venice, we might begin with *Othello*'s subtitle, *Moor of Venice*. Here, Venice functions as a nation, an ideology, and a place of commerce. Othello is a dual citizen: both "of Venice" and an outsider, a Moor, which makes him categorically not-Venetian. Yet as a military general for Venice, he lives and works in that space and fights for its integrity. Similarly, people of color are both inside and outside the places where they live, study, and work.

As a converted infidel, Othello is Venice's entrée to Cyprus, a space that is fought over by both Christian and Turk but which seems in atmosphere closer to Turkey. Othello is a familiar figure to the people of Cyprus, and he has their approval. He has also earned the loyalty and admiration of Montano, the governor of Cyprus and the only speaking Cypriot in the play besides Bianca (see 2.1.31, 35–37.) Thus he is a valuable weapon for the Christian side and makes their occupation of this island easier. Yet this relationship is never completely stable. Othello's status as a converted infidel and therefore an insider to Venetian society is precarious. Since in medieval and early modern culture, black faces often stood as signs of devils, of moral inscrutability, and of resistance to cleansing—both physical and moral—the question always stands whether Othello's conversion has taken.[3] The religious surveillance of Othello also has a larger cultural resonance, since conversos—Moors and Jews who during the Spanish Inquisition converted to Christianity for fear of banishment or death—were heavily scrutinized and watched to see if they were privately practicing their old religious beliefs.[4] Over the course of the play, as Othello falls further and further under the influence of Iago, he loses both his sanity and his confidence in his place in Venice. It would seem, by the end, that he reveals the savage and devilish nature that everyone has feared he has only hidden in the beginning.

Othello's afterlife in visual culture documents the ways in which the Othello icon circulates as a warning in Western culture. In my teaching, I show multiple examples of Othello's presence in visual culture and ask students, Which aspects of Othello's image seem to get repeated most over time? How might these images work in conjunction with the structures of racism of their cultural contexts to confirm "truths" about the black body? In what ways do we see *Othello* seeping beyond its fictive boundaries to become a part of the larger public sphere? Whether captured in paintings; in the frontispieces of *Othello* editions and nineteenth-century burlesques of the play; in the theatrical advertisements that circulated on posters; in newspapers and in magazines, such as the 1930 caricatures of Paul Robeson as Othello ("The Captious Critic"), Othello's body and especially his face are made to bear his potential for violence and destruction. In the 1857 painting *Othello's Lamentation*, signed by W. Salter (from the Folger Shakespeare Library's collection), a dusky Othello is shown humbled and on his knees, surrounded by pointing witnesses. His brow, eyes, and even moustache droop sympathetically with melancholic regret. Yet in many of the visual depictions of act 5, Othello's face, and therefore his humanity, is obscured from our view; especially when Othello is depicted as black. The frontispiece for *Othello* from *The Works of Shakespeare* (1744) depicts a featureless Othello strangling his wife, his face indistinct from his black cloud of hair (see Hanmer). In an eighteenth-century engraving by George Noble, Desdemona lies outstretched on the bed, while Othello hides his eyes with his hands.[5] We witness Othello's shame while being denied access to his face. I situate these illustrations in the larger traditions of depicting the black body in Western art, from the images of muscular black devils in medieval church paintings to Henry Peacham's drawing from *Titus Andronicus* (c. 1595) to early modern portraiture. Recent work on early modern art and culture by Peter Erickson and Kim F. Hall documents numerous early modern portraits whose staging of the power, civility, humanity, and whiteness of their sitters depends on their juxtaposition with the black and brown servants, animals, and even exotic goods that flank them in the background.[6] I also share examples of contemporary art that deconstruct the use of portraiture to stage power, especially to stage it in terms of the black body, like the works of Carrie Mae Weems, Lorna Simpson, Glenn Ligon, and Lyle Ashton Harris. These pieces can open up new possibilities for challenging past images of blackness.[7]

Next, I look at film versions of *Othello*, including those directed by Orson Welles, Stuart Burge, Jonathan Miller, Oliver Parker, and Anthony Davies's 2001 production made by the BBC, to connect them to the everyday experiences of racism, especially those that relate to moving through a fraught public space. How might we link Laurence Olivier's claim that he constructed the makeup for his 1960s version of Othello from watching Caribbean immigrants on the tram to the experience of negotiating public space for people of color in twentieth-century cities?[8] In Miller's widely taught 1982 production, how might we understand Bob Hoskins's alienated working-class Iago as a nod to the increasingly vocal dissatisfaction of the white British working class in the late 1970s and early 1980s—which in some contexts positioned itself against black citizens (A. Smith 35–36)? How does the visual motif of prison bars in Parker's 1995 *Othello* resonate with the surveillance and criminalization of black men and women in twentieth-century America? As Lisa Starks has pointed out, this film's treatment of black violence becomes all the more poignant given that its release coincided with the O. J. Simpson murder trial (68–69).

This discussion of *Othello*, visual culture, and surveillance culminates in a final student project called "Rememorializing Othello." In this exercise, I ask students, What kind of visual commemoration do you think should be launched to symbolize the life and death of Othello? Would you depict him as a warrior, wife murderer, gullible dupe, or victim of a campaign of hate, for example? Would you create a memorial to a fallen man or a warning for the people of Venice? How might you try to capture *Othello*'s complexity in a single set of images? Students might choose a scene that represents a tableau of power from the play: the senate scene in 1.3, for example, or the murder of Desdemona or Othello's suicide. I guide the class by bringing in images from popular culture, but students choose which images to use and how to build the collages. I include some supersaturated images of blackness that I've chosen myself, including some photocopied reproductions of the *Othello* images that I discussed earlier; images from popular culture like those of Tupac Shakur, Emmett Till's funeral, the Simpson Bronco-chase scene, Michael Jackson's dangling his baby from the window; and a stack of popular magazines and recent newspapers. This exercise asks students to translate their analysis of the play into a new visual narrative. In the process, they are reshaping public memory for themselves by negotiating the relation between past images of blackness and contemporary constructions of black masculinity, white womanhood, interracial desire, violence, and danger.

I first had students try this project in fall 2001, in the aftermath of September 11th. Certainly, the issues of surveillance and also fear of public spaces were on their minds. For example, one collage features a sequence of four images of George W. Bush's face, with the phrase "Justice will be done" coming out of his mouth, juxtaposed with words, "Underneath, I'm loveable." Several collages register the increased presence of the military in the public imagination during this period. One uses the advertisements for the armed forces from popular magazines that feature handsome men of color in come-hither poses—a modern version of the warrior as lover also found in the play.

One of the most striking student *Othello* collages features the central image of a suited and well-coiffed black man who happens to be the African American soul singer Luther Vandross. He is connected to a sea of hands that seem to come out of the sky by puppet strings. In his belly burn orange and yellow flames. In the original image, a cover photo from the November 2001 issue of *Savoy* magazine, Vandross is seated in a chair with his legs crossed, singing.

The students have removed the chair from the picture so that his legs appear to be twisted and his face is in an ambiguous rictus that could be either pain or ecstasy. As in the early modern portraits discussed earlier, once Vandross is transformed into Othello, his face and motives become unreadable. At the figure's feet is a cutout of a mousetrap, offering a white cup of tea as its lure—a fresh metaphor for the pleasures and danger that Desdemona might offer for Othello. A white, disembodied hand rests on Othello's shoulder—a symbol of Iago's lethal influence or the hand of the Venetian state, perhaps? From the right corner of the poster lurks an eye, wide open. The eye competes for our attention. It is as big or bigger than Othello's head, and it is cut round, as if peering through a peephole. The eye is topped with the words "Being watched" in black, white, and yellow lettering. This eye, juxtaposed with the image of Othello on strings nicely conveys the dynamic of surveillance in the play and the ways in which Iago's paranoia and the fears of the Venetian state compete with Othello's pain for our sympathy. The poster is mostly in black and white but is interrupted by startling bursts of color, including a cutout of a close-up of a strawberry, its fleshy surface resembling a pink tongue. Other images form the cultural contexts from which we understand *Othello* in the twenty-first century: an African mask, a grouping of black and white World War I soldiers, a smiling and relaxed Michael Jackson chatting on a talk show, and *New Yorker* cartoons depicting the woes of marriage.

Finally, in this exercise I ask the class to strategize how they would use public space in the memorial. Where would they post this work? How do they want their audience to receive it—as part of a ritual like a funeral or wake? in an art museum or a gallery? as a part of their everyday life, in a subway or a supermarket? DePaul students might choose one of the spaces on the border of university space and city-commercial space: Dominick's grocery store. The store is located on a busy corner between Fullerton Avenue and Sheffield Avenue, a few steps from the Fullerton El train station as well as from the DePaul library and classrooms. It is clearly a commercial space—a high-service grocery store with a Starbucks, gourmet deli, salad bar, flower stand, and snack bar. On any given day, one might see mothers with strollers, dentists from the office across the street, and the blue-uniformed train conductors from the Fullerton El stop. The store also clearly courts DePaul students and faculty and staff members as its customers. It sells DePaul T-shirts and mugs, and the ebb and flow of its business mirrors the academic school day. Outside the store, it is common to see different forms of urban display: sellers of *Streetwise*, a newspaper that raises funds for the homeless; petitioners for Greenpeace; people stepping out to smoke or to make a cell-phone call. This store is one of the signs of how urban schools like DePaul use the city as an "extended campus" (Suchar 144). Moreover, because some DePaul students of color have reported being followed or watched by security guards in the store, this setting might provide a rich location for the study of racial surveillance. How would the display of the rememorials reflect both an imagined

Venice and real social spaces? Since the students are working in small groups, they must negotiate with one another about which images best express their vision of the play.

In my own work, documented in my essay "Everyday Use; or, How I Stole Othello and What I Did with Him," I have integrated contemporary public spaces like the mall and grocery store into my analysis of the Othello icon through performance art. I encourage students to participate in a similar form of direct action by posting their pieces in a chosen public space outside the classroom and then documenting the responses to their work. Some possibile locations might include on-campus public spaces like corkboards, and common spaces in the dorm or lunchroom. They could also consider larger public venues like the Web, a subway platform, or a light post. The students should justify their choice of spaces and their expectations of their audience. I ask them to observe and note some of the reactions to their piece over the course of a few hours. How long does it take for someone to notice the piece? What were the reactions? What happens to the meaning of the work when it is separated from the original context of the play and our classroom? The results are then written in the form of personal narrative, journal, or ethnographic report.

While "rememorializing Othello" confirms Shakespeare's iconographic status and continuing influence on contemporary culture, it also puts students in the role of re-creating and shaping public memory. By reaching outside the classroom, this exercise puts Shakespeare in the context of the changing city. More generally, it explores the impact of gentrification and location on the experiences of learning. This is one way teachers of Shakespeare might nurture the experiential knowledge and analysis that their students bring with them.

NOTES

[1]Citations to *Othello* are from Greenblatt's edition.

[2]For a discussion of Desdemona's desire as excessive, see Newman, " 'Wash' " 149–53.

[3]Examples of medieval and early modern paintings and icons depicting devils and demons as black are in Devisse 13, 77, 83, 212. Blackness was not always connected with evil in medieval and early modern visual culture, of course. Peter Erickson points to the tradition of depicting Saint Maurice as both heroic and black skinned (" 'God' " 330), and the many examples of Western art from this period depict a black Saint Gregory and black Madonnas. However, as Erickson also explains, the black Saint Maurice could be read more ambiguously as a means to highlight white heroism by contrast (" 'God' " 330–31). For a general discussion of the connection between blackness and evil in medieval and early modern theater, travel, and religious texts, see Barthelemy, *Black Face* (esp. 1–17) and Jordan 3–43. For analyses of *Othello* in the context of these associations, see Newman, " 'Wash' "; Neill, "Unproper Beds"; Bartels,

"Making More"; and P. Parker. For a thoughtful and comprehensive analysis of the image of blackness as morally and aesthetically unclean, see K. Hall, *Things* 62–122.

[4]On early modern English familiarity with and anxiety around conversos, see Matar, *Turks* 19–42.

[5]Michael Neill includes a reproduction of Noble's engraving in his seminal essay "Unproper Beds" (386).

[6]On the staging of raced nobility in early modern portraiture, see Erickson, " 'God' " 315–45; K. Hall, *Things* 211–53 and " 'Troubling Doubles.' "

[7]For useful resources for reproductions of recent art by African American artists on this topic, see Golden; Willis and Williams; and Willis, *Reflections*.

[8]In a July 1964 interview in *Life*, Olivier tells Richard Merryman, "It's terribly hard to say what they were like, those boys from Morocco. The whole thing will be in the lips and the color. I've been looking at Negroes' lips every time I see them on a train or anywhere, and actually, their lips seem black or blueberry colored, really, rather than red. But of course the variations are enormous. I'll use a tiny touch of lake and a lot more brown and a little mauve" (qtd. in Tynan 88). It is striking that in this interview, the lips are the only body part that Olivier discusses "getting right," lending them the power of a fetish. Olivier's confession that he watches black people's lips on buses evokes M. R. Ridley's often cited comparison of Othello with a Pullman train conductor, in his introduction to the 1958 Arden edition of the play.

"Your Own for Ever":
Revealing Masculine Desire in *Othello*

Nicholas F. Radel

Like *Romeo and Juliet*, *Othello* seems to be easily explained by modern conceptions of sexuality. The play is a love tragedy ostensibly about a heterosexual couple, and to the extent that other kinds of desires factor into the plot, they seem to constitute perverse others to normative heterosexual functioning. Increasingly, popular performances negotiate Iago's opaque motives around modern responses to homosexuality, whether same-sex desire is explicitly dramatized or not. Oliver Parker's 1995 film, for instance, reveals a repressed homosexual desire in Iago that leads him to destroy the salutary coupling of Othello and Desdemona (Burt 241). And on the opposite end of the spectrum, the recent film, *O*, directed by Tim Blake Nelson (2001), simply writes out of the story problematic revelations of desire between Hugo, its Iago character, and O, its Othello, with the result that only heterosexuality seems to qualify as genuinely erotic in either the characters or the film. But such interpretations are not historically accurate, for they attempt to romanticize and stabilize the play's disorderly heteroerotic energies by anachronistically imagining its homoerotic ones as modern homosexuality, marginalized or silenced. It is not homosexuality that is relevant to *Othello*, but sodomy—a category of sexual offense not limited to same-sex activities but referring to almost any sexual misconduct that interferes with usual social alliances and procreative marriage arrangements. Studying the play becomes, then, an excellent way to introduce students to historically accurate understandings of same-sex desire and its place in the early modern period.

To address the historical anachronisms imposed on the play by twentieth-century constructions of homosexuality, I focus on Iago. By stressing the presence and legitimacy of his (potentially) eroticized relations with other men, I try to impress on my students two ideas that only seem paradoxical. First, same-sex desire is fundamental to understanding the social world of the play. As Alan Bray long ago suggested, the early modern period did not recognize a divide between homosexual and heterosexual identities, nor did it separate the sexual and social as scrupulously as we do (*Homosexuality* 69; "Signs" 40, 42–44). The relevance of these ideas for *Othello* has been carefully argued by Robert Matz. Second, homosexuality is not an appropriate concept for describing Iago or anyone else in the play. As Jonathan Dollimore has brilliantly argued, any desire Iago might feel for Othello must be read within the triangulated structures of their relationships both to Desdemona and Cassio, for male sexual behavior in the play is not external to but inscribed in early modern social structures such as male bonding and marriage. Indeed, disorder in sexual behavior, such as Iago's jealousy or envy, destabilizes these structures (158). My goal in teaching *Othello* is to show students that what seem specifically sexual or homosexual issues in the characterization of Iago are best understood as part of a radically different social world. I stress the ways the play attempts to contain within discourses of sodomy the disruptions to its homosocial military bonds occasioned by Iago.

Othello demonstrates cultural notions of masculinity in terms of close (potentially eroticized) bonding between men, a bonding that is often mediated through male-female relationships. Iago abuses and exploits the rules of masculinity and male bonding in his society and so comes to be identified with sodomy, a historically specific discursive category that only seems similar to modern homosexuality. Early modern masculinity was, to quote Bruce Smith, "a matter of contingency, of circumstances, of performance" (4). Its signs were not immutable but open to interpretation. To be a man was to control these signs and, more particularly, as work by both Lorna Hutson and Mark Breitenberg shows, to demonstrate one's masculinity by effectively reading and interpreting one's relation to other men and women (Hutson 64–76; Breitenberg 175–201). Iago becomes associated with sodomy not because he desires other men but because he exploits his superior ability to read and control the signs of masculine identity to serve himself, disrupting, in the process, normative social relations. In teaching the play, I strongly emphasize Bray's point that sodomy did not describe a subject position that one supposedly exercised on one's own behalf (as presumably modern sexualities do). Rather, it was an accusation used to color and tarnish people when their behavior could be interpreted as a threat to appropriate social functioning ("Signs" 51). Sodomy described sexual behavior that actually was or was perceived to be socially disruptive; it was emphatically not a synonym for normative (and always potentially erotic) male bonding. Its appearance as a symbolic construct in *Othello*, in particular its connection to Iago, signifies the anxiety of the play, its creator, or society about the inherent "instability of homosocial bonding" (Dollimore 158).

To introduce these ideas, I rely on Eve Kosofsky Sedgwick's notion of the homosocial triangle, in which relations between men are established through their relations to women (21–27). In her reading of the *Sonnets*, Sedgwick shows that male desire for women does not simply replace affection between men but often provides a ground of competition and alliance that helps define and consolidate male relations and masculinity itself (35). Her work helps students see that male relations in the period do not exclude erotic desire but in fact encode it. I highlight these ideas from the beginning of the play, in the triangular structure of Iago's mercenary relationship to Roderigo.

Careful analysis allows students to see how Iago uses Desdemona in constructing this relationship and, more important, how discursive constructions of women might generally facilitate masculinity, male bonding, and desire in the early modern period. This particular bond is insalubrious, but it reveals one way masculinity is defined in the play. And it is charged with male desire. "Let us be conjunctive in our revenge against [Othello]," Iago tells Roderigo, using a term, "conjunctive," that connotes symmetrical identification through their planned uses of Desdemona (1.3.367–68).[1] What I ask students to see here is that masculine desire emerges as a function of the characters' joint imagining of an act of sexual copulation, one between Roderigo and Desdemona: "If thou canst cuckold [Othello]," Iago says, "thou dost thyself a pleasure, me a sport" (1.3.368–69). Iago and Roderigo's relationship is predicated on an explicit erotic identification of their own masculinity with the uses of Desdemona's body: "Come, be a man!" Iago challenges. "I have profess'd me thy friend, and I confess me knit to thy deserving with cables of perdurable toughness" (1.3.335, 336–38). To be a man is to be conjoined to other men in understanding how to interpret—literally how to know—and use women (Breitenberg 178–84). It is a lesson in the potentially misogynic structure of early modern masculinity that Iago teaches Roderigo throughout these scenes, a lesson that he will use to greater effect later. But even though Iago contorts triangular structures for his own ends, he is able to do so because the privileging of masculine desire and male bonding within these structures was itself a normative and unremarkable sign of masculinity in the period. Indeed, I point out to students similar triangulations that benefit other, less unscrupulous men again and again in *Othello*.

My primary purpose is to show that the relationship between Iago and Roderigo clarifies what only seems counterintuitive: exemplary masculinity in the early modern period did not depend on a paranoid exclusion of desire in relations between men, as it may, perhaps, for us; it depended at least in part on bonds that established a proper distance from women and facilitated men's control of them. Understanding these issues helps students see how masculinity in Shakespeare is constructed along fundamentally different lines from contemporary versions.

I also suggest, of course, that there is something not quite right in the relationship between Iago and Roderigo, something that allows it to be seen as sodomitical. In a normative scheme, a wealthy aristocrat like Roderigo might well assume access (including sexual) to the services of his friend and social inferior, Iago. In the right circumstances, Iago might exploit that access through a mutual understanding that does not transgress social hierarchy, which apparently was the case with King James and his favorites or any number of master-servant relationships in the period. But rather than silently assume his place in a hierarchically composed discourse of masculine friendship, desire, and access, Iago exploits the duller, more gentle man by manipulating the affection Roderigo has for him, the desire Roderigo feels for Desdemona, and any residual loyalty Roderigo may demonstrate toward Othello. Indeed, once Roderigo leaves the stage, Iago titillates the audience by celebrating his complete mastery of this foolish man: "Thus do I ever make my fool my purse" (1.3.383). That the line has its own sexual resonance—"purse" can refer to male or female sex organs—corroborates Iago's emasculation of his superior.

Nevertheless, the social, not the sexual, problem—or at least their overlap—is key. In trying to accommodate his apparently injured sense of manhood by establishing this homosocial bond with Roderigo (which serves as a test for his later bonding with Othello), Iago manipulates the (especially gendered and racial) subject positions of his age to effect a thematics of hierarchical violation that proves, ultimately, to define one world of the play. Iago demeans Othello and marks him as (among other things) alien and effeminate: "These Moors are changeable in their wills"; Othello is "an erring barbarian" (1.3.346–47, 355–56). In doing so, he uses Othello as he had earlier used Desdemona, to mark his own masculinity in his bond with Roderigo. At the same time, Iago uses Roderigo, emasculating him and reading him as if he were a woman. In other words, Iago seeks to establish his own vengeful alliance with Othello by effeminating the dupe, Roderigo. These acts display the astonishing instability of the homosocial bond, which becomes clearer later in the play when Iago successfully effeminates his social superior, Othello, to further reestablish his own masculine validity and, indeed, superiority. I try to help my students see that it is Iago's exploitation of the fungibility of these hierarchical social categories that makes it possible to interpret Iago's actions as sodomy.

Significantly, although he emasculates Roderigo, Iago himself seems to be impregnated by their exchange. The masculine conjunction that is imagined through an act of copulation with Desdemona leads to conception: "There are many events in the womb of time which will be deliver'd" (1.3.369–70). While the metaphor states explicitly that time carries and will deliver a child, Iago nevertheless claims this conception for himself: "I have't," he says. "It is engend'red. Hell and night / Must bring this monstrous birth to the world's light" (1.3.403–04). The image of male conception is monstrous, hermaphroditic, and sodomitical. Interestingly, it aligns Iago with what many critics have seen as the monstrous femininity of Desdemona and the threatening foreignness of Othello (e.g., Newman, *Fashioning*; P. Parker; and Singh), for, like these other two characters, Iago comes to represent in the play a particular kind of threat to early modern English ideals of order and hierarchy. Iago does to Roderigo what men do to construct their own masculinity and authority. The villain reads or interprets Roderigo and his social place. But instead of doing so to establish the usual or conventional sense of place and hierarchy specific to his culture and constitutive of masculinity in the period, Iago dissolves those bonds and uses his superior, Roderigo, to serve his own ends. To the extent that Iago's actions can be seen as socially disrupting normative rules of masculine behavior, they come to be described through language associated in the period with the sodomitical, for sodomy symbolically encodes the fear or anxiety that results when normative social and sexual relations are abused. Iago's inscription into sodomy, then, reflects more than his singular, deviant character. It marks another set of social anxieties in the play.

By strongly marking the place of sodomy in this early homosocial triangle, I hope, paradoxically, to distinguish it from the structure of normative masculinity and the complex place of erotic desire in that construction. Having worked through the seeming paradoxes of Iago's relationship to Roderigo, students may now be in a better position to understand some of the other performances of masculinity and homosocial bonding monstrously or sodomitically disrupted by Iago. Foremost in this regard is Iago's relationship to Cassio. It may be an oversimplification, but I suggest that Cassio represents a norm of masculine erotic desire. As is evident in his relationship to Bianca, which serves his connections with other men (including Iago), Cassio's uses of women may, like Iago's, reveal the misogynic undertones of masculine identification. But Cassio's relationship with Othello satisfies a particular kind of male desire—a desire for a place near and an intimate contact with one's superior, another male. And the bond between them is cemented by his having served as go-between for his general and Desdemona (see 3.3.70–71, 94–105).

Cassio and Othello stand in enviable relation to each other in the early modern period. They are bound in a mutual obligation as men, an obligation that has been negotiated around the love of a woman. It is a bond symbolized in the word "lieutenant" (1.1.9), which literally translates from the French as "one who holds the place of." In the symbolic world of early modern alliance, Cassio is so intimately identified with his general that, after his drunken brawl with Roderigo, he says that he "will rather sue to be despis'd" than to regain Othello's favor (2.3.277). He sees his transgressions as marks on Othello that can only be removed by his absence. Iago jealously discerns the strength and erotics of this connection and seems to understand that the relationship Cassio has with Othello, one which marks the lieutenant's status and position—even his sense of manliness—can have no second. In other words, no other man can attain the connection with Othello that Cassio has gained by helping him to a wife—unless, of course, it is the man who helps him lose her.

The paradoxes of this relationship—and its instabilities—are nowhere better illustrated than in Iago's infamous report to Othello of sharing his bed with Cassio. Few places in Shakespeare imagine homoerotic sexuality so explicitly, and Iago's lines may, indeed, provide a foundation for later, anachronistic attempts to read Iago's motivations as homosexual desire. But I encourage students to adopt an appropriate historical perspective that reveals clearly in these lines the differences between the place of early modern same-sex desire and our own. Iago reports that he recently slept with Cassio. Being troubled with a toothache, he says he lay awake and supposedly overheard Cassio reveal his secret relationship with Desdemona. In his sleep, Iago reports, Cassio gripped his hand, kissed him, and then "laid his leg / [Over] my thigh, and [sigh'd], and [kiss'd], and then / [Cried], 'Cursed fate that gave thee to the Moor!' " (3.3.424–26). Because we know that Desdemona is not having an affair with Cassio, it is obvious that these lines are in some sense a lie.

But in other senses they may be true. It is entirely possible that Iago and Cassio have shared a bed and that such sharing allows for an eroticism in their relations. This kind of ambiguity around male-male intimacy seems to have authorized same-sex desire in the period and seems to be at the heart of Iago's competition with Cassio to become Othello's lieutenant. I remind my students of another point Bray makes: the intimacy of the bedmate confers a well-established position of power in the early modern period, a position that apparently brings with it possibilities of erotic relations, even if these are always articulated as something else ("Signs" 42–43). Students need to understand that Iago's sharing a bed with Cassio and his imagining such a scenario can be read as evidence of something other than his own repressed desire. These acts can be read as part of a social system in which intimate and publicly acknowledged connections between men denote relations of power and status. If any desire revealed by Iago here is genuine, it is a desire that may also be felt by Cassio and would reflect the desire for intimacy and access to power and knowledge both feel for Othello. The anguished line—"Cursed fate that gave thee to the Moor!" (3.3.426)—may reflect not only Iago's jealousy of the relationship he imagines between Cassio and Othello but also Cassio's own fear that Iago may replace him.

When students are asked to read Iago's speech in relation to the triangulated erotics of early modern masculine relations, they can see that the possibilities for desire proliferate in it and cannot be limited to the expression of homoerotic desire by one man. Still, I emphasize that it is not the revelation of same-sex desire per se that is problematic (as it is in a modern context) but Iago's misuses of his superior understanding of the workings of desire and power. This knowledge allows for the lines to be read in a sodomitical imaginary.

To avoid limiting the desire to Iago, I ask students to try to imagine some of the many possibilities of desire revealed in the speech. Does it reflect Iago's desire for Cassio? Cassio's desire for Othello? Both are possible in the normative schemes of male bonding I have been discussing. Does it reflect Cassio's love for Desdemona or, through displacement, Iago's desire for her? Again, two positive answers seem possible, and neither is inconsistent with the homoerotic possibilities revealed. Do the lines imply Iago's desire for Othello? That is, does he figure himself in Desdemona's place as the lover of Othello? These and other possibilities are in play, since the creation of masculine identity through complex triangulations of desire in hierarchical schemes means that there will be multiple locations of desire. In other words, if men bond with men around their relationships with women, desire has to be imagined more complexly than it ostensibly is in a modern scheme, where men's bonding with women may be understood as the defining mark of their masculinity.

Equally important, however, I show students that Iago introduces doubt into the normative system of male-male alliance by reporting Cassio's supposed dream. Iago raises the troubling possibility that Cassio's relationship to Othello may be a cover for more subversive motives—an adulterous desire for Desdemona, an attempt to take Othello's place literally as a man and as a general, or even perhaps a sexually insalubrious desire for Othello (which could stand symbolically to mark these other motivations as sodomy). In short, he suggests Cassio may be using his intimacy with Othello for illegitimate ends, his own self-advancement. If Iago implies adultery, the trouble is obvious. If he suggests there is an irregularity in Cassio's desire for Othello, Iago invokes the tragic dilemma of Marlowe's *Edward II*, in which Gaveston was accused of using his erotic relationship with the king to wield and exert power out of measure with his station. Iago destabilizes normative homosocial bonding by exposing it as a location not only for negotiating social hierarchies but also for transgressing their boundaries. Iago understands the importance of place and position in normative male bonding, and he uses that knowledge to misread Cassio to Othello and, indeed, Othello to himself. Matz argues that Iago renders the friendship between Cassio and Desdemona as adultery or sodomy (266–67). The villain also, however, colors the normative erotics of Cassio's relationship with Othello as a social transgression of place and appropriate male bonding in a way that also qualifies as sodomy. Thus I suggest that the provocative, indeed pornographic, evocation of homoerotic sex in this famous moment in the play signifies more than normative erotic possibilities. It comes to signify complex instabilities around homosocial bonding and masculinity that occupy the discursive terrain of sodomy.

Of course, it is not Cassio but Iago who is involved in the transgression of place and hierarchy. It is, in fact, Iago who sets same-sex desire against other-sex desire in his pursuit of Cassio's place next to Othello and who exploits the possibilities of male-male desire to serve his own social advancement. This is an irony probably not lost on any reader of the play, but to help students grasp its significance, I direct them to one last image of sodomy in the play embodied by Iago himself: the famous moment when Iago and Othello exchange what has often been seen as mock marriage vows. This moment replays the sodomitical tensions of Iago's relationship to Roderigo and literally embodies Iago's false analysis of Cassio's actions. At the end of the so-called temptation scenes, at the climax of the play, with both men kneeling (stage direction, 3.3. 460, 462), the following exchange occurs:

> OTHELLO.   I greet thy love,
>   Not with vain thanks, but with acceptance
>   bounteous,
>   And will upon the instant put thee to't:
>
> . . . .
>   Now art thou my lieutenant.
> IAGO.   I am your own for ever.   (3.3.469–80)

Once again a scene of masculine triangulation—this time between Othello, Desdemona, and Iago—ends inappropriately. Although the tableaulike image of two men marrying seems suitable to the illogicalities (in early modern terms) that dominate these temptation scenes, this so-called marriage symbolizes the dynamics of the scenes made monstrous. If the tableau reveals masculine desire and alliance to be central to the sex-gender system of the play, it signifies simultaneously their preposterous inversion. The mock marriage vow is a sign of the multiple displacements that have occurred: Iago has replaced Cassio as Othello's lieutenant and Desdemona as the focus of Othello's interest and desire. What perhaps renders the moment clearly sodomitical is the way it articulates male desire (usually conceived in terms of place and position) through the ceremonies of marriage. What confirms the monstrosity is the threat such desire poses to marriage and reproductive sexuality. Sodomitical perversion accompanies Iago's violations of hierarchy, particularly when he so deftly reads and then mishandles his superior, Othello. I argue that *Othello* is especially significant in its handling of sodomy and masculine desire because it reveals Iago to be in the sodomitical space of disruption that he has so brilliantly imagined for others. He comes to occupy the discursive terrain he articulates throughout the play.

Othello reveals the ways male same-sex desire is fundamental to the construction of early modern masculinity. It demonstrates as fully as any play in the Shakespeare canon that masculinity is always in the process of being constructed. To be a man means to negotiate a place in a homosocial sphere that is appropriate to one's position and status, and it means knowing how to read and use women to serve those ends. At the same time, the play recognizes the fluidity of such a construction of masculinity and encodes the disastrous results that occur when someone is willing to exploit the conventions by which normative masculinity proceeds. The effect of such exploitation is sodomy, and I show students that Iago's violations against social order disrupt normative structures of gender more than of sex, which makes Iago different from the homosexual character he may seem to be in modern interpretations. That Iago's disruptions occur within a social system in which always-potentially eroticized male bonds served as signs of masculinity signals a key historical difference between the early modern period and our own.

As a final point, I emphasize that the dramatization of Iago's social transgressions in *Othello* reflects tensions similar to (though certainly not the same as) those found in the play's anxiety over Desdemona's aggressive femininity and Othello's difference in skin color. It seems to me important not to allow Iago's particular brand of misconduct to become a locus of sexual transgression that marks the nonsexual difference of race and gender.[2] My aim is to teach students that definitions of race, geographical difference, or gender overlap epistemologically with understandings of sexual behavior in *Othello*. As Karen Newman makes clear, Desdemona's aggressive femininity is marked as a social transgression in *Othello* that helps prescribe the place—sexual and otherwise—appropriate to women (*Fashioning* 86). Desdemona's resistance to patriarchal power overlaps the racial transgression of Othello's marriage to her, the marking of which, Ania Loomba suggests, helps define European cultural boundaries (" 'Delicious Traffick' " 211–12). The transgressions of that marriage also make clear racially conventional sexual boundaries. Like Iago, both Desdemona and Othello embody threats to social order revealed through the axis of the sex-gender system, and both seem open to interpretation within the discourses of sodomy. Matz makes clear that Desdemona's behavior can be interpreted in this way, and the play's increasing association of Othello with animal lust, bestiality, and magic brings him within the bounds of that objectifying category. As I have argued, Iago is associated with sodomy because he transgresses gender norms that mark the boundaries of acceptable and unacceptable sexual behavior, and, in this respect, he is not so different from Desdemona. Nor is he profoundly different from Othello, who transgresses racial or geographic boundaries that also normatively regulate and police sex. The sodomy revealed in Iago does not merely describe a species of same-sex disorder the character is associated with but an array of disorders in the sex-gender system. Iago, Othello, and Desdemona are all linked by an imagery of darkness and monstrosity in the play that suggests their actions may be understood to differ more in degree than in kind.

A profound irony of *Othello* is that Iago is able to translate the alliance of Desdemona and Othello into a socially transgressive match by exploiting his culture's fear that dark-skinned others and monstrous women may usurp places not rightfully theirs. In doing so, he seems to increase his power and place, at least temporarily. But his own transgressions of place mock his efforts and lead him to be associated with darkness, hell, and sodomy. The association of sodomy with Iago marks one more space of paranoia in a play whose dominant metaphor is the threat posed to European Venice by the dark-skinned

Turk. The point of reading Iago's social transgressions through sodomy is not to redeem him. As a character, he remains a remarkable villain, a supreme product of Shakespeare's brilliant negative capability. But he is also a sign of what would and would not be authorized socially and sexually in the period, a marker of the play's tensions about the fluidity of social, sexual, and geographic borders. In linking him to Desdemona and Othello, I guide students through the many complexities of that sign and its role in ensuring that appropriate, orderly alliance is discursively figured both as patriarchal or hierarchical and white.

NOTES

[1]Citations to *Othello* are from Evans's *Riverside Shakespeare*.

[2]As is well known by now, the word *race* and its grammatical derivatives suggest to the modern ear reified or essential categories of people based on physical or phenotypical difference. These categories do not necessarily obtain in early modern English, where the meaning of the word seems much more unstable, although it primarily denotes genealogy or lineage. (See, e.g., Hendricks and Parker 1–2.) In this essay, I use the word advisedly to reference the various subject positions that are made to adhere (especially by characters such as Iago or Roderigo but also in the discourse of the play as a whole) to Othello's real or imagined skin color or his place of origin. In deference to house style, I have omitted quotation marks around *race* and its derivatives in this discussion, but the provisional meaning for the words I have outlined should be assumed throughout. It is important not to reconstruct race as an essential category while working to deconstruct sexuality.

Improvisation and *Othello*:
The Play of Race and Gender

Emily C. Bartels

In *Othello*, just before Iago successfully prods the Moor into a disastrous distrust of Desdemona, Othello and his new wife engage in a domestic dialogue of a sort rarely seen on Shakespeare's stage.[1] After assuring Cassio that she can and will "have my lord and you again / As friendly as you were" (3.3.6–7), that she will "talk [Othello] out of patience" (3.3.23) until she succeeds, Desdemona draws Othello away from Iago and intently pleads Cassio's "cause" (3.3.28).[2] Othello at first resists her many attempts to "name the time" (3.3.62) of a possible reconciliation and then interrupts her advances by giving in. Yet in an extraordinary, seemingly extraneous moment, instead of simply accepting her victory, Desdemona chastises Othello for his interpretation of her request. In response to his assertion that he will "deny [her] nothing," Desdemona retorts that her request is "not a boon" and warns that, when she "mean[s] to touch [his] love indeed," her suit will be "full of poise and difficult weight, / And fearful to be granted" (3.3.75–76, 80–83). Othello reiterates his intent to "deny [her] nothing" (3.3.83) and asks to be left alone. Desdemona then contemplates denial herself ("Shall I deny you?"); rejects that possibility with an emboldened "No" (3.3.86); and exits, proclaiming that, whatever Othello is, she is "obedient" (89).

Desdemona's pursuit of Cassio's cause comes at an opportune moment for Iago, supplying useable ocular proof of the attachment between Desdemona and Cassio that Iago seeks to taint. Shakespeare positions the exchange between the shaky beginnings and the startlingly effective follow-through of Iago's attempts to corrupt the Moor's vision of his wife. Immediately before, Iago tries to excite Othello's suspicions by emphasizing how "guilty-like" Cassio has seemed to "steal away" from Desdemona on Othello's approach (3.3.39). At that point, Othello does not yet latch onto Iago's insidious implications. Instead of obsessing over the suggested "guilty" exit, he gets caught up in confirming whether or not Cassio was indeed the sighted party. Once Othello and Desdemona have sparred over the reconciliation, however, Othello begins to press Iago on the meanings of his barbs. He asks why Iago is so interested in Desdemona's history with Cassio and raises the question of Cassio's "honesty" (3.3.102). Othello returns as well to what he heard Iago say earlier ("I heard thee say even now thou lik'st not that, / When Cassio left my wife" [3.3.110–11]) and seeks to know what has been repressed or suppressed.

Poised in the midst of Iago's escalating invasion of Othello's psyche, the negotiation between Othello and Desdemona thus seems to catalyze the forthcoming change of mind and heart that Iago has plotted. Yet if we read and teach that dialogue solely as fuel for Iago's fire, we flatten its significance to one of the play's central questions: why is Othello, who otherwise loves his wife, willing to believe Iago's lies? To be sure, Desdemona's mediation for Cassio seems to give those lies some substance. But in a world where mediation provides the order of the day, her intervention does not account for the incredible leap of faith, that is, for the astounding lack of faith, necessary for one to imagine that advocating for Cassio means committing illicit sexual acts with him. Moreover, if the dialogue between Desdemona and Othello serves merely to support Iago's fictions, we have no way to make sense of the coda, the superfluous chiding that Desdemona voices after Cassio's suit is resolved.

To my mind, the scene is crucial dramatically not because it furthers Iago's schemes but because it interrupts and supplements his guiding narrative, at once augmenting and challenging its terms. That is, the interaction exceeds the frame of meaning that Iago would impose and emphasizes domestic tensions that he manipulates but neither creates nor controls. For the exchange embodies and amplifies a subtle play of power between Othello and Desdemona that has been emerging with their love. We can interpret the dynamic as a clash between a husband who would dominate his wife and a wife who would express her voice, will, and desire or between a military leader who is uncomfortable with his domestic and erotic roles and a woman who, he fears, might "make a skillet of [his] helm" and require more of his "speculative and officed instrument" than he can flesh out (1.3.268, 266). But however we articulate the conflict, it adds a crucial credibility to Othello's otherwise unfathomable transformation. We may be more willing to suspend our disbelief in Othello's fear that he has lost his wife's chaste body to Cassio if we are first reminded of the ominous, though subtle, disturbances already embedded in the marital relation. It is precisely because Othello's too easy ingestion of the "green-eyed monster" (3.3.168) is framed by the domestic dispute that his transformation appears as the exclusive result neither of an extraordinarily persuasive insider (Iago) nor of an extraordinarily vulnerable outsider (Othello). It derives at least as much from the more ordinary and less predictable phenomenon of domestic dis-ease.

The content of this exchange is obviously essential to an interpretation of the play. But the exchange is also useful pedagogically because it brilliantly illumines the improvisational edges of dramatic speech and action and so provides a ready vehicle for the exploration of dramatic form. Generally, students have access to Shakespeare through printed, ostensibly stable and authoritative texts, such as *The Riverside Shakespeare* or the self-affirming Signet Classics series instead of through theatrical performance. They are therefore likely to approach the plays as if the characters, speeches, and actions exist in a fictional world that is consistent rather than conditional, established rather than evolving. Students are inclined, that is, to imagine that when Othello first appears in act 1, he is as likely to fall for Iago's schemes as he is in act 3 or that, once Iago voices his terms, Desdemona can only play into his script.

Undergraduates may not understand that although we may know in advance what Othello will say after "It is the cause" (or Hamlet after "To be or not to be"), Othello (like Hamlet) does not. Unfamiliar with the spontaneity of performance, they may not see drama's persuasive illusion as a dynamic in the making and not simply a dynamic already inalterably made.[3]

This problem is actively compounded by a play such as *Othello*, some of whose characters market stereotypes as a transparent touchstone of meaning and action. Throughout *Othello*, citizens on the sidelines of Venetian society attempt to color the images of Othello and Desdemona with a prescribed, easily iterable shame. Iago, Roderigo, and Brabantio produce Othello as a "lascivious Moor" (1.1.125), a "Barbary horse" (1.1.111–12), and an "extravagant and wheeling stranger" (1.1.135) who neither comprehends Venice's "country disposition" (3.3.203) nor deserves Venice's women. They simultaneously implicate the outspoken Desdemona as sexually, deceptively, even treasonously complicit with the Moor in "making the beast with two backs" (1.1.116). Instructors might add historical contexts to these impressions to establish more complicated parameters of such features as race and gender. But if we do so without underscoring the partiality and contingency of any given history, our efforts may exacerbate the problem. In an attempt to model their critical strategies on ours, students may reach outside the text at the expense of what's inside. In order to interpret the Moor Othello's strangely deteriorating character, they may rely on a vague or studied set of explanations they assume the Renaissance would have of the Moor as a type. Similarly, students may adhere so strongly to a belief that Desdemona necessarily typifies the chaste, silent, and obedient wife of prescriptive Renaissance discourse that they will overlook her unorthodox insistence on her will and way.

As a starting point, we need to stress that characters and actions are defined first and foremost by particular interactions inside the play, even as those characters and actions take shape against codes and values that circulate outside. Because of its seemingly superfluous coda, the exchange between Desdemona and Othello almost begs to make the point. In announcing itself as supplementary to the requirements of plot, the dialogue compels us to view the story and its inscriptions of race and gender as not given but made—and made not simply by Iago, the master of plot, but also by the unlooked-for interactions that arise, as if spontaneously, from contingency, coincidence, and chance.[4] It teaches us how to read the play against the grain of stereotypes, to read the Moor as a Moor, the wife as a wife. How, then, can we unveil the flexible immediacy of this dramatic moment while bringing it into contact with the larger issues and contexts that give it poignancy and pertinence? How do we create frames of reference that allow for the improvisational underpinnings of this instance, and other instances, of dramatic representation? And how, especially, do we address manifestations of race and gender in *Othello* in a way that preserves the unpredictability of their embodiment and effect?

In the classroom, the easiest way to investigate the impact of the dialogue in question is to imagine the play without it—to imagine Iago accosting Othello without pause and to imagine Othello responding without first confronting his wife. Two films that do precisely that present a convenient, if unintentional, aid. In one, *Othello* (dir. Parker), an exotically tatooed Laurence Fishburne plays a North African Othello, enmeshed in a Venetian culture that, like his new wife Desdemona, is characterized by Mediterranean costume and accent. The other, *O* (dir. Nelson), takes place in an American South still polarized by racial discrimination. Its Othello is Odin James, a black American basketball player and the only black student attending an elite private high school; his desires are drawn catastrophically to the dean's white daughter, Desi. Both films exaggerate the ethnic and racial distance between the Othello figure and the surrounding society, offering that social dissonance as the prevailing cause of his destruction and decline. In these films, Othello is not Shakespeare's "Moor of Venice," complexly embedded in a society that is itself defined and riven by internal cultural differences. Rather, each of these modern Othellos is disastrously out of place in a culturally coherent mainstream, whether as an African in Venice or a black man in the American South.

But as these films press racial issues powerfully to the forefront of their pictures, they do so at the expense of gender and thus, paradoxically, at the expense of race. In their versions of the structurally and ideologically central scene (act 3, scene 3), Desdemona's intervention for Cassio is omitted almost entirely, and Othello's psychological metamorphosis figures solely as the product of his interaction with Iago. Although the interplay of black against white, insider against outsider, fosters a progressive politics demanding that we understand racial prejudice as a source of tragedy, the deletion of the domestic tension in this pivotal scene actually limits the range, integrity, and subtlety of the Moor's characterization. Viewed in isolation, Othello's change of heart appears inherently erratic, if not also slightly mad. Unfortunately, the films offer racial difference as the only explanation we have to fall back on. Moreover, because of the erasure of the domestic complications, Desdemona simultaneously loses her force as a participating subject and becomes the doomed object of a distorted misogynist discourse that, according to the films' unacknowledged message, a black man, and maybe only a black man, would believe. By omitting Desdemona's interventions, these two racially overdetermined representations inadvertently make clear that if we are to sympathize with the Moor or empathize with his wife, we need another frame of reference. Othello's tragedy hinges significantly on a seething racial tension, but his story does not—and, we see from the films, really cannot—stop with race.

If we return then to the omitted exchange between Desdemona and Othello, we can add the missing link of gender to the spectacle of race and recover the contingency of identity that gets acted out most obviously around the issue—and crisis—of gender roles. Across the play, the domestic relations offer a flexible counterpoint to the ostensibly static political environment whose dichotomous terms (Venetians versus Turks) at first seem categorically and racially or ethnically set. If Othello's status as Moor marks him as an isolated subject whom we might read through the established outsides of history and prejudice (and that is a real "if"), his status as husband requires that we view him in relation to his wife, through the volatile insides of domesticity and desire. In the dramatic fiction, *the husband* does not convey meaning in the same way that *Moor* (or, for that matter, *whore*) does; characters do not and, it seems, cannot use the domestic term to stereotype and condemn. In fact, in the role of husband, Othello evades our gaze in the opening act. After being "hotly called" to court (1.2.44) to take up arms against the Turks, he steps aside en route, out of everyone's sight and hearing, to "spend but a word here in the house" (1.2.48). In the meantime, Iago informs Cassio that Othello is "made for ever" (1.2.51)—that is, married—a phrase that Cassio professes not to understand. But at this moment, neither we nor Cassio can "make" Othello, the married man; we are excluded from that scene. The detour suggests what is to come as the domestic challenges the political and the unreadability of the husband complicates the presumed readability of the Moor. When the play allows us to be privy to Othello and Desdemona speaking more than just "a word" in the crucial scene in act 3, it insists on the relation and reactivity of husband to wife, wife to husband, speech act to speech act, consequence to coincidence.

Performance exercises can vividly demonstrate the relational and improvisational edges of that dialogue, as of dramatic action and character generally, suggesting grounds of cause for Othello's forthcoming transformation without boxing him into a set position as either husband or Moor. This approach can also make room for the theatrical flexibility of the script, which allows (I think *had* to allow) a number of plausible interpretations for its actors. In an undergraduate Shakespeare survey, I set up a series of performances of 3.3.41–92.[5] (We notice that Iago and Emilia are present, although we omit their parts.) My initial goal is to have students experience the tension in this scene as something vital to both the content and the performance of the play—something that exceeds the particular question of Cassio and the exposition of plot and provides a malleable crux of character and meaning. We want to confront the negotiation as a negotiation, full of unexpected and unpredictable turns, dangers, and suspense.

Starting with the premise that domestic power provides the source of conflict in the scene, I enlist two pairs of students to take on the roles of Desdemona and Othello. I direct each actor to perform an exaggerated interpretation: in the first pair, Othello is to be totally dominating and aggressive, and Desdemona contrastingly submissive and timid; in the second pair, Othello is to be submissive, next to a dominating Desdemona. From the sidelines, I prompt the actors to manifest their attitudes and relations spatially and physically, to stand or sit, advance or retreat, touch or shield their bodies from touch. As the class then attempts to decipher what motivates these perform-ances, how these characters position themselves against each other begins to register over and against what they say about Cassio. What emerges—and what class discussion then probes—is a subtle but crucial power play that propels our engagement with the scene and, eventually, our understanding of Othello's vulnerability. To emphasize the point, I then ask the actors to replay their parts as exactly as they can next to an alternative partner: the dominating Othello acts against the dominating Desdemona, the submissive Othello against the submissive Desdemona. Without this marital tension, students be-gin to see, the scenes simply do not work.

In taking the characters to extremes, the initial set of performances exposes a potentially disruptive, theatrically essential distance between Othello and Desdemona. At stake for both characters is the ability to stand their ground in the face of an advancing and resisting partner; the implications here extend beyond the practical matter of Othello's reconciliation with Cassio and the negotiation of a "politic distance" (3.3.13) to the very definition of status and self. In reversing the assignment of which partner dominates, the exercise does not dictate a single or set dynamic; it teases out two ends of a spectrum of behavior and attitude as a means of coming to terms with more nuanced possibilities in between. In the end, of course, Othello submits to Desde-mona's request, reiterating that he "will deny [her] nothing," asking to be left alone, and hypothetically anticipating a "chaos" "when" his love might end (3.3.91–92). Yet along the way, when the scene is dramatized through ex-tremes, students can see the exchange as a heated cascade of pressured actions and reactions, rather than as a revelation of foreseeable thought. And they can understand why Othello's ultimate submission to Desdemona's desires does not work here as a point of resolution or closure (despite Othello's at-tempts to make it so) but serves more radically as a poignant but unsustainable pause and as the uneasy starting point of a traumatic domestic upheaval.

The next and equally important step is to add variation in the parts to the variation between them—that is, to identify places in the dialogue where Othello's and Desdemona's roles may fluctuate, the dominant player retreating to a submissive posture, the submissive taking on the dominant. (Again, we exaggerate the performances to make the points clear.) The why here is as crucial as the where. If we are exposing the dialogue as a dynamic work in progress, we need to correlate potentially signal shifts in stance to their prompts. It is here that gender enters in explicitly as the defining, linguistically based axis in the negotiation of domestic power. Following the play's lead, I posit the destabilization of expected gender roles—males as authoritative and controlling, females as subordinate and compliant—as the source of modula-tion and stress.

To draw attention to the places where the language itself seems (on Shake-speare's part) self-consciously gendered, I regender the script: a female actor takes Othello's part, constructing him thus as female, and a male actor plays Desdemona. These new volunteers perform the dialogue again, substituting "lord" for "lady" where needed and altering names (Othella, say, for Othello) but nothing more. The class then identifies lines, phrases, or rhetorical structures that seem especially well suited to the alternatively gendered speakers. Within this frame, Desdemona's insistent iteration of "I," for example, fits comfortably as male discourse, Othello's "I will deny thee nothing," as female. We treat these gender-crossing speech acts as potential points of crisis and consider the reactions they provoke. We notice, for example, that Othello interrupts Desdemona's first barrage of pleas with a language—"I will deny thee nothing" (3.3.76)—that echoes her line, "What would you ask me that I should deny" (3.3.69). His response mimics her position as an obedient wife and points as well to the ultimate sign of her sex, the ever suggestive "nothing." Whatever the tenor of Othello's reaction, the feminization of the language disturbs his masculine presumption and signs his retreat from the competing discourse of a wife who expresses her obedience through an assaulting advance of her own free will. In the end, students inhabit or observe these gendered identities not as readable touchstones but as loaded and malleable postures, improvised constantly (and not always consistently) in relation and reaction to a particular partner or circumstance. To texture the performance further, I ask students to choose specific inflections of tone, volume, and pace as they voice particular lines and to test the impact of viable attitudes (erotic, imperious, imperative, apprehensive, and so on). However these performances take shape, gender makes the difference here, not in any set way but as the explosive undertext of domestic and theatrical tension.

Ultimately, as Shakespeare interrupts Iago's increasingly predictable plot against the Moor with an exchange that announces its own superfluity, he insists that we pay attention to the unpredictable domestic interactions. *Othello* dramatizes the story of the "Moor of Venice" in a way that defies prescription. With a single tempestuous stroke, Shakespeare, after all, remakes history by obliterating the Turks (who were, as we know, holding Cyprus at that time). In so doing, he renders moot the Venetian-Turkish dichotomy that initially defines Venetian politics in the play and underwrites Venice's embrace of the Moor, and he thus requires that we come to the Moor with unscripted brave new terms. In layering domestic complications on top of the political scene, Shakespeare insists that what counts in the world of Venice and Cyprus is not what is already on the books but what is in the making on the stage. And if in *Othello* race seems to provide the cue for the creation of impermeable social and cultural boundaries, gender provides the passion for negotiating between them, in the volatile space of performance where interaction and improvisation are all.

NOTES

[1] I have discussed Desdemona's part in this exchange and its dynamic of submission and assertion in "Strategies of Submission" 426–27.

[2] Citations to *Othello* are from Sanders's edition.

[3] I am indebted to Elin Diamond's articulation of performance as a "doing and a thing done" (4–5).

[4] Compare Greenblatt on the "improvisation of power" (*Renaissance Self-Fashioning* 222–54), which for Greenblatt is "the ability both to capitalize on the unforeseen and to transform given materials into one's own scenario" (227). Tellingly, the exchange I center on here does not figure in his analysis, which reads characters as isolated egos.

[5] These strategies have evolved out of an invaluable collaboration with the Acting Ensemble of the Bread Loaf School of English (Middlebury College). I am extremely grateful to the actors involved, especially Brian McEleney, for teaching me new ways to see, read, and teach Shakespeare.

Orders of Fantasy in *Othello*

Cynthia Marshall

Who would wish to be Othello? Duped into believing he has been cuckolded, he registers as the most unfortunate of tragic heroes. His late effort to explain himself by claiming he loved "not wisely, but too well" (5.2.340) only confirms the domestic rather than heroic scope of the tragedy. Even before his fall into suspicion and jealousy, Othello occupies a compromised position as the outsider in Venetian society, a point recent critical attention to discourses of race and ethnicity has tended to emphasize. Early in the play, Iago seems envious of Othello's success with Desdemona and perhaps of his easy confidence and command under pressure, but Iago's envy is tainted with condescension and gives way to something far more murderous. It is Desdemona herself who wishes, after hearing the story of Othello's life, "[t]hat heaven had made her such a man" (1.3.162).[1] The remark, reported by Othello, prompts inquiry into the gender ideologies shaping identities in the play and the role of fantasy in effecting action.

Othello, near the conclusion of his account of the love affair's genealogy, tells the senate of Desdemona's response to his life story:

> She gave me for my pains a world of sighs:
> She swore, in faith, 'twas strange, 'twas passing
> strange,
> 'Twas pitiful, 'twas wondrous pitiful;
> She wished she had not heard it, yet she wished
> That heaven had made her such a man.
> (1.3.158–62)

The chanting rhythms of Othello's speech do not drown out Desdemona's struggle for a poised response: "strange . . . passing strange . . . pitiful . . . wondrous pitiful." Disavowal ("wished she had not heard it") yields to participation; she craves the adventures and seeks, through imagination, to enter fully into them. Or, as the wish translates into narrative action, she seeks to participate in Othello's life. "Made her such a man" is sometimes understood to mean "created a man of that sort *for her*," and, although most editors consider this a secondary reading, it does not altogether contradict the primary sense of wishing "she had been born" a man of that sort.[2] The two meanings converge, that is, through the mystical sense of marriage as a union of identities, allowing Desdemona to take on Othello's heroism as she takes him as husband.

By giving credit to Othello's report of Desdemona's fantasy, we can make sense of her sudden and uncharacteristically bold decision to elope, what she herself calls "[m]y downright violence and storm of fortunes" (1.3.245). Although she hints that her mother similarly chose a partner independently of paternal approval (addressing Brabantio in the Sagittary, she speaks of her mother "preferring you before her father" [1.3.185]), Desdemona shocks both husband and father with her eagerness to accompany Othello to war. Critics have suggested that her seemingly open acknowledgment of sexual desire ("That I did love the Moor to live with him" [1.3.244]) raises the specter of impropriety in Othello's mind and thus lays the groundwork for his suspicion (see, e.g., Greenblatt, *Renaissance Self-Fashioning* 250). Marrying without her father's consent and promptly traveling to a dangerous outpost, Desdemona has not only "[tied] her duty, beauty, wit, and fortunes / In an extravagant and wheeling stranger / Of here and everywhere" (1.1.134–36), she has become such a "wheeling stranger" herself.

Brabantio certainly thinks so. In his view, Othello must have "enchanted her," for "if she in chains of magic were not bound" (1.2.63, 65), he finds it incomprehensible

> Whether a maid so tender, fair, and happy,
> So opposite to marriage that she shunned
> The wealthy curlèd darlings of our nation,
> Would ever have, t'incur a general mock,
> Run from her guardage to the sooty bosom
> Of such a thing as thou—to fear, not to delight.
> (66–71)

In the senate chamber Brabantio describes his daughter as "A maiden never bold; / Of spirit so still and quiet that her motion / Blushed at herself" (1.3.94–96). Brabantio would not be the first father to be surprised at his daughter's choice of a partner; the issue here goes deeper: he seems not to know her at all. Desdemona, at least as we see her in the first three acts, is not a maiden who "blushed at herself."

Of course, Brabantio could be lying, exaggerating Desdemona's timid gentility with an eye toward heightening the sense of Othello's crime, charging the Moor not only with social impropriety but also with the spiritual evil of witchcraft. Or he could be wrong about his daughter's character, either overtly deceived as he first suspects ("O she deceives me / Past thought!" [1.1.164–65]) or simply ignorant of her wishes and desires. None of these explanations can be ruled out altogether, although the apparent closeness of the relationship between Brabantio and Desdemona, together with the circle of witnessing friends and associates, makes it unlikely that Brabantio is either overtly false or altogether misled about his daughter. Rather, he has awakened to find her not only married but changed, no longer a young woman appreciative of his "guardage" but one who deliberately shucks off Venetian conventions.

In a play so focused on careening changes in character, Desdemona's transformation from timid maiden to "fair warrior" (2.1.174)—as Othello greets her in Cypress—should be considered the first demonstration of how identity can be altered by the force of passion. Her fantasy of being, or becoming, "such a man" as Othello propels Desdemona from her timid devotion to "house affairs" (1.3.146) to the boldness of her marital choice. Shakespeare calls attention to her change by having her engage in slightly risqué banter with Iago early in 2.1, before Othello's arrival in Cypress. She accounts for her behavior as "beguil[ing] / The thing I am by seeming otherwise" (2.1.121–22)—that is, she hides her anxiety about Othello behind a guise of levity. The wit and sophistication exhibited here, together with her spirited defense of the disgraced Cassio, indicate a woman empowered with surprising agency. Unfortunately, they also indicate one who transgresses the boundaries of prescribed behavior.

In *Othello*, as in all Shakespeare's plays, an elaborate code of social expectations and requirements organizes characters' actions along gendered lines. An enforced patriarchy means that men control affairs of state (the Duke and the senators are all male) and the arrangement of marriages. Women are expected to be confined in the home—alerted to his daughter's elopement, Brabantio asks, "How got she out?" (1.1.168 [see Stallybrass, esp. 135–42])—whereas men enjoy freedom of movement and choice, especially a man like Othello, the "wheeling stranger," who explains:

> But that I love the gentle Desdemona,
> I would not my unhousèd free condition
> Put into circumscription and confine
> For the sea's worth.   (1.2.25–28)

A woman who appears too available, like Bianca, or who talks too openly about sexual matters, as Desdemona does in 2.1, calls her chastity into question by suspicious males. Their suspicions reflect a system of gender ideologies—operant in the play and in Shakespeare's England—constructed on inequality and difference on the one hand and on anxiety and separateness on the other.

Psychoanalytic theory can help us understand both the origin of these ideas and how they are enforced. Freud pondered the human riddle of having a rational mind in a mortal, sexed body; as Freud realized, our personal and social arrangements for accommodating this condition have often been imperfect. Attempting to understand what we are, we tend to focus on how others differ from us, and since sex provides both means of reproduction and a source of intense pleasure, sexual difference carries particular significance. In Freud's view, male pride and delight in the penis entail a corresponding perception of female lack; the theory connects a literal sense that women lack visible external genitalia with an assumption of women's cultural, and in some cases emotional and intellectual, deficiency (Freud, "Psychical Consequences"). Although the theory identifies a condition detrimental to women's equality, it initiated conversation about the link between physical differences and social roles. Freud's fixation on the penis, for instance, suggests how the organ carries a freight of anxiety and vulnerability, and Freud himself was explicitly aware that men's concern with identifying their offspring lies behind the impulse to corral women and control their sexual activity.

Later theorists who have built on Freud's ideas provide tools for explaining the potency with which gender ideologies take hold. The French psychoanalyst Jacques Lacan has proved especially useful for students of literature because of his interest in language as a factor in psychology. Developing Freud's concept of how language traverses the split between the conscious and unconscious mind (as evidenced by so-called Freudian slips), Lacan proposes that the symbolic structures of language secure our connection to the social world. Yet the symbolic realm remains to some extent alien; just as we struggle to put our thoughts into words, we struggle to match our normal existence, which Lacan calls the imaginary, with the symbolic networks organizing culture as a whole. Further, Lacan suggests that certain aspects of human experience, which he dubs the real, remain resistant to language altogether. Also crossing the three levels of existence, and often torquing the subject in various directions, are the forces of desire. The psychoanalytic sense of desire entails more than sexuality; it names the various kinds of impetus that motivate the human subject, especially in relation to others. Significantly, the forms of desire are not preordained. Rather, they are shaped by interactions with the environment (Lacan 154–58).

Psychoanalytic theory holds that fantasy is strongly involved in developing or molding the individual subject's desires. On the one hand, Freud suggests that individual fantasies can be a site of imaginative creativity; he holds that creative writing, for instance, involves a crucial component of fantasy ("Creative Writers"). On the other hand, Lacan maintains that desires are rarely, if ever, created by the individual but instead are imposed from without by means of transferable fantasies. "Through fantasy we learn 'how to desire,'" in the words of Slavoj Žižek (118). Fantasy coordinates the individual's desire by hiding his or her submission to "the desire of the other," or the imaginary identification with some person or cause that organizes an individual's existence (Lacan 158). That is, people learn what they want by incorporating scripts of socially organized behaviors, and they make these scenarios their own by playing them out in fantasy. In this sense, a person does not so much create his or her own fantasy scripts as receive them ready-made, promulgated by the dominant forces in society. Consumer advertisements exemplify an insidious form of this sort of ideological fantasy when they attempt to sell not so much a product as an image. Perhaps because sexuality is closely related to fantasy, norms of gender identity and erotic behavior are particularly susceptible to the conditioning influence of cultural ideologies.

Othello, a play structured around erotic fantasies, illustrates their ready transferability. From the opening scene onward, the male characters seem obsessed by the image of Othello and Desdemona's sexual union; as Patricia Parker notes, "fantasies of miscegenation . . . haunt this play from its beginning" (99). Iago tells Brabantio, "An old black ram / Is tupping your white ewe," and, later, "your daughter and the Moor are now making the beast with two backs" (1.1.89–90, 115–16). Brabantio himself confesses to a glimmer of awareness: "[t]his accident is not unlike my dream" (1.1.141). Cassio, even while seeming to express respectful concern for his captain, lapses into sexual implication:

> Great Jove Othello guard
> And swell his sail with thine own powerful breath,
> That he may bless this bay with his tall ship,
> Make love's quick pants in Desdemona's arms. . . .
>   (2.1.77–80).

Later, Iago feeds Cassio's imagination, attributing Othello's retiring at an early hour to eagerness to sleep with Desdemona: "he hath not yet made wanton the night with her, and she is sport for Jove" (2.3.15–16). Iago not only emphasizes her desirability but speaks of her as inciting sexual response: her eye "sounds a parley to provocation," her voice is "an alarum to love" (2.3.20–21, 23).

More destructively, Iago calls up in Othello fantasies of his wife with Cassio. As W. H. Auden notes, "Iago treats Othello as an analyst treats a patient except that, of course, his intention is to kill not to cure. Everything he says is designed to bring to Othello's consciousness what he has already guessed is there" (266). For Auden, the seeds of suspicion already exist in Othello's mind, where they remain latent until activated by Iago's hints. The resulting fantasies are powerful because they take root in Othello's own imagination. Iago prompts:

> Would you, the supervisor, grossly gape on?
> Behold her topped?
>
> . . . .
> It is impossible you should see this,
> Were they as prime as goats, as hot as monkeys,
> As salt as wolves in pride, and fools as gross
> As Ignorance made drunk.   (3.3.396–406)

Iago cunningly introduces Desdemona's handkerchief as a prop or prosthesis to aid Othello's imagination, reporting that he "[saw] Cassio wipe his beard" with it (3.3.440). He even creates a scenario in which Cassio, billeted with Iago, calls out in his sleep for Desdemona (3.3.414–27)—an especially interesting fantasy script because it exposes an element of homoeroticism in the activation of heterosexual jealousy. Ultimately, Iago will inflict on Othello a misogynistic vision of Desdemona's sexuality as disgusting and a racist vision of his sexual union with his own wife as unnatural (on the vicissitudes of Othello's fantasies, see Snow, esp. 391–98). The speed and power with which these visions take hold suggest Othello's vulnerability and his reliance on Iago, who is a member of the majority race, married, evidently experienced in relating to women, and a confident cynic. Yet the visions' virulently contagious quality suggests something about the culture more generally, not just about Othello.

For one thing, the fantasies extend to the audience. *Othello* holds an uncanny power to absorb and move viewers (Pechter 11–12). The play is structured so that the fiction enacted in the theater is shadowed by a further layer of imagined events—the beast with two backs, the supervisor gaping on, the captain panting in his wife's arms, and so forth—that the audience imagines, just as the characters in the play are shown to do. Because the fantasies themselves are crucial to the outcome of the plot, this imagined realm is something more than back story. Accordingly, the theater history is filled with accounts of audience members attempting to stop the action on stage. The critical history too is marked by a slippery loss of objectivity, at its most innocent a simple admiration for Iago's energy and intelligence, but ranging into grimmer notes of condescension toward Othello and indictment of Desdemona. The situation is keenly heightened by racial anxiety and its attendant woes: uneasiness about the status of the other, guilt and resentment about the history of colonialism, a sense of being judged, of being caught in a web of prejudice. Many viewers and readers find themselves, like Othello, accepting Iago's ideas—the marriage was ill advised, Desdemona would be better off with Cassio or perhaps Lodovico—not because of a conscious decision to trust Iago, although a wish to be intellectually in the know may be a factor. Rather, his ideas are accepted because of the coercive quality of ideological fantasy, its capacity to shape and order our desires. Literature, and perhaps drama in particular, holds potency to the extent it can influence audiences in this way.

Also remarkable is the sheer vulnerability exhibited by all the characters in the play to the fantasies Iago suggests: obviously Brabantio, Roderigo, and Cassio are taken in, but, more surprisingly, Emilia and Desdemona too become complicit. Pocketing her mistress's handkerchief, Emilia says, "I nothing but to please his fantasy" (3.3.301). The syntactically incomplete line—as Pechter points out, it wants a verb (116)—corresponds to her self-erasing compliance to her husband's will or, more accurately, as she puts it, to his "fantasy." This word hints that the scene Iago scripts for Othello in 4.1, in which Cassio and Bianca handle the strawberry-spotted handkerchief, originates in Iago's own fantasies involving the item. At the very least, Emilia seems unsurprised that he would crave the cloth, indicating familiarity with her partner's penchant for fetishism.

Desdemona, disturbingly, "seems to dwindle away" (Pechter 120) after Othello's accusations. Excusing him, she takes the blame on herself:

> Beshrew me much, Emilia,
> I was—unhandsome warrior as I am—
> Arraigning his unkindness with my soul;
> But now I find I had suborned the witness
> And he's indicted falsely.   (3.4.144–48)

Although Desdemona contests the charge that she is a whore in 4.1, her decision to lay the wedding sheets on the bed carries a self-sacrificial note. Her last words are ambiguous: she both proclaims her innocence ("O, falsely, falsely murdered! . . . A guiltless death I die" [5.2.118, 123]) and accepts the blame for Othello's deed ("Nobody; I myself" [5.2.125]). The great outward arc of development that takes Desdemona from her father's guardage to her bold warrior role in Cypress collapses back, despite her considerable verve and spirit, into anxious timidity and enforced submission to masculine authority. Character development is traced onto the formal structure of the play as Desdemona boldly exits her father's home and familiar Venice only to find herself trapped within another man's imagined and literal space.[3]

That her fantasy of self-authorization brought her to the space of her death does not mean, however, that the play simply enacts the patriarchal morality lesson Thomas Rymer identified. For if the female characters participate to some extent in patriarchal ideologies, their involvement is contradictory enough to suggest partial resistance. Emilia forcefully contests the charges against Desdemona, who fights for her life in 5.2, even if she does partially excuse Othello. In fact, although the main action establishes a problematic code whereby men must bond together to resist the wiles and sensual excesses of women and although the critical history suggests that this view extends to many readers and viewers, there is also evidence in the play of an altogether different role that fantasy plays for women. The dominant ideology, coercively misogynistic and masculinist, is fostered by Iago and adopted to some degree by most every character in the play, depending on their vulnerability to its fantasy scripts. For the subordinated female characters, however, fantasy functions as an empowering means to resist the established norms and to imagine alternative possibilities.

Nowhere is this clearer than in 4.3, the only scene featuring an extended conversation between two female characters. Although Desdemona puts up a brave front, declaring, "my love doth so approve him / That even his stubbornness, his checks, his frowns . . . have grace and favour in them" (4.3.18–20), her nervousness is almost palpable in her thoughts of death (23–24), in her jumpy response to the wind (50–51), and most of all in her compulsive singing. Beyond being thematically appropriate, the song of Barbary, her mother's maid, extends Desdemona's emotions and her plight back into a seemingly lost and otherwise unacknowledged female history. The recursion of this memory through song, especially a song whose lyrics lapse into echolalia ("willow, willow, willow"), instances the presymbolic language known as the semiotic. Julia Kristeva associates the semiotic realm with bodily forms of communication, such as tears and sighs, as well as with vocalizations without symbolic contact, such as nonsense syllables ("Women's Time" 200). This sort of sound and communication characterizes infants' interactions with their caregivers and is thus associated with women in their capacity as mothers. Kristeva suggests that poetry, in its reliance on vocal patterns, draws heavily on the semiotic ("True-Real" 227), and certainly Othello's poetry is richly inflected with the semiotic register, even breaking with symbolic order at times. Still, it seems significant that a window into Desdemona's past, melancholy though it may be, is opened by the memory of Barbary's song (see P. Berry 45–46, 56–57). The memory returns Desdemona to an innocent posture, and she then questions Emilia about adultery, both in moral and theoretical terms:

> Dost thou in conscience think—tell me, Emilia—
> That there be women do abuse their husbands
> In such gross kind?   (4.3.58–60)

and in practical, experiential ones:

> Wouldst thou do such a deed for all the world?"
>   (4.3.61)

Evidently the adventures Desdemona contemplated when she eloped did not include betrayal and moral opprobrium or a spouse who would strike her. The world turns out to be larger and more complicated than she could imagine when she "wished that heaven had made her such a man." Defensively, her mind returns to childhood.

If Desdemona's imagination fails her confrontation with evil, Emilia's can rise to the challenge:

> DESDEMONA.   Wouldst thou do such a deed for all the world?
> EMILIA.   The world's a huge thing; it is a great price
>   For a small vice.   (4.3.65–67)

The moral relativism exhibited in Emilia's suggestion that everything and everyone has a price—"who would not make her husband a cuckold, to make him a monarch?" (4.3.72–73)—has proved controversial. For some, hers is simply a brief for adultery; she demonstrates herself to be no better than the procuress Othello pretends her to be in the previous scene (4.2.88–93). Auden's case against Desdemona as a protoadulteress depends on his perception of Emilia's prurience: "Given a few more years of Othello and of Emilia's influence and she might well, one feels, have taken a lover" (269). The blame here is badly misassigned. Othello, after all, has called Desdemona a whore, struck her, ordered her to dismiss her attendant, and so intimidated her that she fears for her life, a life rapidly constricting to the bed she has shared with Othello. By proposing alternative moralities, Emilia opens a space for continued consideration of the play's key issues. In imagining a different set of arrangements between men and women (4.3.82–99), she anticipates arguments advanced by modern feminists.[4] Far from leading her mistress into sin, Emilia wishes to save her life. Tragically for all involved, Emilia's subversive fantasy of a world in which women and men hold equal status has no power against the encompassing patriarchal ideology guiding the relations in the play. Her fantasy comes too late in the play, too early in the history of social reform. Yet for all that, by prompting interest, discussion, and consideration, it is not worthless.

Othello thus exhibits two orders of fantasy, one affiliated with the dominant male social group and used to enforce ideologies supportive of its continued privilege, the other associated with the disempowered female characters and key to their ability to generate new possibilities for themselves and for society in general. "Nay, this was but his dream" (3.3.428), Iago facetiously cautions Othello—yet that supposed dream turns out to hold immense power. By showing the extent to which masculine power rests on ideological fantasy, the play undercuts male autonomy and self-determinism. It illustrates the murderous potential of an indulgence in imagined truths. But *Othello* does not indict fantasy per se, for Shakespeare apparently recognized that to do so would militate against drama itself and against a potent means for envisioning personal and social change. I am suggesting a recuperation of the discourse of character, fueled by psychoanalytic theory, not out of sympathy with traditionalist or formalist approaches but because it can suggest to students a means of personal agency in the face of seemingly all-encompassing social ideologies. Just as important as learning to recognize ideological fantasies for what they are is nurturing the ability to dream up methods of resistance and reinvention.

NOTES

[1]Citations to *Othello* are from Sanders's edition.

[2]Norman Sanders glosses the line, "she had been born" (75n162). M. R. Ridley considers the grammatical issues fully: "Is *her* accusative or dative? The supporters of either view are apt to regard those of the other as obtuse. The straightforward accusative seems to me certainly right. With the dative the wish not only is unexpectedly 'forward,' but also makes the following 'hint' quite needless; and further, the use of the word *made* gives the wish an arrogance which is still more out of character, since heaven is then thought of not as just bringing such a man across her path, but as manufacturing such a man for her alone" (*Othello* 1.3.163n).

[3]In Stallybrass's terms, "the play constructs two different Desdemonas: the first, a woman capable of 'downright violence' (1.3.249); the second, 'A maiden, never bold' (1.3.94). Desdemona's subservience, enforced by her death, has already been enforced by the play's structure" (141). Although I agree that the play's structure enforces her subservience, evidence in the play suggests a changing rather than a double Desdemona.

[4]As Valerie Wayne observes, "instead of affirming an opposition between women and men, Emilia proposes that women, like men, are not so constituted as to permit sexual control by their spouses. The emergent character of her approach is espcially difficult for us to read now because our own emergent discourses ask us to be alert to gender differences and to difference within genders; yet during the Renaissance, asserting a likeness with men was an important means by which women justified some of their claims to power" (168). See also Neely, *Broken Nuptials*.

Othello as an Adventure Play

Jean E. Howard

In the one hundred years between 1550 and 1650, England vastly expanded its contact with people who were neither part of the British isles nor part of Europe but who lived in North Africa, in the eastern Mediterranean dominated by the Ottoman Turks, in India, in present-day Indonesia, and in the Americas. There had long been "strangers" (as foreigners were called) in London and the seaports along England's coasts. They were mostly Europeans who conducted trade with England or refugees seeking a haven from religious warfare in their home countries. For example, Italian merchants had long imported luxury textile goods into England, and French Protestants, or Huguenots, increasingly settled in London in the sixteenth century to escape Protestant-Catholic antagonism at home. English merchants also traveled abroad. Throughout the Middle Ages, England's biggest export was woolen cloth, which it traded for everything from pepper from Java to port wine from Spain and Portugal. Much of the trading was done at Antwerp, one of the largest international markets in northern Europe. In the 1570s, however, this market was disrupted by the increasingly virulent religious wars.

In the late sixteenth century, England began to pursue new kinds of economic activity. It sought direct access to luxury goods such as silks, furs, pepper, nutmeg, and other spices, rather than import them through middlemen. The richest and most successful members of the traditional London guilds joined together to form what were called joint stock companies, in which investors pooled resources to get a share of profits in voyages and overland journeys to far-flung ports and cities where English traders had not previously gone.[1] The names of some of the companies indicate just how adventuresome the English became. The Muscovy Company was set up in 1555 to find an overland route to import silks and spices from Persia through Russia (Brenner 13). In 1580 the Turkey Company began to trade directly through the Mediterranean to reach ports in North Africa and the Levant. The amalgamation in 1592 of the Turkey and Venice companies formed the Levant Company, the most successful and lucrative English trading company through much of the seventeenth century. In 1599 powerful members of this company helped establish the famous East Indian Company, which consolidated trade to India and the Far East (Brenner 3–23). These companies made huge profits importing Eastern luxury goods into Europe through the Mediterranean or around the African Cape of Good Hope. At the same time, the establishment of the Virginia Company in 1609 marked England's initial attempts to develop colonies in the Americas.

These developments had an immediate material effect on the London in which William Shakespeare wrote his plays. Clothing changed since townsmen and merchants increasingly had access to the silks and velvets once reserved for members of the aristocracy. Diet changed as sugar, currants, and spices became available to more and more people (see K. Hall, "Culinary Spaces"). In Shakespeare's play *The Winter's Tale*, a rustic man is sent by his sister to buy items for their sheepshearing feast. On the shopping list are currants, rice, sugar, saffron, dates, nutmeg, and ginger (4.3.35–45)—all imported foodstuffs with which Shakespeare obviously assumed his audience would have been familiar.[2] The population of London was also changing. While Italian, Dutch, German, and French merchants had long been in the city, now there were people from much farther afield. In 1600 a Moroccan ambassador, Hamid Xarife, arrived in England to solidify military and trade agreements with Queen Elizabeth's government. Morocco at the time supplied England with North African sugar as well as gold and other items from sub-Saharan Africa. This ambassador and his entourage stayed six months and became a familiar sight in the streets of London (Matar, *Turks* 33–34). A picture of this imposing man, dressed in robes and a turban and wearing an ornate sword, is now owned by the Shakespeare Institute in Birmingham, England. It has been suggested that he was one model for Shakespeare's Moorish hero, Othello.

But elite strangers were not the only ones occasionally appearing in English streets. When English ships set out for the ports of Tunis, Alexandria, Bantam, or Madras, they may have carried an English crew, but they returned with a different one. Mortality on long voyages was high, and at each port new sailors were taken on board. Eventually these men—some of them Egyptian, some Sumatran, some Indian—landed in London. Ports were notoriously multicultural spaces. Moreover, English seamen sometimes jumped ship in foreign ports or were captured by Ottoman Turks or Spanish rivals.[3] If these men ever returned to England, they did so full of tales of life among alien cultures. Some, in captivity, "turned Turk," that is, assumed the Islamic religion and even underwent circumcision, either because they had to or because they actively sought a place in their new culture (Vitkus, " 'Turning Turk' "). Some Englishmen, who could never be part of the wealthy elite who headed up the joint stock companies, saw their best opportunity for advancement to lie in piracy, preying on the ships of the many European powers, including the English, who were competing for pieces of foreign trade, especially in the Mediterranean where piracy had long been established (Andrews, *Elizabethan Privateering*, esp. 26–30).

Among the people responding to these developments were the playwrights of London. Always looking for popular tales to dramatize, toward the end of the sixteenth century they found a rich vein of material in stories about real or imagined adventures in the places where English trade and piracy had been expanding, especially the Mediterranean world where the cultures of Europe met and mingled with the cultures of North Africa and the Ottoman Empire. Some of these plays were about real people. For example, the extremely colorful life of an Elizabethan named Thomas Stukeley was dramatized in an anonymous play called *The Famous History of Sir Thomas Stukeley*, and his death was portrayed in George Peele's *The Battle of Alcazar*. Stukeley, who wanted to win favor at court and advance his fortunes, was a gentleman but had little money and a reputation for hotheadedness.[4] To promote himself, he joined the English forces fighting to subdue the Irish, but Queen Elizabeth was afraid to give him too much responsibility and even suspected him of double-dealing with the Irish. Refusing to come back to court when Elizabeth demanded, Stukeley fled to the court of Spain, England's great rival and Catholic enemy, where he was knighted. Later he went to Rome and finally ended up fighting for the king of Portugal in a battle in North Africa between two members of the Moroccan royal family. He died at that battle, the battle of Alcazar, as did the king of Portugal. This life, with its journeys across Europe and into Africa, with its cast of Irish foot soldiers, Catholic kings, and racialized black Africans, easily formed the stuff of which adventure drama was made.

There were more plays about actual people who journeyed beyond England's shores. *The Travels of the Three English Brothers* of 1607 (by John Day, William Rowley, and George Wilkins) staged some of the adventures of the Shirley brothers, Anthony, Robert, and Thomas, who between them traveled to Italy, Moscow, Persia, and many points between. Robert married the niece of the sophy of Persia, and the play ends with the child of that union being christened in the Christian faith. Equally exotic was a play called *A Christian Turned Turk* (by Robert Daborne), which depicts the life of a real English sailor, John Ward, who left his life as a fisherman to become a pirate and operate a ring out of the North African city of Tunis. In this role he sells captured Christians into slavery, cuts deals through a Jewish middleman with the Ottoman powers in Tunis, and eventually undergoes a ritual conversion to Islam so he can marry a Muslim woman.

Besides these dramatizations of actual people, a number of plays create fictional characters who follow similar paths of adventure. One of my favorites, Thomas Heywood's *Fair Maid of the West, Part 1*, dramatizes the life of a fictional woman, Bess Bridges. A barmaid who through hard work and good fortune becomes the captain of a ship, Bess fights the Spanish in the Azores and eventually sails to Morocco. There she conquers the heart of the Moroccan king before being reunited with her English lover and returned to a "safe" position as his betrothed.

A number of features distinguish these English adventure plays (Howard, "Gender," esp. 345–49). First, they portray characters venturing beyond the shores of England, sometimes within Europe to Ireland, Spain, or Italy, sometimes beyond Europe to port cities such as Tangiers, Tunis, Alexandria, or Aleppo. In the Shirleys' case, one brother even travels to Persia. These are places to which English trading ventures were increasingly drawing attention (Cohen, esp. 131–35). Moreover, when these characters travel abroad, they encounter strangers of all types: Italian, Irish, French, and Spanish soldiers, sailors, and merchants. They also encounter non-Christians: Jews serving as middlemen in the trading centers of the Near East and the Maghreb; Turks who rule the far-flung Ottoman Empire and practice the Muslim religion; and Moors from Africa, some of whom are described as "tawny," perhaps Berbers, others as "blackamoors," who share the dark skin of sub-Saharan Africans. Often these Moors, tawny or black, practice Islam; sometimes their religion is indeterminate. In each case, the Europeans in these plays are confronted with cultural difference. For example, in *Fair Maid of the West*, Mullisheg, the Moroccan king, has a harem and eunuchs to guard that harem; in *The Travels of the Three English Brothers*, Thomas Shirley is imprisoned by the Great Turk and threatened with death if he will not divulge his name and convert to Islam; in *A Christian Turned Turk*, John Ward actually does undergo conversion and renounces his Christian faith.

All these plays, even those with happy endings, present their European heroes as endangered by travel among foreign people and as often unable correctly to interpret their actions. John Ward, for example, cannot recognize that Voada has contempt, not love, for him; Thomas Stukeley seems oblivious that he is backing the wrong Moroccan ruler, a man depicted as a kin murderer, usurper, and tyrant. Sometimes the danger to the European adventurer takes the form of physical torture, as we see in *The Travels of the Three English Brothers* when Thomas Shirley is put on the rack; other times forced conversion to Islam is the threat, and with it the trauma of circumcision, a permanent transformation of the male body that is often confused and conflated with castration (Vitkus, *Three Turk Plays* 5). In *Fair Maid of the West*, where the adventurer is a woman, there are hints that Mullisheg will deprive Bess of her cherished chastity (Howard, "English Lass" 113–16). In each case, loss of identity is at the heart of the plays' anxieties. What will travel to foreign lands do to the European who undertakes it? Will he or she retain a Christian identity? Or will he or she choose or be forced to assume a new identity and with it new customs, clothing, diet, and religious practices?

In many plays, the threat to identity is posed through a foreign woman (Loomba, "Shakespeare and Cultural Difference" 177–79). In *A Christian*

Turned Turk, John Ward only turns Turk when there is the possibility that by doing so he can marry Voada, a Muslim woman. In *The Travels of the Three English Brothers*, Robert Shirley's decision to marry the sophy's niece likewise imperils his Christian identity. The final scene where Robert's newborn child is christened into the Christian faith seems designed to allay that fear. Whatever the ending—whether the encounter with foreign difference leads to death and conversion or to the triumph of the European over the temptations of otherness—few of the heroes of these adventure dramas are shown returning home. Stukeley dies in the sands of North Africa; John Ward commits suicide in Tunis; Robert Shirley is last seen in Persia; Bess Bridges in Fez, in *The Fair Maid of the West, Part 1*. The same is true for Europeans in other plays linked to the adventure genre such as *The Renegado* (by Philip Massinger), *The Island Princess* (by John Fletcher), or *The Four Apprentices of London* (by Thomas Heywood). In the adventure genre a European leaves home, committing himself and occasionally herself to the perils of a sea voyage and the encounter with alien cultures. From this experience, there is no simple coming home.

I argue that the popularity of adventure drama in the late sixteenth and early seventeenth century on the London stage was closely tied to England's commercial expansion during this period. These plays, of course, did not accurately represent English trading activities; in fact, the details of trade are often absent or expressed obliquely as a general desire for advancement or for growing wealthy through piracy. Rather, what these plays represent is the ambition of the English to assert themselves in distant arenas and the anxieties that attend that ambition. And they provide ordinary English people, the Londoners who went to the public theater, with powerful representations of alien cultures and people, using distinctive costumes and props: Turks wore turbans and robes and carried curved swords or scimitars; Moors were also often turbaned, and the faces of white actors were blackened to simulate black skin.

Shakespeare never wrote a play that directly reproduced the conventions of adventure drama, but he must have been familiar with them. *Antony and Cleopatra* comes closest to imitating the adventure paradigm. In it, the noble Roman warrior, Antony, falls in love with the tawny Egyptian, Cleopatra. He never abandons her, although his love affair diminishes him in the eyes of his Roman peers and holds him physically in Egypt when duty calls him back to Rome. Antony ends up defeated by a Roman army and commits suicide in Egypt. It is possible thus to read the play as reproducing the conventions of adventure drama, Cleopatra being cast as the exotic alien woman who causes Antony to forfeit his Roman identity. Shakespeare, however, distances his story from contemporary events by setting it in ancient Rome; more important, he troubles the assumption that Rome represents a standard of value to which Antony should adhere. Shakespeare's Cleopatra is something more than a seductress, and Antony is arguably enlarged, not diminished, by his encounter with her (Adelman, *Common Liar*).

However, Shakespeare's most profound engagement with the adventure paradigm occurs in *Othello*. If one reads the play with the conventions of adventure drama in mind, one is immediately struck with how the play works with and transforms those conventions, mainly by changing the direction of the adventurer's journey and with it the whole orientation of the genre. Othello is not a white European but an African Moor; he does not move from Europe into North Africa but from North Africa into Europe, specifically to Venice, a leading Italian center for international trade. He does not "turn Turk"; instead, he has at some point "turned Christian" and to that extent been absorbed into European culture (Greenblatt, *Renaissance Self-Fashioning* 241–42; Vitkus, " 'Turning Turk' "). He does not marry an exotic North African woman of color; instead, he marries what to him is an equally exotic European white woman. Shakespeare's genius in this play is to imagine what it might be like to make a black man the hero of a tragic tale of cross-cultural encounter, to imagine, so to speak, what the process Englishmen were undergoing might look like from the other side. An interesting way to teach this play is to compare it with one of the adventure dramas in which an Englishman goes to North Africa. The contrast reveals a great deal about what is unique in Shakespeare's recasting of the adventure paradigm and about how thoroughly Shakespeare was in conversation with plays being produced in this genre by other dramatists.

I want to identify some of the consequences of Shakespeare's inversion of the adventure paradigm. First, and perhaps most striking, is that this inversion puts Othello, a Moor and an outsider to European society, in the position of tragic protagonist. It is he on whom audience attention is focused, he who speaks soliloquies of inexpressible beauty, and he whose mistakes evoke the terror and pity traditionally associated with tragic action. If, as I argue, Othello's outsider status is intimately bound with his downfall, that status in no way bars him, in Shakespeare's dramatic universe, from commanding the preeminent position in a tragic action.

Second, an emphasis on the play's inversion of the European adventure narrative draws attention to Othello's status as an alien in Venice, just as John Ward or Robert Shirley were aliens in the cultures to which they traveled. No matter how useful Othello may be to Venice's ruling class, his outsider status affects his ability to understand and negotiate the culture in which he finds himself. What the play reveals about Othello's prior life comes mostly from his own mouth. When he tells Desdemona and her father about his past, he emphasizes his suffering and—to Europeans—the exotic nature of his encounters in distant places:

> I spoke of most disastrous chances,
> Of moving accidents by flood and field,
> Of hair-breadth scapes i'th' imminent deadly
>   breach,

> Of being taken by the insolent foe
> And sold to slavery, of my redemption thence,
> And portance in my traveller's history,
> Wherein of antres vast and deserts idle,
> Rough quarries, rocks, and hills whose heads
>   touch heaven,
> It was my hint to speak. Such was my process,
> And of the cannibals that each other eat,
> The Anthropophagi, and men whose heads
> Do grow beneath their shoulders.
>   (1.3.133–44)

The details of Othello's narrative derive from medieval and early modern travel books, some of which describe fantastic or fearful creatures such as the cannibalistic anthropophagi. These books also often recount tales of enslavement. Europeans might become enslaved to Turks. Africans might be enslaved by other Africans or fall into the hands of white slave traders. A number of adventure plays of the period, such as *A Christian Turned Turk*, depict slave markets where Europeans and Moors are equally subject to purchase. We do not know who enslaved Othello: Christian, Turk, or African. We do not know where he saw the tall mountains that kissed the sky. It could have been in sub-Saharan Africa, in the Atlas range in southern Morocco, or elsewhere. All we can glean for sure is that Othello presents himself as a man whose prior experiences lay far beyond the shores of Italy. He is an outsider, someone whose past is opaque but whose narratives of difference rivet the attention of the Venetians to whom he tells his tales. Desdemona consumes them with "a greedy ear" (1.3.148); her father often invited the Moor to his home to listen to these stories. Othello, of course, is not the only one to label himself as an outsider in Venice. If the Moor stresses his difference in terms of the cultures he has encountered and the experiences he has had, Iago crudely focuses on Othello's color and his supposed bestiality. Famously, he compares Othello to a "barbary horse" (1.1.113) and "an old black ram" (1.1.88), and he characterizes the sexual union of the Moor and Desdemona as "making the beast with two backs" (1.1.118). This racializing discourse interprets difference as inferiority.

Othello, like many adventure dramas, thus makes clear that contact between cultures can be a fraught affair. Iago's vile denigration of Othello suggests that Othello is in peril in Venetian society, no matter how powerful and necessary he may appear to be. There are men like Iago who would destroy him and use the fact of his difference to incite violence against him. Even Brabantio does not want him to marry his daughter. Contact with the exotic storyteller can go only so far. Useful as soldier and entertainer, Othello cannot be a son-in-law (Neill, "Unproper Beds").

More crucial to the course of the play is how Othello's perception of his difference affects his actions. Above all, it makes him unsure of his ability accurately to decipher Venetian culture and especially Venetian women; and it partly explains his dependence on Iago for advice about personal matters. An insider, Iago offers the promise of transparency. He can make the foreign customs of Venetian women intelligible, as he does when he tempts Othello to doubt Desdemona's chastity:

> I know our country disposition well.
> In Venice they do let God see the pranks
> They dare not show their husbands; their best conscience
> Is not to leave't undone, but keep't unknown.
>
> (3.3.205–08)

Under Iago's tutelage, Othello comes to doubt his instinctive responses to Desdemona, reading her through the suspicious eyes of his Venetian interpreter.

In most adventure drama, the foreign woman is a treacherous seductress who pulls the hero to his downfall. In *A Christian Turned Turk*, Voada promises to marry John Ward if he will convert to Islam, but she secretly loves another man and never consummates her union with the English pirate. Shakespeare follows the adventure genre in having tragedy arise from the love between a foreign man and a woman native to the culture to which the adventurer travels. However, he experiments with this template, making the woman a faithful spouse able to love across a cultural divide but destroyed by her husband's inability to understand her chastity for what it is. Like John Ward, Othello cannot accurately read the woman he loves, but instead of overvaluing the alien woman, he undervalues her. Shakespeare explores with unprecedented subtlety an epistemological problem central to the adventure genre, namely, how can one properly interpret the actions of persons from another culture?

In *Othello* the handkerchief concretizes the problems arising from the cross-cultural union. It is the play's most notorious stage prop and its most contested site of interpretation. As much criticism of the play has shown, the handkerchief takes on different meanings at different points in the play, registering the shifting degrees of trust and distrust, fear and desire, distance and closeness felt by the Moorish Othello and his Venetian wife. At first, Desdemona speaks of the handkerchief simply as a token of affection given to her by her husband and loved by her for that reason. In English culture, handkerchiefs were often given as betrothal gifts (Green 1090–91). Moreover, the strawberry pattern on the handkerchief was one found in many English textile designs from the period (Korda 125). The handkerchief, then, is easily read by the European woman simply as a love token from her husband and nothing more.

However, when Desdemona cannot find the handkerchief, which she dropped while she was using it to soothe her husband's aching head, Othello creates a story about the handkerchief's origins and significance that places it firmly outside Desdemona's realm of experience:

> That handkerchief
> Did an Egyptian to my mother give.
> She was a charmer, and could almost read
> The thoughts of people. She told her, while she kept it
> 'Twould make her amiable, and subdue my father
> Entirely to her love; but if she lost it,
> Or made a gift of it, my father's eye
> Should hold her loathèd, and his spirits should hunt
> After new fancies. She, dying, gave it me,
> And bid me, when my fate would have me wived,
> To give it her. I did so, and take heed on't.
> Make it a darling, like your precious eye.
> To lose't or give't away were such perdition
> As nothing else could match.   (3.4.53–66)

A moment later, he intensifies the aura of mystery and magic surrounding the object:

> There's magic in the web of it.
> A sibyl that had numbered in the world
> The sun to course two hundred compasses
> In her prophetic fury sewed the work.
> The worms were hallowed that did breed the silk,
> And it was dyed in mummy, which the skilful
> Conserved of maidens' hearts.   (3.4.67–73)

Whether or not this is a true story, it locates Othello outside the parameters of European common sense. Sibyls, mummy (liquid taken from mummified bodies), magic—suddenly the Othello who in act 1 had denied using magic to win Desdemona aligns himself with charms and magic objects. The history Othello gives the handkerchief makes both him and it uncomprehensible to Desdemona. Wishing she had never seen the newly toxic handkerchief, Desdemona tries to steady herself in the face of the unfamiliar. In the later part of the play, realizing that she has lost the favor of her lord, she too turns to Iago for advice about how to win him back (4.2.152–55). In the play's kaleidoscope of possibilities, the handkerchief is at times a symbol of hope—the hope that a foreigner and a native can bridge the cultural and racial gap that makes their marriage seem an impossibility to members of the Venetian community such as Brabantio. But it also becomes a symbol of seemingly unbridgeable cultural difference—a love token freighted with a threat if its unfathomable (to Desdemona) codes of passage and preservation are violated. Significantly, it is on another important piece of cloth, the couple's wedding sheets, that Othello strangles Desdemona. Unable to read the sheets as a sign of their chaste union, Othello remakes them into a burial cloth.

In the context of the early modern fascination with the far reaches of the globe, *Othello* stands out as Shakespeare's most profound exploration of the perils and possibilities of crossing the boundaries between cultures, religions, and races. In writing *Othello*, Shakespeare drew on the conventions of adventure drama established by his fellow dramatists. From them he learned to think about the transformations of identity to which the adventurer was subject and about the role of sexuality as the arena where desire for and suspicion of the other could be most tragically worked out. But the fact remains, Shakespeare's hero is not a European imperiled by Ottoman culture but a Moor imperiled by European culture, a man who in his turn puts in jeopardy those to whom he comes closest. But like Stukeley, Ward, and Antony, Othello never goes home. He too commits suicide in a distant country. In Othello's case, even at the moment of death he speaks of himself as a creature of two cultures, being both the circumcised Turkish dog who deserves to die and the servant of the Venetian state who slays him (5.2.360–65). In their different ways, both *Othello* and a play such as *A Christian Turned Turk*, with their profoundly divided heroes, are fictions that speak directly to the anxieties that the English faced as they themselves increasingly became border crossers in their attempts to play an expanded role on the world's stage.

NOTES

[1] For the best account of the development of England's overseas trade in the sixteenth and seventeenth centuries and the rise of the joint stock companies see Brenner; see also Ramsay; Andrews, *Trade*.

[2] Citations to Shakespeare's plays are from Greenblatt's *Norton Shakespeare*.

[3] Linda Colley estimates that between 1600 and the early 1640s alone, more than 12,000 English, Welsh, Scottish, and Irish sailors were captured by Ottoman Turks (43–44).

[4] For information on the life of Stukeley, I am indebted to "The Biography of Sir Thomas Stucley," prepared by Richard Simpson. For an account of the life much embellished by literary flourishes, see Izon.

Teaching *Othello* as Tragedy and Comedy

Douglas Bruster

When *Othello* was published—initially as a quarto, in 1622, then in the First Folio a year later—its full title read *The Tragedie of Othello, the Moore of Venice*. Many readers are familiar with the generic categories that the First Folio uses to frame its collection of Shakespeare's plays: *Mr. William Shakespeare's Comedies, Histories, and Tragedies*. Titling the First Folio this way may have been his publisher's way of avoiding the difficult choice between "works" and "plays" that Ben Jonson had faced some seven years earlier when bringing out his own dramas. But genre was much more than nomenclature to Shakespeare and his contemporaries. More than a method of advertising literary works, genre constituted a way of seeing the world and a language for describing the worlds it imagined.

Like many plays from Shakespeare's time, *Othello* fits, and does not fit, the primary genre first assigned it. As commentators have long pointed out, *Othello* seems part tragedy and part comedy. As much as any of Shakespeare's plays, it draws on both these genres for its characters, language, and plot. Far from being a problem in the classroom, the two generic faces of *Othello* can prove a useful way for instructors to introduce not only the idea and function of dramatic genres but also their history. The commercial theaters of Shakespeare's day habitually blended genres and contributed an important chapter in this history. The enhanced variety and effect that arose from these playhouses' generic mixing everywhere inform *Othello*.

Genre and the Classroom

What role can genre play in teaching *Othello* today? Few plays of Shakespeare's have benefited more than *Othello* from recent criticism's interest in race, culture, and postcoloniality—topics that do not always bring to mind issues of literary form. Indeed, the play's almost textbook interest in an other and in cross-cultural frictions makes it easy to see why Geraldo de Sousa has described *Othello* as a study in "the dynamics of ethnographical representation" (118). Even as postcolonial criticism has energized much recent discussion of *Othello*, it implicitly asks us to justify certain traditional ways of approaching not only the play but also drama generally. Compared with such topics as race and culture, for instance, the notion of genre can seem curiously antiquated and unlikely to lead to invigorating discussions. While this essay does not afford room for a full justification of genre in the classroom, a few remarks in its support are in order.

Genre can be defined as a literary type or kind, although the term's reference to categorization is not confined to literary works. Whether they use this term, students today are actually extremely well versed in the workings of various genres. Usually their knowledge comes not from the theater but from the ready availability of narrative through electronic media. Whether in the form of film conventions, television formats, classification schemas in video and DVD stores, or fantasy-game rules, genre remains central to all fictional world making and its reception. On average, our students have already consumed more stories through television and film than any of Shakespeare's contemporaries would have experienced in a lifetime of reading, listening, and play going. Today's role-playing computer games, in particular, foreground the workings of genre by accustoming students to scripts that, while allowing a measure of freedom and creativity, establish parameters for characters and action. Students tend to recognize that genres involve the rules of fictional games and thus offer templates for the play worlds that dramatists create. Genres can also be understood as providing what Rosalie Colie has dubbed "the resources of kind": instructions and tools for the fabrication of fictional environments and even the materials for such environments.

Instructors may emphasize genre's foundational importance to all storytelling and story analysis. Students can be made aware of their proficiency with genre through a simple exercise. An instructor asks for a provisional definition of the word. Students are then canvassed for how entertainment products are categorized, including film, television shows, and music. They are then asked, What categories are such products conventionally divided into, and what defines those categories? Content? Style? Characters? Language? Plot? Structure? Audience? Which of these elements is most important in determining the genre of the object in question? Which of the elements can be changed without changing the object's genre? Where artists bend or break the rules they have inherited, for instance, can tell the class something as significant about the work in question as the rules themselves. An instructor may solicit mention of a recent film that defies the students' expectations of genre. The endings of films are particularly relevant here: when a character dies unexpectedly or makes the wrong romantic choice, one's sense of generic rules is foregrounded precisely because a rule has been broken.

Once genre has been introduced, defined, and discussed, an instructor may move on to consider *Othello* as both tragedy and comedy. Although these two genres most influenced the play's structure, and the way it has been understood through time, *Othello*, like all Shakespeare's plays, draws on a host of resources for its compositional structure, including such nontheatrical literary genres as the prose romance and novella. Students interested in such resources may find them discussed as sources in some of the collected editions of Shakespeare's works, such as *The Riverside Shakespeare* and David Bevington's *The Complete Works*, as well as in such single-volume editions as the Arden, second series, and Oxford and in the section on *Othello* in Geoffrey Bullough's *Narrative and Dramatic Sources of Shakespeare*, which contains relevant extracts from a number of literary sources and analogues.

Othello *as Tragedy*

Othello is a tragedy, which is evident from the play's original title, from the number of unfortunate deaths that occur in its narrative, and from the way one of its characters describes the play world in which he participates. Lodovico closes the play by ordering Iago to "Look on the tragic loading of this bed" (5.2.363).[1] Other than the play's original title, this reference remains the only form of the word *tragedy* in *Othello*.

What did Shakespeare understand tragedy to be and to mean? Dramatists of his era had a number of models for tragedy, perhaps central among them the works of the Roman dramatist Seneca, which were available in both Latin and English during the later sixteenth century. From plays like *Medea* and *Hercules* Shakespeare would have understood tragedy to entail aristocratic characters involved in (and often brought low by) horrific violence and suffering, elevated rhetoric punctuated by epigrammatic moralizing, iterated imagery, and the use of the supernatural. The biblical tradition would have offered Shakespeare the examples of Job and Christ as good men suffering tremendously in a vicious world, as well as tragic figures like Samson and Herod. Continental resources such as Boccaccio's *De casibus virorum illustrium* ("On the Fall of Illustrious Men") influenced Chaucer, Lydgate, and later the writing of English history in *A Mirror for Magistrates* and worked to define tragedy morally. The characters of the *de casibus* genre understand too late their true relation to fortune's wheel, which, in its inexorable turning, takes its tragic figures from the height of success (usually political) to the depths of misfortune and death.

Some of Shakespeare's contemporary playwrights offered conventional definitions of tragedy in prefatory material to their plays. In his epistle "to the readers" before *Sejanus*, Ben Jonson characterizes the "offices of a *Tragick* writer" as including "truth of Argument, dignity of Persons, gravity and height of Elocution, fulnesse and frequencie of Sentence" (*Works* 4: 350, lines 18–25). By "truth of Argument" Jonson seems to refer to the moral consistency of the subject matter (including theme and plot) of the tragedy in question; "dignity of Persons" implies not just the moral worthiness of a play's characters but their social elevation; the "gravity and height of Elocution" suggests an equally elevated register of speech; and the "fulnesse and frequencie of Sentence" involves the compressed, gnomic wisdom—the encapsulated morals and insights—that readers would have been familiar with from the biblical and native proverb tradition as well as from the Senecan example of tragedy. We find George Chapman echoing Jonson's definition in the preface epistle to the 1613 quarto of *The Revenge of Bussy D'Ambois*, when he takes it on himself to represent the genre: "materiall instruction, elegant and sententious excitation to Vertue, and deflection from her contrary; being the soule, lims, and limits of an autenticall Tragedie" (442; lines 27–29).

Unlike many of his contemporaries, Shakespeare rarely provided this kind of discursive commentary on his publications. In his plays, however, Shakespeare's characters often define the tragic in relation to moments of great emotional distress. Alexander Schmidt's *Shakespeare Lexicon and Quotation Dictionary* examines the playwright's use of the word *tragedy* in his works and defines it as meaning both "a dramatic representation of a serious action" and "a mournful and dreadful event" (2: 1250). We could note that when, in *Titus Andronicus*, Tamora speaks of Bassanius's death as a "timeless tragedy" (2.3.265), he uses "timeless" in the sense of premature, unnatural, or untimely. This phrase is redundant, since all tragedies are timeless or untimely in that they steal time from the dead by robbing them of life and from the living by robbing them of the company they enjoyed.

Shakespeare tended to use the word *tragedy* and its variants to describe situations that profoundly and negatively affected the bodies and spirits of those involved. In *A Lover's Complaint*, for instance, his speaker indicts one who feigns "To blush at speeches rank, to weep at woes, / Or to turn white and sound at tragic shows" (307–08). Here Shakespeare describes one who becomes pale and swoons at tragic spectacles; these spectacles are defined by their effect on the viewer. We may take a definition of Shakespearean tragedy from Horatio's description of seeing the Ghost in *Hamlet*: "it [harrows] me with fear and wonder" (1.1.44). This line describes the Senecan mode of tragedy that had influenced Shakespeare even as it confirms the playwright's understanding of tragedy as something that changes the bodies of those who watch it: to "harrow" a field is to violently pulverize it with a rakelike object made up of a heavy frame and sharp teeth or tines. For Horatio to depict the sight of the Ghost as harrowing him—in the quartos the word is "horrors"—is, like the description we have seen in *A Lover's Complaint*, to hint at tragedy's claims on the body.

Students may come to *Othello* with a perception of tragedy based on its use in today's media and on its definition in Aristotle's *Poetics*. Instructors may feel that neither definition is sufficient for understanding *Othello*, but an approach to the genres of the play cannot afford to ignore them. *Tragedy* and *tragic* are used in newspaper, Internet, or television journalism to refer to surprise deaths, usually multiple in number. Soldiers killed by friendly fire, a tourist's car hit by a train, a boat sinking with numerous people on board—these are a few of the events described with the word *tragedy* in a sampling of news stories as I write this paragraph. One of the biggest differences between this modern understanding of tragedy and the definitions circulating among such playwrights as Jonson and Chapman, then, lies in what Jonson called the "dignity of Persons" involved in the tragic event. As George Steiner noted in *The Death of Tragedy*, modern democracy cannot accommodate itself easily to definitions—or examples—of tragedy that insist on elevated protagonists. Likewise, conventional elements of tragedy sometimes fit awkwardly with protagonists from a homogeneous social order. One assumption of

Boccaccio's *de casibus* tragedies is that the fall of elevated protagonists means more because they have further to fall. Students today may not share this view but can benefit from imagining audiences who might have accepted the premises behind it.

In addition to assumptions concerning social class and merit, the moral interpretation of tragedy can prove an important issue in the classroom. Students may come to Shakespearean tragedy from Aristotle's *Poetics*, still widely taught as offering a moralistic framework for tragedy. This approach comes from a long-standing mistranslation of the Greek word *hamartia* as referring to a tragic flaw in the personality of the play's central character. Humphrey House describes the problem:

> [I]t may be said by some writers to be the "tragic flaw" of Oedipus that he was hasty in temper; of Samson that he was sensually uxorious; of Macbeth that he was ambitious; of Othello that he was proud and jealous—and so on . . . but these things do not constitute the "hamartiai" of those characters in Aristotle's sense.   (94)

In a perceptive essay on the concept of *hamartia* in the *Poetics*, Nancy Sherman notes that *hamartia* as a word is "rooted in the notion of missing the mark (*hamartanein*), and covers a broad spectrum that includes accident and mistake, as well as wrongdoing, error, or sin" (178). Eschewing the definition of *hamartia* as "tragic flaw," Sherman insists that we recognize the "range of ways in which tragic characters can err" in Greek drama (180); *hamartia*, Sherman notes, "focuses on agency" and asks us to recognize that the "mistake" is actively made by a protagonist (178).

Classroom exercises dealing with *Othello* and the genre of tragedy could begin by asking students to compare and contrast various definitions of tragedy, ranging from the classical era to Shakespeare's time and our own as well. How do these definitions differ? What do they have in common? Further questions could pursue the implications of these definitions. Borrowing Aristotle's term, what error (*hamartia*) or errors (*hamartiai*) can we perceive in the tragedy? Who makes them, and why? Do such errors ask for a moral or a practical explanation? a personal or social one? What "materiall instruction," to use George Chapman's definition, can we locate in *Othello*? Is such instruction the same for us as it would have been for Shakespeare's audience? In that regard, how would a modern newspaper or television news program describe the events of the drama? Further, what does it mean to see Othello as the tragic figure here? Could we call this *The Tragedy of Desdemona*? of Cassio? Emilia? Iago? Brabantio? What difference would such renaming make to our reading of the play? Another, and by no means a final, question to ask concerns the play's understanding of tragedy. That is, if we took *Othello* as a template for tragedy, what would its template mean for other plays? What kind of standard would the play suggest for tragic action, speech, and characters?

Othello *as Comedy*

Othello is a comedy, which is apparent from the play's focus on an older man married to an attractive younger woman and his subsequent fears of cuckoldry, from its frank and frequent mention of sexuality, and from the machinations of Iago, its imaginative trickster figure. In his *Short View of Tragedy* (1693), Thomas Rymer offers what remains the most notorious comments on *Othello*, which he reads as inappropriately comedic—a "Bloody Farce" ([ed. Zimansky] 163). Desdemona's handkerchief and the structurally comedic fuss made over it, Rymer claims, are not suitable for tragedy. In *Othello*, he says, Shakespeare makes "a Tragedy of this Trifle": "Had it been Desdemona's Garter, the Sagacious Moor might have smelt a Rat: but the Handkerchief is so remote a trifle, no Booby, on this side Mauritania, cou'd make any consequence from it" ([ed. Zimansky] 164, 160). Although it does not follow Rymer's indictment of *Othello*, much criticism on the play echoes his feeling that the play mingles comedy and tragedy—at the very least, that *Othello* achieves its tragic end through what is essentially a comedic plot.

Comedy lends itself less well to genre theorizing than tragedy does. Perhaps it is enough to say that many of Shakespeare's contemporaries would have understood a stage comedy to entail a focus on love or at least on erotic intrigue, often involving the middle or lower orders of society and usually featuring a significant misunderstanding or series of mistakes relating to identity and character. In its emphasis on mistakes or errors, comedy shares something important with tragedy. However, the two genres differ in the disposition of characters' bodies: comedy typically ends with safe and satisfied (or soon-to-be satisfied) bodies, tragedy with dead, maimed, and grieving bodies.

Equivalence of partners satisfies bodies in comedy and audiences attending a comedy. One norm of romantic comedy involves pairing off linguistic, physical, and intellectual equals. Thus in the logic of comedy, when an older man marries a younger woman, that woman will gravitate to suitors her own age and sometimes cuckold her husband. Such is a common story line in the medieval fabliaux, in prose tales like Boccaccio's *Decameron*; and in Chaucer's Miller's Tale, with its story of Alison and Nicholas, and the Merchant's Tale, with its story of January cuckolded by May.

In addition to the January-May relationship in *Othello*—we will remember that Iago tells Desdemona's father "an *old* black ram / Is tupping your white ewe" (1.1.88–9; emphasis added)—an abundance of love talk occurs in the dialogue. Sex, often discussed, is among the play's dominating concerns. *Othello* can be read as an investigation of the erotic—a usual focus of comedies.

What creates and fosters passionate feelings for another? What can excessive erotic passion do to existing relationships, whether familial (Desdemona's relationship to her father, for instance) or marital (Othello's relationship to Desdemona)? These are just a few of the questions the plot of *Othello* addresses.

Seeing *Othello* as a comedy helps explain many things in the play that, as Rymer recognizes, are nonconventional elements in tragedy. Among these things are Iago's scenes with Roderigo, a conventional gull (that is, an easily fooled person) from the era's jestbooks, prose narratives, and stage comedies; the "bold show of courtesy" and "old fond paradoxes" that ensue when Desdemona and Emilia land at the seaport in Cyprus (2.1.99, 138); the drinking and tavern songs of 2.3; Othello's comedic if painful descent into jealousy beginning with Iago's simple "Hah? I like not that" as Cassio exits the stage (3.3.35); Cassio's scenes with Bianca (3.4.169–201; 4.1.146–61), as well as Iago's and Cassio's characterizations of Bianca in 4.1 as a "huswife" (94), "strumpet" (96), "customer" (119), "monkey" (127), and "bauble" (135); and, finally, Desdemona and Emilia's quiet conversation about handsome men and marital infidelity just after wedding sheets are laid on Desdemona's bed (4.3.11–105).

In the context of the deaths in *Othello*, these examples may not seem to deserve the name of comedy—which is just the point. Although the murders that Iago's trickery inspires in the play suggest otherwise, the above examples and the central role that Iago and his deceptions take in *Othello* support defining *Othello* as a comedy. Most critics note that Iago is a playwright figure who gleefully imagines, scripts, casts, and directs a play of his own conception in the drama. One could argue that *Othello* is a comedy written from within by a playwright—that is, Iago—who refuses to accept the conventional understanding of comedy as excluding death and in fact understands death as the best evidence of his farcical revenge on a pompous superior.

A class devoted to *Othello*'s comedic subtext could start with the question, what would need to be done to make the play into an instance of comedy? A list of such transformations typically begins with preventing the murders in the play. But an instructor could also ask whether a new comedy of *Othello* would need to dole out some kind of punishment for various inequities that transpire in its plot. That is, would "The Comedy of Othello" have to punish Iago for his deception or Othello for his jealousy or Cassio for his ungentlemanly treatment of Bianca? Emilia for implicitly lying to Desdemona? Would such a comedy mandate a new structure of power in the marriages of Othello and Desdemona, Iago and Emilia? Would it include a marriage between Cassio and Bianca? Would it need to have Brabantio forgive Desdemona or ask her forgiveness? Would Brabantio and Othello reconcile? Othello and Iago? Iago and the others his deception injured? These questions, which could be answered in various ways, will foreground in the classroom the assumptions we make about comedy and its relation to justice, romance, power, and forgiveness.

Further Reading on Othello *and Genre*

Students interested in pursuing the question of genre could start with Heather Dubrow's *Genre* before moving on to Alastair Fowler's *Kinds of Literature: An Introduction to the Theory of Genre and Modes* and Rosalie L. Colie's *The Resources of Kind: Genre-Theory in the Renaissance*. In addition to some of the critical works on tragedy mentioned earlier in this essay, students may find compelling Raymond Williams's *Modern Tragedy*, as well as the generous selection of definitions and discussions of tragedy from Aristotle to Antonin Artaud provided in Oscar Lee Brownstein and Darlene M. Daubert's *Analytical Sourcebook of Concepts in Dramatic Theory*. Aristotle's *Poetics* has of course come to dominate theories of tragedy, and there are many critical debates about just what his theory is and what his terms mean. I have found helpful Gerald F. Else's *Aristotle's* Poetics: *The Argument* (especially useful for its discussion of controversial passages) and various pieces in *Essays on Aristotle's* Poetics, edited by Amélie Oksenberg Rorty, particularly those of Rorty ("The Psychology of Aristotelian Tragedy"), Sherman ("*Hamartia* and Virtue"), and Jonathan Lear ("Katharsis"). A useful overview concerning the way Shakespeare's contemporaries conceived of tragedy appears in Marjorie Donker and George M. Muldrow's *Dictionary of Literary-Rhetorical Conventions of the English Renaissance*, which excerpts definitions from dozens of sources and provides an extensive bibliography. Works on Shakespeare's relation to genre are numerous; students could start with Stephen Orgel's "Shakespeare and the Kinds of Drama" and Lawrence Danson's recent *Shakespeare's Dramatic Genres*. Foundational pieces on *Othello* and genre include A. C. Bradley's famous remarks on the play in his *Shakespearean Tragedy* and Susan Snyder's *The Comic Matrix of Shakespeare's Tragedies*. More recently, critics have stressed *Othello*'s roots in the subgenre of domestic tragedy; see Peter L. Rudnytsky's "*A Woman Killed with Kindness* as a Subtext for *Othello*" and Brian W. Shaffer's " 'To Manage Private and Domestic Quarrels': Shakespeare's *Othello* and the Genre of Elizabethan Domestic Tragedy."

NOTE

[1]Citations to Shakespeare's plays are from Evans's *Riverside Shakespeare*.

" 'Tis but a Man Gone":
Teaching *Othello* as an (Anti)Revenge Play

Cynthia Lewis

Imagine what students—high school, college, or continuing education students—might respond if you, their teacher, asked them whether Cassio should follow Lodovico's injunction at the end of *Othello*: "To you, Lord Governor, / Remains the censure of this hellish villain, / The time, the place, the torture, O, enforce it!" (5.2.367–69).[1] Chances are they would screw up their faces in disbelief that you would even ask such a question. If any character deserves Cassio's "censure," they might think, surely it is Iago. As I intend to show, however, the question of how Cassio should respond to Iago is not only valid and open but also key to understanding *Othello* in the company of its immediate predecessor, *Hamlet*. The truest statement about *Othello* in the Senecan tragedy of blood tradition, that it is an antirevenge play, is also the least interesting.[2] Far more engaging for students are the questions of how it displays its antirevenge sentiment and of how that display may elucidate antirevenge strains in *Hamlet*, thereby linking the two plays.

At the play's end, Cassio cannot possibly be expected to maintain an objective view toward the treatment Iago deserves. Although Cassio is, by default, newly appointed governor of Cypress, Iago has done him almost as much personal injury as he has Othello. Cassio's judgment is as clouded by a desire for private vengeance toward his enemy as Othello's by the mere suspicion of Desdemona's infidelity. The "cause" for Othello's revenge on Desdemona provides the play's most salient argument against private vengeance (5.2.1–3); Othello's arrogant confidence in his own judgment results in unjustifiable murder. Repeated versions of that arrogance, which blinds other characters to their own vices as it emboldens them to identify vices in others, result in unwarranted violence, whether literal or figurative. Much as physical violence in *Othello* can cause bodily harm, so can language savagely violate identity by turning a subject into an object.

Most obviously, Iago's epithets for Cassio reduce his character to one trait and negate its complexity. When Iago expresses his frustration at having been overlooked by Othello, he styles Cassio as a "great arithmetician" and a "counter-caster" (1.1.19, 31). Later, when he convinces Roderigo that Cassio and Desdemona could be sexually involved, he completely rewrites Cassio's character to suit his needs. Instead of the retiring student of "bookish theoric" (1.1.24), Cassio now becomes a lecher, "rash and very sudden in choler" (2.1.257, 272). Although both characterizations may have some validity, they are opposed, and neither, from what the audience observes about Cassio, rings completely true, as even the dull Roderigo realizes (e.g., 2.1.256). Iago's manipulations of others' images for his own purposes extend to Desdemona (e.g.,

2.1.245–48); Emilia (e.g., 2.1.100–02, 103–07); and even, through Iago's abuse of him, Roderigo. In turn, Roderigo, infected with Iago's drive to satisfy his desires, readily discounts human life. While hiding in 5.1 to ambush Cassio, his presumed rival for Desdemona, he confesses his disregard for humanity in Iago's earshot: "I have no great devotion to the deed, / And yet he [Iago] hath given me satisfying reasons. / 'Tis but a man gone. Forth my sword; he dies" (8–10). The supreme irony of this moment lies in Iago's minimizing Roderigo's character to suit his own fancies as Roderigo has just minimized Cassio's: "Now, whether he kill Cassio, / Or Cassio him, or each do kill the other, / Every way makes my gain" (5.1.12–14).

Such irony permeates scene after scene in which the complexity of individual character asserts itself despite other characters' efforts to suppress it. One example, the passage at the close of 5.1, where Bianca and Emilia verbally scuffle, epitomizes the characters' obliviousness to their hypocrisy in judging others. Once Cassio has been wounded earlier in the scene and Iago has expressed hollow sympathy (69–73), Bianca enters and voices her woe: "O my dear Cassio, my sweet Cassio! / O Cassio, Cassio, Cassio!" (76–77). The irony here is thick. Shrill as she is, Bianca, of the white name and dark profession, truly cares for Cassio, although she seems less sincere than Iago. Bianca is honest, but Emilia nonetheless classifies her solely in terms of her profession, as if prostitution disqualifies her from loving Cassio and qualifies her to attempt his murder:

EMILIA. O fie upon thee, strumpet!
BIANCA. I am no strumpet, but of life as honest
         As you that thus abuse me.
EMILIA.   As I? [Fough], fie upon thee!
                                                (121–23)

The irony thickens. Bianca's denial that she is a strumpet is downright funny. Still, Emilia's label overlooks her own willingness, expressed in the preceding scene, to cuckold her husband "for all the world" (4.3.64). That Emilia's fee is higher than Bianca's does not exempt her from the category of strumpet.

This passage works well in class discussion partly because students tend to identify with Emilia until they are urged to reconsider. Once they learn to see the episode from Bianca's viewpoint, many of them understand Emilia's injustice toward Bianca and thus become more receptive to the same dynamic, in which one character hypocritically judges another, throughout the play.

The conclusion of 5.1 also sends students back to previous scenes that reveal how much Emilia and Bianca have in common. What begins in 4.3 as Emilia's lighthearted fantasy about trading her chastity for the whole world, which she would then lay at Iago's feet, quickly gives way to spleen venting about faithless husbands:

> Let husbands know
> Their wives have sense like them; they see, and smell,
> And have their palates both for sweet and sour,
> As husbands have. . . .
>   have not we affections,
> Desires for sport, and frailty, as men have?
> Then let them use us well; else let them know,
> The ills we do, their ills instruct us so.
>   (93–96, 100–03)

Now Emilia's motive for cuckolding Iago shifts from self-sacrifice to avenging her pain. In terms reminiscent of Shylock's to his Venetian hecklers, Emilia complains of Iago's failure to appreciate her humanity, treatment to which, one scene later, she will subject Bianca and to which Iago apparently subjects her regularly. Iago publicly humiliates her by calling her a nag and a fool (2.1.100–15), much as Cassio ridicules Bianca behind her back (4.1.107–45). Moreover, Iago cows Emilia into stealing the handkerchief—the axis on which the tragedy will turn—merely "to please his fantasy" and then verbally abuses her (3.3.299, 300–15). Similarly, Cassio later prevails on Bianca to copy the handkerchief's work and then scorns her (3.4.179–91, 4.1.139–40, 144).

In truth, both Emilia and Bianca strive to curry favor with men who mistreat them. Desdemona too has her price. To avoid Othello's wrath in 3.4, she understandably tells him the white lie that the handkerchief is not lost (80–85). The point, of course, is not that all the women in *Othello* can be bought but that each is fully rounded to belie the absolutist terms that all the characters, most especially Iago, adore applying to one another. To this language of black and white the play calls famously elaborate, insistent attention. With the exception of Desdemona and, eventually, Emilia, the characters lack the sympathetic imagination to feel any pain or desire but their own, and they avoid doing so partly by collapsing one another's depth.

More important for exploring *Othello* as a revenge tragedy, however, is that, in their moral roundedness, none of the characters is completely blameless. Hence, none is completely entitled to pass judgment on another. No element of the play makes this idea clearer than the epithet "honest Iago." Applied with almost risible frequency, as even beginning students notice, it points to the other characters' complicity in Iago's deception of them, deception to which they sometimes seem led like lambs to the slaughter. *Othello* does offer instances of clear perception, as indicated by the early episode in which the Venetians' discern the intention of the Turkish fleet by careful observation and reasoning (1.3.1–47). In the same scene, Othello, with the help of the Duke, shakes off the negative epithets Brabantio hurls at him by patiently explaining himself and by appealing to reason.[3] Slurs like "mountebank" and allegations of "witchcraft" do not have to stick (1.3.61, 64). As the Duke pronounces, "[t]o vouch" these insults is "no proof" (1.3.106). That the characters slip into vouching for Iago, then, is a choice, albeit a choice difficult to avoid when emotions begin to run high. Still, such a lapse of will—even on the part of Iago's mistreated wife, Emilia—makes the tragedy a communal affair. All are responsible. All are punished.

And that includes Cassio, whose repeated appeals to "honest Iago" implicate him in Othello's tragedy and in his own misfortunes (2.3.335).[4] The question of how Cassio should respond to Iago as the play ends, once he has power over him, is thus problematic. Were Cassio to pass judgment on Iago at this point, he would likely ignore the tragic role he himself has played. Does the play imply that Cassio has the right to "censure . . . this hellish villain" (5.2.368)? I would like to suggest that the question is left open-ended, through Cassio's silence, for a good reason. At the same time, I would like to point out two ways in which the play's conclusion discourages the audience from approving of Cassio's rush to judgment.

The first and more obvious way involves the modeling of characters like Desdemona, Othello, and even Emilia. Desdemona apparently resists the temptation to judge Othello's character on what little she understands about his behavior. Her perplexing, if not contradictory, final speeches combine honest (though vague) revelation of Othello's mistaken judgment—"O, falsely, falsely murder'd!" (5.2.117)—with her refusal to judge Othello. Protesting her innocence—"A guiltless death I die" (5.2.122)—she assumes the responsibility for her death rather than blame Othello. When Emilia asks her, "O, who hath done this deed?" Desdemona responds only, "Nobody; I myself" (5.2.123–24). Finally imploring Emilia to "commend" her to her "kind lord," Desdemona may be expressing faith in the man she has married beyond whatever lunacy currently has him in its grip (125).

By contrast, Emilia foists some damning words on Othello, "murd'rous coxcomb," "fool" (5.2.233), "gull," and "dolt" (163), as well as on Iago, "Villainy, villainy, villainy" (190). But, although reeling from her previously repressed awareness of her husband's capacity for hatred and exulting in her newfound freedom to expose it publicly, Emilia stops short of punishing Iago. Before dying at his hand, she more or less turns him over to the state—that is, to a higher authority. As for Othello, his closing speeches not only reveal his humiliation for his overconfidence in the "just grounds" for Desdemona's murder—"O fool, fool, fool!"—but also remind his audience that human virtue is mixed and that assigning blame is a complicated prospect (5.2.138, 323):

> I pray you, in your letters,
> When you shall these unlucky deeds relate,
> Speak of me as I am; nothing extenuate,
> Nor set down aught in malice. Then must you speak
> Of one that lov'd not wisely but too well;

> Of one not easily jealous, but being wrought,
> Perplexed in the extreme.   (5.2.340–46)

Much as Cassio's responsibility is entangled with Iago's, where Othello's own perplexity begins and his "being wrought" by Iago ends is enigmatic.

The second of the two ways in which the ending of *Othello* cautions against hasty "censure" is an alternative offered to Cassio's punishment of Iago, an alternative at once potentially satisfying and possibly obscure to a modern audience. It hinges on Iago's final silence. Perhaps what most disturbs any audience about Iago's last moments is his refusal to divulge the motives for his behavior, from his point of view. Othello, seemingly unable to stomach directly addressing Iago, asks Lodovico and others to inquire why this "demi-devil" has "ensnar'd" his "soul and body"; Iago responds, "Demand me nothing; what you know, you know: / From this time forth I never will speak word" (5.2.301–04). Having "part confess'd his villainy," Iago makes one final play for control in the only way available to him: withholding all other information (5.2.296). At last, however, his efforts to bedevil others may only turn in on himself, as suggested by Lodovico's reaction to Iago's vow never again to "speak word": "What? not to pray?" (5.2.304–05). Without fully confessing, Iago condemns himself spiritually while ironically transferring the matter of his punishment from Cassio, or any other worldly arbiter, to heaven. What need Cassio's physical "torture" when Iago brings the inner torture of conscience on himself (5.2.369)?

At the very least, *Othello* displays the excruciating consequences of committing vengeance based on error, such as Othello's "great revenge" on Cassio and his delusion that he is the one appointed to prevent Desdemona from "betray[ing] more men" (5.2.74, 116, 6). In addition, the play shows perceptual error to be so common as to query whether grounds for revenge are ever certain.[5] To suppose that the play discounts relativism and therefore rejects degrees of guilt is wrong. Some characters—like Emilia and Cassio—are morally superior to Iago, even if they are flawed. Still, everywhere the play reminds the audience of its characters' mixed virtue; everywhere it is booby-trapped to expose the presumption of one's own correctness as folly, whether in the instance of the tragic protagonist Othello or the otherwise appealing Emilia. In its broad warning against assuming one's right to private vengeance, the play distinguishes itself from *Hamlet*, which is more exploratory than conclusive in regard to the same issue. *Hamlet* stretches over the entire arc of the play the same dilemma that Cassio faces at the end of *Othello*. Hamlet's duty, like Cassio's, is divided: privately, Hamlet believes he owes his father revenge on Claudius; publicly, he must put the state right, if Claudius has indeed deposed Hamlet's father and usurped the crown from his son (5.2.62–68). While in both plays essential ethical questions about revenge loom large, in *Othello* the danger of enacting private vengeance produces a strong antirevenge current from start to finish. That strong trend reflects back on

Hamlet in unexpected ways when the two plays are studied together from the standpoint of revenge.

More particularly, *Othello* and *Hamlet* link up intriguingly as revenge plays through the issue of human control—how much control Cassio is finally entitled to and how much Hamlet seizes as an avenger.[6] The question of whether Iago's ultimate silence sends him from Cassio's hands to God's parallels that of whether Hamlet is ever justified, as he for several reasons protests, in taking Claudius's life (not to mention the lives of Polonius, Rosencrantz, and Guildenstern). Hamlet's claim that he is God's "scourge and minister," although it condemns him to God's wrath for being a scourge, nevertheless neatly displaces responsibility for murdering both Polonius and Claudius from himself to "heaven" (3.4.173–75).[7]

One reason among many to distrust Hamlet's self-description as "scourge and minister" is that he later justifies killing Claudius, as well as Rosencrantz and Guildenstern, on the wholly different basis of "conscience," thus implying that his violence is his own choice rather than one scripted for him. Hamlet tells Horatio of his having killed Rosencrantz and Guildenstern that they "are not near" his "conscience" because "they did make love to this employment"— that is, they committed to spying on him for Gertrude and Claudius and thus betrayed him (5.2.57–58). In the same passage, he supports his right to kill Claudius with a litany of moral reasons:

> Does it not, think thee, stand me now upon—
> He that hath kill'd my king and whor'd my mother,
> Popp'd in between th' election and my hopes,
> Thrown out his angle for my proper life,
> And with such coz'nage—is't not perfect conscience
> To quit him with this arm? And is't not to be damn'd,
> To let this canker of our nature come
> In further evil?   (5.2.63–70)

If killing Claudius with his own arm were as conscionable as Hamlet asserts, he would hardly need to ask the moral question or to apologize for the act. This speech reveals a parallel between Hamlet and Othello that raises the further question of whether Hamlet is unrightfully usurping power: both see themselves as guarding public good by killing evil people (see *Othello* 5.2.6).

That Claudius has committed evil and Desdemona has not is insufficient reason to condone Hamlet's vengeance and to condemn Othello's. For in fact, although Hamlet may be convinced of Claudius's guilt, he is never objectively sure of it, as is the audience, who hears Claudius confess to the elder Hamlet's murder (3.3.36–38). Hamlet's strongest evidence is Claudius's reaction to the play in 3.2, but, because Hamlet ill-advisedly identifies the murderer of Gonzago as "one Lucianus, nephew to the king," he is never certain whether Claudius reacts badly to the play from seeing his own sin reenacted or from seeing his nephew Hamlet threaten him with murder (244). After the play is interrupted, Hamlet believes he has trapped his mouse, but his ironic self-assurance mirrors other instances where he is less clear-sighted than another character or the audience. One such example occurs when Hamlet narrowly misses Claudius's confession in 3.3 and pauses to weigh whether he should kill Claudius at his prayers: that decision, he says, "would be scann'd" (75). What should be scanned before the issue of controlling Claudius's hope of salvation, however, are the matters of his guilt and Hamlet's right to retaliation.[8] Accurate perception is every bit as problematically bound up with the ethics of revenge in *Hamlet* as in *Othello*. But in *Hamlet*, it is handled, like the ethics of revenge in general, more subtly. One result is that many of the perceptual problems in *Hamlet* challenge the audience, as well as the characters.[9]

Most challenging of all, I think, is the play's way of making the audience so impatient with Hamlet's delay that revenge can seem to be the ethical—indeed, the only—course of action available to him. But that effect of the play too, like the seemingly obvious matter of Cassio's final response to Iago (5.2), "would be scann'd." What may be the greatest critical divide about *Hamlet* emerges from its ability to make questioning the ethics of revenge seem silly in relation to the urgency of Hamlet's just getting on with it. In his seminal *Elizabethan Revenge Tragedy*, Fredson Bowers argues that original audiences of revenge plays like *Hamlet* cheered on the avenger because they recognized that his or her death would be "expiation for the violent motives which had forced him to override the rules of God" (184). But among plays that center on the act of revenge, *Hamlet*'s capacity to excite the audience's thirst for violence is exceptional, if not pathological, and the ethics of that capacity are more intricate than Bowers allows. Although Charles Hallett and Elaine Hallett are surprised to find critics taking revengers (all of whom they believe to be mad) at their word, relatively few critics have stepped back from Hamlet's desire for revenge to ask whether it is valid. Kenneth Branagh's film version of the play illustrates well the heroism that audiences often attach to Hamlet's aggression—for example, in 4.4, where he embraces, rather than shuns or examines, Fortinbras's gratuitous violence. The black-clad, square-shouldered Hamlet stands firmly between two rocks, the blue sky and mountain range rising behind him as the background music swells triumphantly. Thrusting a determined arm skyward, Branagh shows what is, for him, Hamlet's turning point; though it will cost him his life and perhaps his soul, he will at least prove his courage as an avenger: "O, from this time forth, / My thoughts be bloody, or be nothing worth!" (4.4.65–66).

A small group of critics also view this scene as a turning point, but a negative one. They locate Hamlet's tragedy not in his being fated to fulfill the role of "scourge and minister" but in the degeneration of his conscience over the play's course. One of the earliest such critics, Harold Skulsky, writes of the protagonist: "The tragedy of Hamlet . . . is the tragedy of spiritual decline"

(87). More recently, R. A. Foakes has analyzed Hamlet's delay as a result of his being "trapped . . . between two codes" of conduct: the pagan revenge code and the Christian prohibition against killing (98). Like Skulsky, Foakes reads Hamlet's growing tolerance of violence as troubling: "Hamlet increasingly displays a sardonic acceptance of the idea of death, and learns to distance himself from what he has done by claiming he is an agent of providence, and that his conscience is untroubled" (96). What we might think of as a minority report about antirevenge elements in *Hamlet* has a wider sweep across Elizabethan tragedies of blood. For a variety of reasons—the influence of feminist criticism and the current state of world affairs perhaps among them—scholars of these plays are more frequently reading them as discouraging revenge, even if the protagonist has just cause for complaint.[10] *Othello*, whose stature in Shakespeare's canon and importance in our culture derive from its countless merits, has much to teach students at all levels about Elizabethan (anti)revenge tragedy.

NOTES

[1]Citations to Shakespeare's plays are from Evans's *Riverside Shakespeare*.

[2]The subgenre of revenge tragedy, as originally defined by Fredson Bowers and explored thereafter by several others, may be due for revisitation, if not revision. But this short essay is not the appropriate venue for querying a generic category. This essay takes for granted that a group of identifiable Renaissance tragedies—among them *Titus Andronicus*, *The Spanish Tragedy*, and *Hamlet*—shows clear signs of Senecan influence and that a preoccupation with bloody vengeance finds its way well into the seventeenth century in plays like *The Duchess of Malfi*, *The Changeling*, and *'Tis Pity She's a Whore*.

[3]I realize that my second example of "clear perception"—Othello's temporarily successful defense of his virtuous intents—is a tricky one. It leads me into the very trap I am discussing in connection with the play's characters: making simple, black-and-white judgments about complex matters and human beings. Brabantio's assessment of Othello's evil nature in 1.3, although almost childishly simplistic, turns out to have its own validity. My point is only that Othello is clearly shown in the course of the play to be capable of a wide range of morality.

[4]The degree of Cassio's responsibility compared to Iago's is not my main concern here—only that Cassio shares in the responsibility. But the question of relative guilt arises throughout the play, most crucially in 3.3 and at the play's end.

[5]In teaching *Othello* from this angle, I often think of it as a sophisticated argument against capital punishment in our society.

[6]The issue of control may be one explanation for revenge plays' popularity at the time. Historically, the number of homicides in England seems to have dwindled between the years 1580 and 1700 (Sharpe 60–61); crime in general decreased as the state's power centralized and gained strength (Anderson 14). Although pockets of gentry were wont to organize themselves by 1550 to exact revenge on those they perceived to have injured them, the practice waned as concepts of courtly behavior became fashionable through such works as Baldassare Castiglione's *Courtier* (Sharpe 96–99).

Despite Francis Bacon's having seen fit to write an essay entitled "Of Revenge"—whence comes that famous phrase "Reuenge is a kinde of Wilde Iustice" (18)—private revenge does not seem to have been a critical social problem of the age. The theological debate over the limits of human control was another matter. It had broken out before Henry VIII split from the Catholic Church, and it continued to rage until the Civil War. In the early sixteenth century, Luther and Erasmus wrote contrary treatises on the question of free will. As the Reformation progressed, the Calvinist insistence on the bondage of the human will was the single most controversial concept for a culture whose Catholic heritage took root in the belief that individual sinners had some control over their own salvation through confession and penance. The historian Nicholas Tyacke has gone so far as to argue that the origins of the Civil War trace back to the Arminian controversy about the nature of grace—whether it is merely predestined or in any sense willed—that grew steadily from about the turn of the century. Whether a revenger is acting at God's behest or according to his or her choice reflects this controversy.

[7]Bowers eventually argued that the roles of scourge and minister were separate and distinct and that Hamlet transformed from a scourge to a minister over the course of the play. As scourge, he would be subject to God's punishment; as minister, to God's reward ("Hamlet").

[8]An example of a gap between Hamlet's perception and that of another character arises in Horatio's response to Claudius's call for "light" during the play (3.2.269); because Horatio's response is more reserved than Hamlet's is, it suggests that Horatio is less sure than Hamlet about what Claudius's reaction means. When Hamlet asks Horatio if he "[d]idst perceive" Claudius "[u]pon the talk of the pois'ning," expressing his own interpretation that Claudius has now revealed his guilt, Horatio is noncommittal: "I did very well note him" (287–90).

[9]Lily B. Campbell, discussing Renaissance theories of revenge, identifies a key epistemological problem for the audience in revenge tragedies. How does the audience know that the protagonist-avenger is the instrument of God that he proclaims himself to be?

[10]Two recent studies of Shakespeare's *Titus Andronicus* are relevant here. Although it is usually considered a play that revels in blood-letting and sympathizes with its title character's blood lust, its antirevenge strains have been diagnosed by Deborah Willis in " 'The Gnawing Vulture': Revenge, Trauma Theory, and *Titus Andronicus*." With an eye to Julie Taymor's complex response to the play's violence and to the violence ushered into American culture by September 11th, David McCandless studies both Taymor's staged production and her film *Titus*.

Teaching the Texts of *Othello*

Michael Warren

In recent years the study of the nature of the texts of Shakespeare's plays has changed from being the arcane pursuit of a few to a major topic of general scholarly interest. The publication in such standard classroom editions as the *Norton Shakespeare* and the New Pelican Shakespeare series of separate texts of the Quarto and the Folio *King Lear*, as well as a traditional conflated text, has made teachers and students aware of important issues here, even though they may not choose to explore them. In the classroom teachers usually give priority to the interpretation of the published text according to various historical or theoretical approaches. Nevertheless, it is advantageous and productive for teachers to give consideration to the nature of the text that is studied; the chosen edition is not an object of uncorrupted transmission from an unimpeachable authorial source but rather a product of history and theory. *Othello*, like *Lear*, presents opportunities for introducing students to the intellectual problems concerning the derivation and presentation of the texts of plays in modern editions and for considering what one means when one says "*Othello*." Attention to those problems can lead to a fresh approach to interpretive issues; it may also provoke new insights into the play.

A modern edition of any Shakespeare play is the product of the examination, discrimination, and evaluation of the data that the earliest printed editions of the play provide. Whether there is just one surviving text or many, the task involves the attempt to understand what the extant documentary evidence reveals. Traditional textual criticism aims to establish from the material data an approximation of the state of the play that the author would have regarded as its finished form. To do that requires a narrative concerning authorship, the transmission of a text from the playhouse to the printer, and the practice in the printing house. Recent thinking about texts has challenged the dominant twentieth-century narrative concerning origins and transmission and has questioned the possibility of establishing the authorial original. Yet in seeking to create an edition, any editor must still aim to present a state of the text that represents some perceived moment in the historical life of the play. Moreover, when two or more authoritative texts survive, the establishment of a single text may require editors to make choices between variant readings based on some hypothetical relation between the texts. *Othello* provides such an example.

Othello survives in two authoritative texts. It was first published in quarto in 1622, eighteen years after its first recorded performance at court, on 1 November 1604. The title page reads "The Tragœdy of Othello, The Moore of Venice. As it hath beene diuerse times acted at the Globe, and at the Black-Friers, by his Maiesties Seruants. Written by William Shakespeare." It was the last of Shakespeare's plays to be published for the first time before the First Folio. The next year, 1623, *Othello* appeared in the First Folio, *Mr. William Shakespeares Comedies, Histories, & Tragedies*, the collection of thirty-six plays compiled for publication by Shakespeare's colleagues in the King's Men, John Heminge and Henry Condell. It is not unusual to find that the folio text of a play already published in quarto is remarkably similar to it; in some cases the derivation of the folio from the quarto can be demonstrated. With *Othello*, however, the texts are very different. There are over a thousand verbal variants between the two texts. The 1622 Quarto text (Q1) contains more than fifty oaths that are not present in the First Folio (F1). Particularly noteworthy is the presence in F1 of approximately 160 lines that are not present in Q1, including significant material relating to major roles such as Desdemona, Emilia, and Othello; there are also a few passages that are specific to Q1 only.

Most editions of *Othello* are created by the modernization of the fuller F1 text and the selective introduction of individual readings from Q1. Various narratives of textual transmission have justified this procedure, but no one hypothesis currently has general assent. The New Bibliography, the system of thought about texts that dominated Shakespeare textual criticism and editing throughout most of the twentieth century, operated on the premise that most printed texts derived, directly or in the form of transcripts, from either the foul papers (an authorial late draft, but imperfect) or the prompt book (the licensed book of the play in the playhouse), which reflected the text in a more finished state than the foul papers since it had been prepared for performance. W. W. Greg worked within this framework but found that the texts of *Othello* presented challenges that were hard to explain. For instance, if, as Greg thought, Q1 was a text that had been cut for performance and yet derived from foul papers, then cuts related to performance must have been made in the foul papers—an anomalous act, since foul papers were assumed to have no direct connection to performance. In *The Shakespeare First Folio*, he wrote that "evidence for the textual history of *Othello* remains contradictory and ambiguous" (370). A few years later two other scholars independently provided new ways of thinking about the differences between the two texts. In *Shakespeare's Professional Skills*, Nevill Coghill, who was not a bibliographer, proposed that the F1-only passages are material added by a revising author rather than material cut from foul papers or an early prompt book. E. A. J. Honigmann proposed in *The Stability of Shakespeare's Text* that the large number of individual variant words and phrases could be explained as the consequence of "second thoughts" (2) on the part of the author, who, having completed his foul papers, modified individual words of his text persistently while making the fair copy for the playhouse. In 1982, in the context of discussions then current concerning revision in *King Lear*, Honigmann discussed Coghill's arguments and, extending the scope of Coghill's thinking, identified "strategies of revision" ("Revised Plays" 158) between Q1 and F1 *Othello*. In A *Textual Companion*, published in conjunction with the Oxford Shakespeare, Stanley Wells and Gary Taylor accepted the idea of authorial revision between Q1 and F1 and proposed that Q1 derives from a transcript of foul papers whereas F1 represents a transcript of Shakespeare's own revised manuscript (477). The text in the Oxford *Complete Works* was therefore based on F1 as closer to Shakespeare's final text. However, the presence of authorial revision in F1 has since been challenged. In *The Texts of* Othello *and Shakespearian Revision*, Honigmann abandoned his endorsement of Coghill's views and rejected his own earlier support for the idea of systematic revision, presenting the position that Q1 and F1 derive from two preperformance authorial manuscripts (foul papers and fair copy), both of which originally contained all the material found in F1 (*Texts* 21). The text of his Arden edition reflects his new views. More recently, Scott McMillin has argued that Q1 and F1 derive from two separate performance scripts prepared in the playhouse from the prompt book at some point during the period 1604–22. For McMillin, the two texts are a pair of surviving textual moments in the history of the play *Othello* and should be considered as theatrical documents detached from their authorial origins (421).

Knowledge of the intricacies of these arguments is beyond the need of undergraduate students, but it is appropriate that they should learn how uncertain scholars are about the nature of the surviving documents and how the text that they study corresponds to neither of its sources exactly. This discrepancy may become apparent casually in the classroom if some students are using an edition other than that which the instructor and the rest of the class are using; small variants can lead to inquiry since they provoke students to different, even conflicting, interpretations. Moreover, if, as most scholars believe, the two texts reflect two different states of the play as it probably was performed between 1604 and 1622, it is instructive to examine the major and even some of the minor differences between the texts. I discuss three linked topics: act 4, scene 3, especially the willow-song sequence; the role of Emilia; and some individual verbal variants.

The conversation between Desdemona and Emilia in 4.3 is an extraordinary moment not only in the play but in the whole of the Shakespeare corpus. As a serving woman helps her lady prepare for bed, they converse informally. No other scene in Shakespeare has this sort of intimate setting and tone; located in a private space, it contrasts with the public violence and distress of the previous scene. Yet the audience knows that an attempt is about to be made on Cassio's life and that Othello plans to kill Desdemona in her bed. It is a scene of potential nuances and tones, and so it permits a wide range of possible interpretations. For instance, one need only consider what level of anxiety Desdemona should display in conversation immediately after Othello's abrupt commands to her; that decision will influence the interpretation of all that follows.

The scene in the received text (based on F1) is notable for Desdemona's recollection of the old song, a traditional song and not an original composition by Shakespeare, that her mother's maid, Barbary, sang. Her recollection of the betrayed Barbary, who died singing, occurs just after she has expressed thoughts of death and has refused to criticize Othello:

> My mother had a maid called Barbary,
> She was in love, and he she loved proved mad
> And did forsake her. She had a song of "willow,"
> An old thing 'twas, but it expressed her fortune
> And she died singing it. That song tonight
> Will not go from my mind.   (4.3.24–29)[1]

Students and spectators of the play are well acquainted with the sequence that succeeds these lines: the discussion of Lodovico, Desdemona's singing of the song, her interruptions of the song, her intermittent instructions to Emilia that refer to the preparation for bed, all ending with the reference to her eyes itching. However, this material derives from F1 alone and is not present in Q1, which continues as follows:

> Will not goe from my mind—harke, who's that knocks?
> *Em.*   It is the wind.
> *Des.*   Now get thee gone, good night:
>   Mine eyes do itch, does that bode weeping?
>   (L2v; *Shakespeare's Plays* 827)

Textual scholars debate whether these two states of the sequence result from cutting for performance or from addition in the process of revision. Critical opinion has regularly entertained the possibility that the absence of the song from Q1 was occasioned by the lack of a boy actor with the capacity to sing the song; meanwhile, those who suspect the addition of the song in the process of revision need no explanation beyond the assumption of desire on the part of the author (or someone else?) to amplify the scene as it appears in Q1.

In the classroom the sequence provides the opportunity to discuss questions that each text raises. For example, in F1, what is Desdemona's response to Emilia's comment on Lodovico? What does the singing of the song reveal about Desdemona? What is the significance of her getting the words out of order? What relationship with Emilia is evident in her series of instructions concerning getting ready for bed? What are the theatrical effects of the singing of the song (how does it "play")? How should the performer of the role of Desdemona perform the song?

Having pursued these inquiries that are specific to F1, one should next ask what the distinctive qualities of the Q1 text are. How does one interpret Desdemona without the song? Does the part read differently, providing different opportunities for the performer? Is she calmer or more anxious? Does the absence of the song produce a less pathetic experience of Desdemona's predicament? What is the significance of her mentioning the song and not singing it and of her move to dismiss Emilia immediately after the reference to the wind? What are the characteristics of Desdemona's behavior in the sequence in Q1? What is the potential theatrical effect of the scene's swiftness? (Performers of the willow song usually sing it slowly.) How does the absence of instructions to Emilia affect the interpretation or the performance of the sequence?

One can then approach the two versions comparatively. How is the relationship of Desdemona and Emilia portrayed in the variant states? How does Emilia respond to Desdemona's behavior in either version? With such approaches one soon arrives at two fundamental questions: how different is the scene in Q1 and F1 and what are the interpretive strategies that one is employing as one examines that difference? The comparison of the two states sharpens the perception of each and renders the received text strange and fresh.

Classroom discussion of the willow-song sequence will usually focus on Desdemona and the structure of her role. However, discussion of the rest of the scene should focus on Emilia's role. After the song, Desdemona wonders whether there really are adulterous wives. Her question is abruptly delivered in Q1. To Emilia's statement, "Tis neither here nor there," Desdemona responds, "Wouldst thou doe such a deed, for all the world?" (L2v; *Shakespeare's Plays* 827). In F1 and the received text (4.3.58, 63), her question emerges more gradually. To her protestation in both texts that "I do not think there is any such woman," Emilia replies, "Yes, a dozen, and as many to th' vantage as would store the world they played for" (4.3.82–84). In F1, Emilia follows her brief prose sentence with a bold speech of eighteen lines of verse that addresses the rights of women in relation to their husbands' sexual inattentiveness:

> But I do believe it is their husbands' faults
> If wives do fall. Say they slack their duties . . .
> . . . .
> Then let them use us well: else let them know,
> The ills we do, their ills instruct us so.
>   (4.3.85–86, 101–02)

Emilia's notable protest, in which she is heard clearly as an independent thinker, is unanticipated in the play; although Desdemona has the final couplet, theatrically Emilia provides the climax to the scene with a speech that challenges the patience audible in the line of Desdemona's song, "Let nobody blame him, his scorn I approve" (4.3.51). In Q1, however, this verse speech does not appear. In both texts the scene concludes with the couplet, "Good night, good night. God me such usage send / Not to pick bad from bad, but by bad mend" (4.3.103–04; for "God," F1 reads "Heaven"). In the classroom it is common to discuss the power of Emilia's speech, but how is the role of Emilia to be regarded without it? How does the scene work without it?

. After studying two versions of a scene, students should be aware that different textual states enable different reading and theatrical experiences. However, the juxtaposition of this material in 4.3 with F1-only passages elsewhere in the play can raise further questions about the distinctive nature of the two texts and their possible relations. First, in the previous scene there is another speech of similar length that appears in F1 and not in Q1: Desdemona's protestation of total fidelity to Othello as she kneels in the presence of Iago and Emilia: "Here I kneel . . . To do the act that might the addition earn / Not the world's mass of vanity could make me" (4.2.153, 165–66). The speech appears to be a complement to Emilia's protest—chastity and submission to the husband's will in one case, a demand for equality and sexual rights in marriage in the other. Theatrically, Desdemona's kneeling in Iago's presence relates visually to two places where the text is shorter in Q1 than in F1, in both of which Othello is either kneeling or prostrate in the presence of Iago (the relevant lines are 3.3.456–63 and 4.1.38–43). Second, Emilia has other F1-only speeches in 5.2. In both texts she is the agent who exposes Iago's deceptions. In the process of the revelation, Emilia participates in the dialogue in F1 (5.2.147–50; 181–90) but not in Q1; her presentation of the evidence that incriminates Iago provides greater opportunities for vehemence in F1 than in Q1. Finally, whereas in her dying speech in Q1 she begins, "Moor, she was chaste," in F1 she prefaces that statement with a recollection of the willow song: "What did thy song bode, lady? / Hark, canst thou hear me? I will play the swan / And die in music. Willow, willow, willow" (5.2.247, 244–

46). Obviously the presence or absence of these lines relates to the presence or absence of the willow song in 4.3. Although it is a matter of scholarly debate whether the cause of variation is cutting or addition, there can be no debate that these variants establish different patterns in the construction and dramatic action of the two roles.

The presence and absence of passages are the most conspicuous signals of textual variation, but the *Othello* texts repeatedly vary at the local level. Most edited texts introduce the oaths and references to God rather than heaven that are characteristic of Q1. Since their omission from F1 may well indicate that the F1 text derives from after 1606 when the Statute against Abuses prohibited the uttering of oaths and blasphemies on stage, editors conclude that in this respect the Q1 text antedates F1 and is closer to the authorial original. But there are hundreds of other individual variants that present editors with challenges if they are not just to follow one text exclusively: for instance Q1: "provulgate," F1: "promulgate" (1.2.21); Q1: "acerb," F1: "bitter" (1.3.350); Q1: "enscerped," F1: "ensteep'd" (2.1.70). Although such variants constitute the verbal texture of each state of the play and are important in that regard, most do not individually produce significant challenges to the interpretation of the speaking role or the action. However, there are at least two passages in which the brief verbal variants create a major interpretive issue, and they can demonstrate for students the implications of local editorial decisions. In Othello's speech to the Senate about the process of his wooing of Desdemona, most editions print the line "She gave me for my pains a world of sighs" (1.3.160). Here "sighs" is the reading of Q1; F1 reads "kisses." Later in the scene Desdemona declares in most editions that her "heart's subdued / Even to the very quality of my lord" (1.3.251–52). Q1 is the source of "very quality"; F1 reads "utmost pleasure." Editors who adopt the Q1 readings do so on the grounds that "kisses" and "utmost pleasure" are not compatible with other features of the role of Desdemona; the individual editor thereby exercises judgment based on personal interpretation. It is not unprofitable to ask students how they interpret the variant states, which readings they would adopt if they were establishing a text, and how they would justify their decisions.

Such a basic introduction to textual criticism as I am proposing requires access to information and the ability to make that information available to students. Facsimiles of Q1 and F1 are available in libraries but are expensive for individual purchasers. A facsimile of the First Folio is available on CD-ROM in the Octavo Digital Editions series (Shakespeare, *Comedies*). Facsimiles of F1 are available on the Web, but at the time of writing no facsimile of Q1 is available. However, downloadable diplomatic transcriptions of Q1 and F1 that can be used in teaching are available at the *Internet Shakespeare Editions* site (http://ise.uvic.ca). The Q1 text has been published in an inexpensive diplomatic reprint edited by Andrew Murphy in the series Shakespearean Originals: First Editions (*Tragœdy of Othello*). Scott McMillin has published an edition of Q1 in the New Cambridge Shakespeare: The Early Quartos series (*First Quarto*). Major editions of the play such as Arden 3 and the New Cambridge include an essay concerning the textual and editorial issues and also present below the text a textual apparatus that indicates the variants. Collected editions usually present lists of variants either before or after the play, where they are not easy to consult. Individual classroom editions do the same, but Barbara A. Mowat and Paul Werstine's New Folger Library edition, based on F1, facilitates study by marking all F1-only passages of a line or more with square brackets and signaling all adoptions of readings from Q1 with pointed brackets (see *Tragedy of Othello*).

NOTE

[1]Citations from *Othello* are from Honigmann's Arden 3 edition unless otherwise noted; it is representative of the received text as it appears in most editions. The two passages quoted from Q1 reproduce the text of the facsimile of the Huntington copy as it appears in *Shakespeare's Plays in Quarto*.

Motivating Iago

Maurice Hunt

Strictly speaking, one cannot say that Iago has any motivation in *Othello*. "[A]s a character in a play, not a person, Iago has no motivation. His entire existence consists of words on a page: he has no psychology, no character or personality, no history (he had no past before the play began, and has no future after it ends)." This opinion of Stanley Edgar Hyman (4–5) has been effectively refuted by James Calderwood: "One problem with this otherwise admirable proclamation is that it endows motivation with an illusionary status no more peculiar to it than to anything else in the theater" (117). "In fact," Calderwood concludes, "Hyman should have titled his book not *Iago* but *The Illusion of Iago* because like everything else in the play Iago is, as he admits, not what he is" (118). In defense of Hyman, one could point out that Calderwood fails to mention Hyman's subsequent admission that every dramatist creates characters who must act and speak as though they had "a psychology, a personality, a history going back to birth, and so forth, in order to make [their] behavior, or [their] share of the play's action, credible and dramatically effective" (5). Undergraduate students are especially attuned to looking for motives in drama, nowhere more so than in Shakespeare's plays, because of students' training in the novel and other kinds of literature. Hyman's authority for his commonsense assertion that dramatists must assign, or associate, motives with their characterizations is Aristotle, in the fifteenth section of his *Poetics*, where he implies that, by assigning moral or immoral purposes to characters and by striving to make them true to life, dramatists necessarily create characters with motives. To be credible likenesses of human beings, dramatic characters must appear to have motives for their actions. Since Iago represents the most vexed case of motivation in all Shakespeare, prefacing a class period solely devoted to "motivating Iago" with a brief presentation and discussion of Aristotle's section fifteen proves useful.

More so than any other Shakespeare character, Iago seems to have too many motives for his evil and thus, paradoxically, no motives for it at all. This strange impression appears to have originated with E. H. Seymour and Samuel Taylor Coleridge in the early nineteenth century. In 1805, Seymour pronounced, concerning Iago's soliloquy at the end of act 2, scene 1 of *Othello*, "there are no sufficient motives apparent for this excess of malignity," a judgment echoed famously by Coleridge when, focused on the same passage, he exclaimed, "[Iago's] last Speech, the motive-hunting of motive-less Malignity—how awful! In itself fiendish . . ." (qtd. in Shakespeare, *Othello* [ed. Honigmann] 33–34; Pechter 58). The problem both critics identify stems from the perception that Iago's stated motive for evil in this second-act soliloquy (sexual jealousy) seems to bear no relation to his stated motive at the beginning of the play (professional envy and resentment). Furthermore, the belief that Iago never reiterates his first motive reinforces the impression of this disjunction. As a result, some commentators adopt the view that Iago, as the tragedy unfolds, had to make up additional motives for wanting to destroy Othello, Cassio, and Desdemona in order to fill in a gap. Since students may have this impression too, devoting a class period to motive identifying and delimiting Iago's motives is time well spent.

What does Iago specifically say his motives are for wanting to destroy Cassio and Othello, and later Desdemona? First, Iago tells Roderigo that he hates Othello because the Moor passed over Iago and promoted Cassio instead, a Florentine whom Iago considers inferior to himself professionally as a soldier (1.1.6–39).[1] Second, Iago states in a soliloquy that he hates Othello because he suspects the general of committing adultery with his wife, Emilia (1.3.385–403, 2.1.291–300). Third, he hates Cassio not only because Iago thinks he deserves Cassio's promotion but also because he suspects Cassio has been committing adultery with Emilia as well. (Instructors will want to tell students that the play offers no evidence supporting Iago's suspicions of adultery). Fourth, he hates Cassio because, to use Iago's words, Cassio "hath a daily beauty in his life / That makes me ugly" (5.1.19–20). Beyond these four stated motives, all is inference.

One could easily infer that Iago hates Desdemona too, because she, more than Cassio, has a daily beauty in her life that might make a man like Iago feel ugly. Or one could infer that he hates her because he loves her and is thus jealous of her affection for and marriage to Othello. The basis for this last inference are these problematic verses about Desdemona in Iago's second-act soliloquy:

> Now I do love her too,
> Not out of absolute lust—though peradventure
> I stand accountant for as great a sin—
> But partly led to diet my revenge,
> For that I do suspect the lusty Moor
> Hath leaped into my seat, the thought whereof
> Doth like a poisonous mineral gnaw my inwards . . .
> And nothing can or shall content my soul
> Till I am evened with him, wife for wife. . . .
> (2.1.289–97)

In these halting verses, Iago reveals that he lusts after (not loves) Desdemona and that he partly does so not out of real passion but out of an act of will, to be "evened" with Othello, adulterous wife for adulterous wife. The great sin to which he alludes is usually taken to be revenge, which in this context displaces the sin of lust. This qualification weakens the likelihood that his motive for hating Desdemona involves a love for her.

E. A. J. Honigmann has shown that Iago's original motive for hating Othello, his resentment over Cassio's promotion, is repeated in different but related terms throughout the play and thus not dropped as Coleridge and others believed (Honigmann, *Shakespeare: Seven Tragedies* 77–88; Shakespeare, *Othello* [ed. Honigmann] 34–35). Still, Iago's first motive and the others, which are closely related by his preoccupation with sexual infidelity, continue to appear incompatible. Furthermore, certain remarks of Iago's suggest that some or all of his explicit motives may be fabricated and thus that other more genuine secret motives may undergird them. Utterances such as the following create this impression: "I know not if [Othello's rumored adultery with Emilia] be true, / But I for mere suspicion in that kind / Will do as if for surety" (1.3.387–89). In this vein, Edward Pechter and Bryan Reynolds and Joseph Fitzpatrick, along with other critics, have noted the paratactic rather than causal structure of motivational assertions of Iago's such as "I hate the Moor / And it is thought abroad that 'twixt my sheets / He's done my office" (1.3.385–87). Reynolds and Fitzgerald argue that if adultery were a motive for hating Othello, Iago would have said that he hates the Moor because it is thought abroad that Othello is committing adultery with Emilia (214). As it is, Iago's "And" makes the suspected adultery logically, causally unconnected with his hatred of Othello (Pechter 62).

An instructor can lead a class to understand this point during discussion. At this juncture, it is fruitful to introduce students to the idea that Iago's motives derive from the kind of person he is, as many commentators assert, rather than the specific injuries he claims. Iago "is malicious, and pleased at the misfortunes of others, envious, hard, and unmoved by pity, at the same time cunning, shrewd, and calculating, a master of dissimulation, in every way a *faux bonhomme*" (Schücking 64). Both A. C. Bradley and Honigmann argue that Iago's tremendous malice toward others springs from his regret that he is not a gentleman, from his resentment of social privilege, from his artistic delight in manipulating others to gain power over them, and from his thwarted sense of superiority and his consequent contempt for others (Bradley 179–92; Shakespeare, *Othello* [ed. Honigmann] 34–35). The list is not exhaustive. Jane Adamson traces Iago's motives to his excessive sadism, to his need to inflict on others the gnawing pain that his envy, jealousy, and sense of inferiority make him feel always. A class discussion of how Iago's motives are associated with other personality traits is helpful but risks obscuring, or dismissing, his stated motives for evil.

This risk is compounded by the multitude of critical studies of *Othello* that suggest that Iago's motives can be explained by his conforming to one or more (mainly literary) character types. Hyman has conveniently assembled the most often mentioned of these types. In *Iago: Some Approaches to the Illusion of His Motivation*, we find chapters in which Hyman quotes language from *Othello* that purportedly establishes Iago as stage villain (vice figure) (8–28), as Satan (29–60), as criminal artist (61–76), as latent homosexual (101–21), and as the Machiavel (122–36). At one or more moments in the tragedy, Iago's words and deeds could authorize the application of these paradigms to his characterization. Each of these types entails its own motivation. The stage villain as vice figure entails, in Leah Scragg's words, "the allegorical represen- tation of an inner moral frailty" (61), a frailty that spreads destruction through the vice's amoral glee in spreading mischief and ruin. This differs from the Luciferan motive of destroying representations of humankind envied for their bliss or beauty, of attempting to thwart God by damning his creation. Leading a class into this kind of consideration of Iago's motives runs the risk that the motive discussed belongs to the type and not to Iago, or not to Iago at dif- ferent moments in the play. One has difficulty imagining, for example, that the traits of the English stage version of the Machiavel can explain the inten- sity of Iago's hatred for specific persons whose ruin would not guarantee Iago the material, political advancement the Machiavel typically desires. Nor can Iago as criminal artist, enjoying his ruthless power as puppet master of Othello, Cassio, and Desdemona, account for the life-and-death personal risk he runs in satisfying his artistic craving or for the intensity and specificity of his hatred (however, cf. Calderwood 118–20).

Scragg has persuasively shown that Shakespeare's contemporaries fre- quently conflated the stage villain or vice and the satanic figure or stage devil. She claims that a conflated type would have been Shakespeare's contempo- raries' perception of Iago. In classroom discussions that consider Iago's mo- tives as the result of conflated character types, the two most important Iagos are Iago as Satan and Iago as latent homosexual. Herein, however, lies the rub, for one represents a symbol and the other represents a man. Despite Hyman's and Robert Heilman's claims otherwise (Hyman 137–47, esp. 140; Heilman 227–29), Iago cannot be both Satan and latent homosexual at any one moment in the play. If he is Satan, a possibility dismissed by Honigmann and many other commentators on *Othello*, he cannot play all the mortal roles usually advanced for Iago. Admittedly, Iago as Satan could at different dra- matic moments play the roles of criminal artist and the Machiavel. It may be possible to find a medieval or early modern precedent for claiming that Satan adopts the role of sodomite. But Iago's homosexuality is latent; Iago, seemingly unconscious of it, is the victim of it. One could say that his latent homosex- uality leads directly to his ruin. Shakespeare would have been aware of the historical tendency to regard Satan as an evil Proteus, a devil who can assume any shape or form to work his evil, even though it, unbeknownst to him, operates to advance God's Providence. (But in *Othello*, one cannot imagine how Providence is furthered by Iago's overwhelming, successful evil). In his vulnerability to his latent homosexuality, Iago is a man—not Satan or a devil. An instructor only confuses a class to say that Iago is both a man and Satan. The challenge in teaching Iago's motivation involves solving this conundrum.

Let us consider more fully the possibility that Iago is a devil type. Hyman demonstrates the abundant evidence in *Othello* for regarding Iago as Satan or a figuration of Satan and thus for considering Iago's destructive motives to be

Satan's (29–60). The plausibility of Hyman's view comes from considering the passages that Hyman cites. When Iago, summarizing his duplicity for Roderigo, pronounces, "I am not what I am" (1.1.64), he implies that he is the archetypal adversary of God, who revealed himself to Moses by pronouncing, "I am that I am" (Exod. 3.14). When Iago tells Roderigo to "plague" Othello "with flies" (1.1.70), the Lord of the Flies may be giving diabolical advice. When he tells Roderigo that he hates Othello "as I do hell-pains" (1.1.152), he seems to be speaking, when his words are reconsidered in the light of the whole play, from firsthand experience. These allusions are consistent with Iago's repeatedly equating himself with the devil. "[Y]ou are one of those that will not serve God, if the devil bid you" (1.1.107–08), Iago tells Roderigo. During the brawl between the drunken Cassio and Montano, Iago shouts, "Who's that which rings the bell? Diablo, ho!" (2.3.157). By uttering the Spanish form of the word "devil," Iago equates the devil with himself, for Iago is a Spanish version of the English name James. Iago exclaims in a soliloquy:

> Divinity of hell!
> When devils will the blackest sins put on
> They do suggest at first with heavenly shows
> As I do now.   (2.3.345–48)

For many readers and playgoers, this exclamation and following utterance amount to Iago's revelation of diabolic identity.

The above examples come from only the first two acts of *Othello*. The most memorable identification of Iago as Satan occurs near the end of the play, when Othello, aware of Iago's deception and his own crime, addresses Iago: "I look down towards his feet, but that's a fable. / If that thou be'st a devil, I cannot kill thee" (5.2.283–84). Othello looks for the devil's fabled cloven hoof. When he immediately stabs Iago, his victim triumphantly says, "I bleed, sir, but not killed" (5.2.285). Iago may lack the devil's cloven hoof and may copiously bleed stage (pig's) blood, but, judged by the terms of Othello's assumption, he *is* the devil: the Moor's apparently mortal thrust does not kill him. Iago's resolute commitment to silence concerning his motives for destroying Othello and Desdemona is consistent with diabolical pride and defiance of pain and torture.

This satanic reading of Iago's motives finds its place in the viable morality-play allegory inherent in *Othello*, wherein Othello is Judas, Desdemona Christ, and Iago Satan or, alternatively, wherein Othello is an everyman figure forced to choose between angelic Desdemona and satanic Iago. (For a listing of critical accounts of these allegories, see Hunt, "Predestination" 373n63). Othello, believing Desdemona dead, does say, "Methinks it should be now a huge eclipse / Of sun and moon" (5.2.98–99), thus likening her death to Christ's, when darkness covered the earth. And if Othello in his final speech likens himself to "the base [Judean]" who "threw a pearl away / Richer than all his tribe" (5.2.345–46), he likens himself to Judas, the betrayer of the great pearl Christ. Shakespeare possibly never worried about the fissure that exists between a morality reading and a naturalistic reading of *Othello*. The tragedy certainly can be read allegorically through five acts, just as it can be read naturalistically through five acts. But, to repeat myself, it cannot be read both ways at the same moment. I have argued elsewhere that Othello, Iago, and Cassio create the morality-play reading of the events in *Othello* and that they do so to vilify and blame others as well as to excuse their own behavior or rationalize their own desires ("Predestination" 375n64). The language creating the theological allegories of *Othello* is theirs before it is Shakespeare's, or it is theirs instead of Shakespeare's (even though he wrote this language).

Cassio's dream as told by Iago represents the key piece of evidence for those commentators who believe that Iago's latent homosexuality explains his motives for wishing to destroy the Moor, his wife, and Cassio. Janet Adelman reminds us that "[I]ago's own erotic life takes place only in his head" ("Alter Ego" 129). To whet Othello's jealousy, Iago fabricates a story of a night in which, as soldiers, he and Cassio lay together. "In his sleep," Iago claims,

> I heard him say "Sweet Desdemona,
> Let us be wary, let us hide our loves,"
> And then, sir, would he gripe and wring my hand,
> Cry, "O sweet creature!" and then kiss me hard
> As if he plucked up kisses by the roots
> That grew upon my lips, lay his leg o'er my thigh,
> And sigh, and kiss, and then cry "Cursed fate
> That gave thee to the Moor!"   (3.3.421–28)

Ostensibly told to inflame Othello's jealousy and stir up hatred of Desdemona and Cassio, Iago's fantasy also, according to this account of his motives, conveys his barely repressed sexual desire for Cassio—and for Othello. If one cites Iago's latent homosexuality to explain his motives, his protestations of love for Othello carry genuine weight: "My lord, you know I love you" (3.3.119); "I humbly do beseech you of your pardon / For too much loving you" (3.3.215–16). Judged in the light of these protestations, Iago's kneeling with Othello at the end of act 3, scene 3, to pledge himself completely to the Moor's service, amounts to a forbidden wedding of love that he has secretly desired (3.3.465–82). Othello's response to Iago's fervent pledge—"I greet thy love" (3.3.472)—identifies the motive possibly fueling this pledge. This approach explains Iago's uniformly low view of women, including his wife, Emilia, and his hatred of his competitor Desdemona in particular. His wish to destroy Othello, and possibly Cassio too, stems from his need to remove temptations creating an unbearable inner conflict.

What makes this portrayal of Iago's motives plausible is its ability to explain the intensity and pathological compass of Iago's suspicions of cuckoldry. The

Freudian dynamics underlying Iago's suspicions suggest that his paranoid jealousy amounts to a male reaction formation to homosexual urges (see Ernest Jones, "Case" 52–53 and *Years* 270–71). This defense mechanism—at least in theory—deflects the threat of these urges by partly satisfying them in pornographic imaginings of the man secretly desired in sexual intercourse with a woman, often a wife. The reaction formation involves the unconscious deceit, "I don't desire him, she does." Its defense, protecting the consciousness from full knowledge of the urge, is pathological, promiscuous sexual jealousy (Freud, "Neurotic Mechanisms"). The best account of this Freudian dynamic in Shakespeare criticism is that of J. I. M. Stewart, who analyzes Leontes's strong bond with Polixenes and his consequent deluded belief that his friend and his wife, Hermione, are committing adultery (30–37). Leontes's role in *The Winter's Tale* is often thought of as a later, romance reprisal of Othello's. But it also has relevance for evaluating Iago's motivation. Shakespeare, like Spenser and other early modern writers, incorporated number symbolism into his works. No one—to my knowledge—has noticed that Iago and Leontes (at the beginning of *The Winter's Tale*) are the same age: twenty-eight (1.3.312–15; Hunt, "Three Seasons" 300–01). Oddly, Stewart never explicitly associates the motivation he assigns to Leontes to Iago, but he could have done so, for it can account for Iago's belief that the Moor and Cassio are having sexual intercourse with his wife.

Introducing students to this explanation for Iago's hatred has the advantage of subsequently being able to suggest that Iago is not Satan or a devil but a tormented man acting out a delusion of sexual repression. One could claim that Iago's impulse to play Satan amounts to compensation for profound feelings of inadequacy, one feeling of which derives from his failure to know himself and control his passions. Moreover, this approach to Iago's motivation provides an explanation for the secondary status of the villain's motive of envy over Cassio's promotion and the impression that the envy motive is only weakly sustained. Furthermore, viewing his motivation thusly can help instructors explain difficult changes in Othello's motivation. If Othello loves Desdemona as much as he says he does, why does he talk so quickly, for little reason, of not loving her at all? Iago has scarcely insinuated anything improper in Cassio and Desdemona's relationship before Othello erupts:

> Excellent wretch! perdition catch my soul
> But I do love thee! and when I love thee not
> Chaos is come again.   (3.3.90–92)

One way to explain Othello's strange, sudden inclination not to love Desdemona as well as the savagery of his sexual jealousy is to suggest that the Moor, like Iago but to a much lesser degree, feels an unconscious but definite attraction to men, to Iago himself. Thus Othello's unknowing words to Iago, "I greet thy love" (3.3.472). Othello and Iago are complementary halves of a whole in this respect, a whole later refigured in *The Winter's Tale* when Leontes internally plays Iago to his own Othello.

Iago's motivation may be the most vexed case in the Shakespeare canon. But sorting through and logically delimiting possibilities of interpretation nevertheless remain possible for instructors determined to provide a consistent, coherent account of his motivation. Still, instructors attracted by the inclusiveness of the Freudian model for accounting for Iago's manifold motivation should introduce it in a broader psychoanalytic context. This context would include an explanation that, at this moment in the development of psychoanalytic theory and practice, the Freudian oedipal paradigm amounts to a historical phenomenon, useful at times for literary analysis but only when supplemented by post-Freudian psychoanalytic theory and methodology, which have superseded it. Meredith Skura's *The Literary Use of Psychoanalytic Process* offers teachers of *Othello* the best overall discussion of post-Freudian psychoanalytic literary interpretation, and Adelman's *Suffocating Mothers: Fantasies of Maternal Origin in Shakespeare's Plays*, Hamlet *to the* Tempest gives them a fine example of that style of psychoanalytic reading.

In her article "Iago's Alter Ego: Race as Projection in *Othello*," Adelman constructs an alternative reading of Iago's psychopathology based on the theories of Melanie Klein, which necessarily engages the issue of his motivation. Nicholas Radel, in his essay in this volume, also offers a post-Freudian reading of Iago's masculine desire, a nonpathological approach to this subject. Because Freud's account of a reaction formation to a male's latent sexual desire for another man makes that desire pathological, the source of an illness, teaching an approach to Iago's motivation based on Freudian theory runs the risk today of seeming antihomosocial, the equivalent of seeming racist, of seeming to endorse the equivalent of Roderigo's ugly idea of Othello. If instructors teach a Freudian-based approach to Iago's motivation, they need, I believe, to discuss the limitations of Freudian theory with students and the negative impressions those limitations can potentially produce. Rather than as sciences or even methods, Freudian and post-Freudian psychoanalytic dynamics are prudently taught in the *Othello* classroom as metaphors for giving the instructor and his or her students the language to complete the taxonomy of Iago's complex motivation. Otherwise, teachers of the play are restricted to partial readings, most likely to the old approach that Iago's evil is an irreducible theological mystery, the closest Shakespeare ever came to making Lucifer's unknowable fault a character trait.

NOTE

[1]Citations to *Othello* are from Honigmann's edition.

Unhoused in *Othello*

Geraldo U. de Sousa

I teach *Othello* in a variety of undergraduate and graduate courses and always enjoy doing so because the play never fails to engage my students' interest and imagination. I have been teaching the play in a theoretically eclectic way, although historical and anthropological approaches, combined with close reading of text and performance, predominate. In my upper-level Shakespeare survey for majors, however, we explore the phenomenology of the house.[1] I help my students discover the extent to which *Othello* connects racial and cultural difference with a sense of homelessness.

In preparation for our discussion, I assign a questionnaire for homework, which is due on the day we begin discussion of the play.[2] I assign a written group report (homework or in-class project) in which the students have to enumerate in detail Iago's malicious moves in his course of revenge and destruction. The report takes as its point of departure two passages. The first is Roderigo's reference to Othello as "an extravagant and wheeling stranger / Of here and everywhere" (1.1.134–35), punning on Othello's foreign status, lack of a permanent residence, and shifty nature. The second is Othello's own description of what he refers to as an "unhousèd free condition" (1.2.26), which he says he gave up when he married Desdemona.[3] My students look up the word *unhoused*, a rare and curious usage, which C. T. Onions's *A Shakespeare Glossary* defines as "having no household ties or cares, unrestricted" and the *Oxford English Dictionary* as "not provided with, not lodged in, a house; homeless." In two to three class periods, we explore the meaning and implications of Othello's self-defined homelessness. What I offer below is a sketch and a blueprint of our discussions.

Proofs or Illusions of Stability

My students' personal definitions of *home*, which serve as our point of departure, focus on home as an actual place (a house), a social institution, a cultural construct, and an ideal. Students also explain how such a place differs from other more temporary or transient dwelling places such as their dorm rooms or apartments. For my students, home signifies different things: the house where their parents live or where they grew up, a place of security and shelter; a familiar resting place; a sense of belonging; memories of meaningful family events; or, as one student said, "a place where I could walk around blindfolded without stumbling."

After this initial free-flowing discussion, I introduce the house as a philosophical and anthropological concept and explain how houses acquire experiential dimensions in their transformation into homes. Robert M. Rakoff puts it best when he writes:

> A house is a meaningful cultural object. People—builders who envision the end result, dwellers who inhabit and use its spaces, observers who seek to understand its cultural role—endow the house with meaning according to their culture's world view and ethos. As part of an ordered human world, houses are used to demarcate space, to express feelings, ways of thinking, and social processes, and to provide areas for culturally defined activity as well as to provide physical shelter.   (85)

Further, the idea of the house also serves to express the "uses and purposes of intimate space" (85). In *Poetics of Space*, Gaston Bachelard suggests that culturally, psychologically, spiritually,

> a house constitutes a body of images that gives mankind proofs or illusions of stability. We are constantly re-imagining its reality: to distinguish all these images would be to describe the soul of the house; it would mean developing a veritable psychology of the house.   (17)

Indeed, as a specific kind of place, home signifies the house or dwelling in which one habitually lives and the place to which one properly belongs and in which one's affections center or where one finds rest, refuge, or satisfaction.[4] In one class in 2003, the question whether houses give us "proofs or illusions of stability" generated a lively debate because at the time the television networks were bombarding the airwaves with images of hurricane Isabel's devastation along the Atlantic coast.

Next, we explore the different meanings of Othello's "unhousèd free condition." Students are puzzled by Othello's statement that he would not have put that "unhousèd free condition" "into circumscription and confine / For the sea's worth" (1.2.26–28) except for Desdemona's sake. One student remarked that, unlike Desdemona, Othello never felt connected to a place, another that he never had stability or a permanent place, and yet a third that Othello lived on the road. I steer the discussion to what Othello says about his past in act 1, scene 3. My students readily figure out that Othello refers in part to his experience as a slave, exile, traveler, and soldier. To focus on textual analysis, I ask students to read aloud the passages in act 1, scene 3, in which Othello recounts the story of his life, a story of tribulation, wandering, and homelessness: "disastrous chances," "accidents by flood and field," "hairbreadth scapes," slavery, and his "traveler's history" through "[r]ough quarries, rocks, and hills whose heads touch heaven" and dangerous and strange tribes, or as Othello states, the "dangers" for which Desdemona fell in love with him (1.3.128–70). Marriage to Desdemona implies an attempt to overcome a personal history of restlessness and wandering. Further, I point out an earlier textual detail that students tend to miss. Even while residing in Venice, Othello does not have a permanent home, as Cassio indicates: "You have been hotly called for; / When being not at your *lodging* to be found, / The Senate hath sent about three several quests / To search you out" (1.2.44–47; my emphasis). "Lodging" suggests temporary quarters, such as one finds in a boarding house, where Othello presumably lived before he married Desdemona.

However their decision to elope came about, Othello takes Desdemona from her father's house and seeks shelter for the night not in his usual Venetian lodging but somewhere else, as Othello's statement to Cassio implies: " 'Tis well I am found by you. / I will but spend a word here in the house, / And go with you" (1.2.47–49). He will go inside the house, tell Desdemona that the Duke and the senators require his presence, and then proceed to the Senate. The text makes clear that this house provides only temporary accommodation. When the Senate orders Othello to set sail for Cyprus, for he best knows "the fortitude of the place" (1.3.222), Desdemona's own "unhousèd" condition becomes apparent. Desdemona has no place to stay during his absence (see 1.3.240–43). Having defied her father and severed her ties to her family, she cannot return to her father's house, and Othello has neither bought nor rented a house in Venice; therefore, she has little option but to follow him to Cyprus. For all practical purposes, she has become unhoused, homeless. Othello's military duties and urgent commission expose a lack of plan beyond the elopement.

Next I ask the students to trace through the text various instances of unhousing and instability, starting with the representation of Brabantio's house. Brabantio's house offered Desdemona only the illusion of stability, not a real home. The dark empty house, as represented in the play's opening scene, contrasts sharply with the warm, hospitable house of the past, as described in the third scene. In the past the house functioned as the center of home life, hospitality, and love. A student remarked that Brabantio's house must have been a special place, since it was here that Othello and Desdemona fell in love. We catch glimpses of what the house used to be like, especially in Othello's description of his experience as a frequent dinner guest in Brabantio's house (1.3.128–70). "Her father loved me, oft invited me," says Othello, suggesting warm hospitality, love, and family life. As host, Brabantio provided food and drink, whereas Othello, as guest, provided entertainment, primarily in terms of narratives about his life experience. Desdemona took an interest in his life, eventually encouraging him to woo her. In its warmth, stability, hospitality, and domestic life, Brabantio's house may have come as close to a home as anything that Othello had ever experienced.

But Brabantio's house offered Othello and Desdemona only an illusion of stability and acceptance. By the end of the play's opening scene, that illusion has already been irrevocably shattered. The stage direction at the beginning of act 1, scene 1, reads, *"Enter Roderigo and Iago,"* but does not specify their location. Only when Iago instructs Roderigo, "Call up her father, / Rouse him"

(66–67), does Roderigo identify the location (73). Iago shouts: "Awake! What, ho, Brabantio! Thieves! thieves! / Look to your house, your daughter, and your bags!" (78–79). To shock Brabantio, Iago refers to Othello and Desdemona as copulating animals. Brabantio counters that his "house is not a grange" (105). Lurking in the shadows, Roderigo insists, "Straight satisfy yourself. / If she be in her chamber, or your house, / Let loose on me the justice of the state / For thus deluding you" (135-38). Darkness hides the emptiness of the house, but as Brabantio lights candles to search for his missing daughter, we sense a dark, empty house, robbed of something precious. This provides a sharp contrast to the same house in the past. Once Brabantio discovers that his daughter has eloped with Othello, he offers no acceptance of her marriage. To be together, Desdemona and Othello must escape her father's house and the forces of racism and hatred that Iago's revenge unleashes.

The move to Cyprus may offer new opportunities for happiness, but it leaves behind the shattered foundation of Desdemona's relationship to her father and the dark and empty house of her father. A wide gap becomes apparent as the scene shifts to Cyprus. The storm scatters and destroys the Turkish fleet, and the sea voyage separates Desdemona from Othello and places her in Iago's company. Ironically, Othello, sent on a military mission, engages in no military activity; yet the destruction of the Turkish armada opens the path for Iago, who wages a war in Othello's inner world. Far away from Brabantio's house, Othello and Desdemona seemingly will have another opportunity to start a life together in Cyprus. Yet Montano and the gentlemen suggest in act 2, scene 1, that a violent storm can shake even the strongest fortification, a fitting reminder that Iago's malice could undermine and destroy the foundation of Othello and Desdemona's marriage.

Turmoil temporarily gives way to calm. When Othello finally arrives in act 2, scene 1, allaying fears that he might have perished at sea, and observes Desdemona, his heart fills with joy: "If after every tempest come such calms, / May the winds blow till they have wakened death!" (2.1.184–85); he adds: "Come, let us to the castle" (200). In scene 2, through the herald, Othello decrees a general double celebration of his nuptial and of the defeat of the Turks, ordering that "every man put himself into triumph; some to dance, some to make bonfires, each man to what sport and revels his addition [rank] leads him" (2.2.3–6). By scene 3, Othello and Desdemona have already retired to bed. The play's attention turns to this inner sanctum of their marriage.

The Bedroom

In *Othello*, the Cyprus scenes reflect a shift in focus from military to conjugal matters, exterior to interior space, public to private life. Michael Neill's essay "Unproper Beds: Race, Adultery, and the Hideous in *Othello*" supplements our discussion of the bedroom.[5] As Neill suggests, Othello and Desdemona's conjugal bed, kept hidden offstage, begins to occupy the consciousness of the characters and of the audience. Neill argues that the bed in *Othello* symbolizes the play's preoccupation with a sensational, scandalous biracial marriage; therefore, a "lurid vision of the bed" ([Young] 133) looms large in the audience's imagination throughout the play, until the bed is finally revealed in act 5, amid the distorting shadows cast by the light of a single candle burning in the darkness. In my classes, I either summarize the main points of Neill's essay or assign it as an oral report. In one of my graduate classes, for example, my students began their presentation by asking their classmates to identify good things they associate with beds—such as comfort, rest, sleep, security, lovemaking; then they traced references to the bed in the play and explained how Iago perverts all these, turning the conjugal bed into its diabolical double.

References to the bed abound, from Desdemona's empty bed in the opening scene to the conjugal bed as crime scene at the end of the play. Using Neill's essay, the class can trace together all these references, especially Iago's role in rousing other characters out of the comfort of their beds and slumber. For example, act 2, scene 3, echoes the opening scene. Once again, the scene takes place at night. But instead of Brabantio, Othello and Desdemona now stir out of their bed because of the brawl between the drunken Cassio and Montano. Othello finds himself in a situation reminiscent of the play's opening scene, when Iago and Roderigo woke up Brabantio in the middle of the night. Iago couches his language in nuptial metaphors. One minute Cassio and Montano were the best of friends, "like bride and groom / Devesting them for bed" (2.3.169–70); the next Cassio turned into a "night brawler" (185). Othello fears that others will question his ability "[t]o manage private and domestic quarrel" (204), and hence he must set an example by cashiering Cassio. When Desdemona also comes outside, Othello complains, "Look if my gentle love be not raised up!" (239); and turning to Desdemona, he states, "All's well, sweeting. / Come away to bed" (241–42). The disturbance has its intended consequence. As he dismisses Cassio, Othello reveals flawed judgment and seemingly loses control over his emotions: "My blood begins my safer guides to rule" (194)—certainly an ominous sign of another storm to come in the terror of the night.

Iago's evil strategy centers on Othello and Desdemona's bedroom. Act 3, scene 3, a pivotal scene in the domestic tragedy, begins with Cassio's departure from a private conference with Desdemona and ends with plans for the double murder of Desdemona and Cassio. By the end of the scene, Iago has contaminated the temple of Othello and Desdemona's marriage and transformed it into its diabolical opposite: a nightmarish vision represented in the narrative that Iago fabricates about Cassio's erotic dreams (3.3.410–26). Before the scene is over, Othello and Iago make a pact to each other, in language reminiscent of marriage vows: one of them will suffocate Desdemona in her bed; the other will kill Cassio. Ironically, Iago seals the new marriage with a false promise: "I am your own forever" (480).

Act 4 takes place at night. As bedtime approaches, Othello and Desdemona turn their attention to the conjugal bed. In the first scene, Lodovico arrives with letters from Venice commanding Othello's return home and deputing Cassio in the government of Cyprus. In scene 2, Desdemona instructs Emilia to "[L]ay on my bed my wedding sheets" (4.2.105); in the next scene, Emilia reports that she has done so (4.3.22). As Desdemona undresses for bed, she and Emilia talk about domestic life. Desdemona remembers her mother's house and servant Barbary, who was in love, but whose lover "proved mad / And did forsake her" (4.3.27–28).[6] Barbary died, singing the willow song about another "poor soul" (4.3.40) who lamented her fate under a sycamore tree. Desdemona wonders whether there are women who betray their husbands; Emilia thinks that there are many, arguing that "it is their husbands' faults / If wives do fall" (4.3.86–87). Desdemona remembers her mother's house, as a site not of joy and hospitality but of tragedy and conjugal strife—a sad, grotesque parallel to her own house in Cyprus. So she remembers another unhappy time and other people, whereas Emilia speaks of the harsh and violent reality of domestic life.

The focus on the bed coincides with a narrowing in Othello's field of vision. In fact, the 1999 Royal Shakespeare Company production of *Othello* in Stratford-upon-Avon, England, underscored how Othello's physical world symbolically shrinks. Several doors in earlier scenes gradually disappeared until only one door remained: the door that Othello closes behind himself as he enters the conjugal bedroom to kill his wife in act 5, scene 2. The bedroom door symbolizes his isolation from the outside world and from the truth. Othello's entire life has now been reduced to one dark room, one dark night. Othello approaches the conjugal bed, as he had done before; yet this time he has come to "Put out the light, and then put out the light" (5.2.7). For the first twenty-two lines, he seems on the verge of turning his murderous errand into lovemaking. Only after he has stifled Desdemona does the whole truth finally emerge. Although most of the characters that are still alive eventually converge on the bedroom, nothing remains except a profound sense of emptiness, disturbingly reminiscent of Brabantio's house in the opening scene of the play. Othello realizes that he has reached his "journey's end" (5.2.268), and he asks himself, "Where should Othello go?" (272). He has no place to which to return.

Finally, I take my students to the principal source of the play, Giraldi Cinthio's *Hecatommithi*. Cinthio depicts the characters' experience of home in a memorable way. He explains that Disdemona and the Moor felt a strong mutual bond of love and were united in marriage, although "the Lady's relatives did all they could to make her take another husband" (242). After a period of marital bliss in Venice, the Moor becomes commandant of the soldiers in Cyprus, where he and his wife settle down in a house. The Corporal, Cassio's prototype, regularly frequents their house as a dinner guest. Iago's counterpart, the wicked Ensign, falls in love with Disdemona, who rejects his advances. In turn, the Ensign, imagining that Disdemona loved the Corporal, sets out on a path of revenge against the Corporal and Disdemona. When she comes to the Corporal's defense, the Ensign suggests to the Moor that "Perhaps Disdemona has good cause to look on him so favourably," advising the Moor, "if you keep your eyes open you will see for yourself" (244). The Ensign steals the handkerchief from Disdemona and persuades the Moor to use a sand-filled stocking to beat Disdemona to death, and then, since "the house where you are staying is very old, and the ceiling of your room has many cracks in it," he adds, "when she is dead, we shall make part of the ceiling fall; and we'll break the Lady's head, making it seem that a rafter has injured it in falling, and killed her" (250). That is precisely what they do. After her funeral, the Moor searches the empty house for his Disdemona. Filled with regret and kindling his hatred for the Ensign, the Moor can no longer contain his feelings. In the source, "unhousèd" has a much more literal meaning: the ceiling of the house comes tumbling down, as does the Moor's marriage. The specter of this unhousing haunts Shakespeare's representation of space in *Othello* and defines the central character's identity.

In Shakespeare's play, Othello neither searches the empty house for his dead wife nor returns to Venice to be punished. Yet Othello seems linked to a house, at first in Iago's imagination, as the guest turned thief who steals the most precious possession of the house, and then as a noble but extremely jealous exile who robs himself of the home that he and Desdemona tried to build together. Not in a literal but in a figurative sense, Othello's house comes tumbling down as he unhouses himself with the help of Iago. His family, home, past experiences, and childhood memories have become a blur of half-remembered, half-forgotten images, full of fundamental contradictions and fantasies. To tragic ends, Iago recognizes that Othello's emotional realm revolves around Desdemona; their bedroom is Othello's anchor in the European world.

NOTES

[1]I borrow ideas from Maurice Merleau-Ponty and Gaston Bachelard about the cultural, psychological, and philosophical meanings of the house, but I do not focus on phenomenology proper. I have used a similar teaching approach in my graduate Shakespeare class, but for the purposes of this essay I focus on my experience in the undergraduate class.

[2]This homework assignment consists of two parts. Part 1, based on the students' personal experience, asks them to define home, to explain how a dwelling becomes home and how such a place differs from temporary or transient places such as their dorm room or apartment, and to explain what they associate with home and what connects them emotionally to what they consider home. Part 2, based on preliminary analysis of *Othello*, asks the students to enumerate the details that the text of *Othello* gives about Brabantio's house, to explain what Othello and Desdemona remember or

associate with it, to describe and give details about Othello and Desdemona's residence in Cyprus, and finally to explain in detail what Othello means when he describes his life before he eloped with Desdemona as an "unhousèd free condition." The report ensures thorough preparation for classroom discussion and obviates quizzes.

³Citations to *Othello* are from Orgel and Braunmuller's *Complete Pelican Shakespeare*.

⁴This definition paraphrases and combines several *Oxford English Dictionary* definitions. *Home* may also refer to a region, state, or country.

⁵This interpretation is consistent with Neely's "Circumscription" 306.

⁶Desdemona's account of the events in her mother's house contrasts with the seemingly loving relationship between Othello's parents, although Othello offers contradictory narratives about the origin of the handkerchief (see 3.4.55–75 and 5.2.217–18), which I discuss in *Shakespeare's Cross-Cultural Encounters* (125–28).

Teaching Teachers:
Othello in a Graduate Seminar

Martha Tuck Rozett

My graduate seminar, called Teaching Shakespeare, is intended to prepare prospective and veteran teachers to teach Shakespeare in high school and college. The atmosphere is different in a classroom where the students are teachers. Teachers are not only accustomed to being the sources of authority in their own classrooms but also may feel that their ways of teaching, honed through experience, are best left unchanged. I have learned that the most productive way to begin Teaching Shakespeare is to acknowledge that I have never taught high school students. This admission decenters the classroom; veteran high school teachers, and even students with a semester of student teaching under their belts, can point to an experience that I lack. Much of the course's success, however, depends on the fact that not all the graduate students are prospective or practicing high school teachers. The participants in Teaching Shakespeare have included doctoral candidates in English who have gone on to teach my department's 100-level Reading Shakespeare course; faculty members from other two- or four-year colleges; instructors in prisons or residential facilities for young offenders; and teachers of theater courses, ESL courses, or night-school courses for adults with low-level reading and writing skills. What we share is the experience of having studied Shakespeare in high school and college and varying degrees of conviction that Shakespeare can be taught successfully to first-time readers as well as more experienced ones.

Although the forty-minute high school class and the college lecture course do not lend themselves readily to a performance-based approach, my course begins from the premise that teaching Shakespeare must include some elements of performance. I have students work in groups on a staged reading project, often performing different versions of the same scene. We also experiment with teaching strategies I have encountered, through observation and participation, in several New York City arts-in-education programs that focus on Shakespeare, where talented teachers-artists work with middle and high school students and their teachers. Our texts are the Shakespeare Set Free series published by the Folger Library, the Cambridge School and Folger editions of the plays, and collections like Ronald E. Salomone and James E. Davis's *Teaching Shakespeare into the Twenty-First Century* and Milla Cozart Riggio's *Teaching Shakespeare through Performance*. They describe activities ranging from vocal warm-up exercises and improvisations that serve as anticipatory lessons to two-, three-, or four-week units in which the class mounts a fully staged performance.

We also begin from the premise that students' first readings are a legitimate form of interpretation that reflects the social and educational culture students inhabit. In *Talking Back to Shakespeare*, I argued that first-time readers "try to make the text 'mean' something, using what they know best, which frequently consists of received truths and rather prescriptive formulas about human behavior" (17). In papers on *Othello*, for example,

> [s]tudents adopted the posture of advice-givers, proffering bits of received wisdom and personal opinions in a remarkably prescriptive tone of voice: hence they took Othello to task for "acting hastily, without first consulting several people," for not "communicating better with his wife," and for "being so foolish as to let jealousy get the better of him." They frequently assumed the authoritative voice of an advice columnist: "Communication is a vital part of sustaining a relationship" one young woman declared, after asserting that "in Othello's position I can safely say I would have consulted others, but not without consulting Desdemona." (27)

Many of the graduate students in the Teaching Shakespeare seminar acknowledge that they too, as first-time readers, engaged in this kind of talking back. Indeed, some are reading *Othello* for the first time, and their responses to the play, although certainly more complicated and less formulaic than the ones I quote in *Talking Back*, confirmed my sense that first-time student readers and teachers approach a Shakespeare play quite differently. First-time student readers often want to "demystify the text," to draw lessons from it and use it as "a solid object against which they, as young adults, [can] test the moral and social assumptions they [are] in the process of formulating" (*Talking* 31). Teachers, including the more experienced teachers in my seminar, are more likely to focus on the play's multiplicities and contradictions.

Teaching Shakespeare culminates in a final project that is at once a collection of resources and an annotated teaching unit designed for a high school or college course. Through their projects, the students participate in an ongoing discussion of Shakespeare pedagogy. They become familiar with journals like *Shakespeare Quarterly*, *Shakespeare Bulletin*, the *Shakespeare Newsletter*, *Shakespeare and the Classroom*, and the *Upstart Crow* and with the many online resources for teachers of Shakespeare. My instructions for the final project limit the practicing or prospective high school teachers in the course to a fifteen-to-twenty–day teaching unit (or the equivalent for high schools that use block scheduling) that includes tests and writing assignments. For college teachers, the unit cannot exceed two weeks. Since there won't be time for everything, all choices need to be discussed and justified.

The final-project assignment has produced a remarkable range of teaching strategies. One student decided to focus on six scenes from *Othello* in her fifteen-day unit for eleventh graders, although she asked students to read other scenes on their own. Another designed her *Othello* unit for ten eighty-five-minute classes (two or three each week) in the second semester of an introduction to theater course for upper-middle-class students in the ninth through twelfth grades. The plan culminated in a group project that included a director's notebook (adapted from O'Brien 272–73) and performances of fourteen scenes between fifty and one hundred lines each. The list of scenes contained some interesting choices; for example, the student's excerpt from 1.1 starts with Brabantio's entrance, and the only excerpt from 4.2 is Roderigo and Iago's conversation at the end of the scene. Although I disagree with some of her choices (she includes 3.1, where I would opt instead for the first ninety lines of 3.3), the very process of paring the text to fourteen short scenes was an important part of the learning experience. As she remarks at the end of her project, "I need to realize that I just can't get through every single part and need to focus on the theatrical concepts I want to teach, using the play as the medium to do it."

Well before the students embark on their final projects, time management emerges as a recurrent theme in Teaching Shakespeare, since the success of the teaching units depends on making the best use of class time. As my students explore new teaching strategies, I remind them that with roughly 450 minutes to teach a play, they need to make hard decisions and plan well in advance. They, in turn, remind me that some of the most interesting-sounding activities we try out in our classroom could lead to rowdiness and classroom chaos in theirs. Throughout the course, we agree to disagree. I recall a spirited discussion about using Tim Blake Nelson's teen film *O* in a unit devoted to *Othello*, in which some of the teachers argued that the film would make resistant students receptive to Shakespeare and that it was worth the ninety minutes or so of class time. I argued, instead, for devoting those minutes to short film clips from two or more film versions of the play, so that students could see how different directors and actors approached the text. The teacher who argued most energetically for showing *O* in its entirety, as I recall, was teaching a night-school class for young adults who had dropped out of high school. She undoubtedly knew how to make them want to read the play better than I possibly could.

We also debate about reading aloud in class versus assigning reading at home; on this vexed issue, having college and high school teachers in the same classroom helps reinforce the importance of acclimating high school students to the culture of college. Can the students be sent home after reading 1.1 of *Othello* in class to read the rest of act 1 on their own? Should we direct their reading with study questions, synopses, or other preparatory devices? With only a limited number of class sessions for discussing the play, how do you explain your choices regarding which scenes or parts of scenes to pass over? As part of this discussion, I show my class a working script of *Othello*, which I devised for an arts-in-education program for seventh graders in the Bronx.

My script, which changed few words but reduced the number of lines by about forty percent, underwent further revision as the teachers-artists and students rehearsed.

During our discussions of innovative teaching strategies, students return frequently to three essays from Salomone and Davis's *Teaching Shakespeare into the Twenty-First Century*. Many students come to my course believing that Shakespeare's lines need to be translated to be understood. William Liston's essay "Paraphrasing Shakespeare" and an exercise I developed to accompany it get us thinking about how carefully you have to read a speech, such as Othello's "It is the cause" (5.1.1–22) or "Behold I have a weapon" (5.1.259–81) or "Soft you, a word or two before you go" (5.1.338–56) in order to find alternative words that make sense of its complexities. Marie Plasse's "An Inquiry-Based Approach" describes an assignment called "seed papers" based on "productive questions" (as opposed to "dead-end questions"), which students develop and then respond to. Variations on this assignment are now being used in classes taught by several teaching assistants in my department and by local high school teachers. And Leila Christenbury's "Problems with *Othello* in the High School Classroom" poses the provocative question, "to what degree does race matter in *Othello*?" (183). It then offers two alternative interpretations: "race does not matter" (184) and "race does matter" (185). This approach has been enthusiastically received by high school teachers who use classroom debates as a pedagogical strategy. In addition to assigning these three popular essays, I ask students to read Russ McDonald's "The Flaw in the Flaw," which meets with a mixed response, since many teachers, sad to say, are still wedded to the notion that the protagonist's tragic flaw brings about his downfall.

Toward the end of Teaching Shakespeare, we address various ways of testing high school or college students' grasp of a Shakespeare play. Using the unit tests in *Shakespeare Set Free* as models, the graduate students select quotations from *Othello* to use for "identify and discuss" questions, and we talk about how the choice of a quotation emerges from the themes emphasized in class. Among the passages a recent class selected were several excerpts from Iago's plotting soliloquies and asides, such as

> I have't. It is engend'red. Hell and night
> Must bring this monstrous birth to the world's light.
> (1.3.403–04)
>
> He takes her by the palm; ay, well said, whisper.
> With as little a web as this will I ensnare as great
> a fly as Cassio.   (2.1.167–69)[1]

We talked at length about the distinctive Iago voice that draws the readers or audience in, making them complicit in the plotting and scheming. Other quotations students have chosen come from a model forty-five-minute lecture on act 1 that I give, accompanied by running commentary on my reasons for emphasizing certain lines. A good example is Brabantio's warning couplet:

> Look to her, Moor, if thou hast eyes to see;
> She has deceiv'd her father, and may thee.
> (1.3.292–93)

The students often gravitate to speeches by women, even when we have not discussed them; Emilia's soliloquy about the handkerchief (3.3.290–99) is a popular choice.

About thirteen years ago, I decided to give open-book exams to my undergraduates, on the premise that the play text belongs in the exam room just as the periodic table or the calculator does. The students in Teaching Shakespeare have often had difficulty accepting this idea, even when a serendipitous event demonstrated its usefulness. I had distributed some of my own test questions from an introductory Shakespeare course, and a veteran high school teacher confused Nerissa and Jessica when composing a short response to the question, What do Emilia in *Othello* and Nerissa in *The Merchant of Venice* have in common? A doctoral student well versed in postmodern theory argued that the answer was creative and should be given full credit; other class members and I felt otherwise. I pointed out that, if this had been an actual open-book exam, the test taker's decision to trust her memory rather than consult the cast list would, in effect, be part of the test. In the long run, the life skill of knowing how and when to use the tools at your disposal is just as important as the reading comprehension and analytic skills we assess in our exams and paper assignments. Another spirited debate occurred when a student proposed the following test question for a hypothetical class of seventh graders: How does Desdemona explain her "divided duty" in 1.3? Some of us felt that students who had read act 1 of *Othello* only once might not recall or be able to decode the phrase "divided duty"; others advised recasting the question as, What does Desdemona mean by her "divided duty?" to help elicit the expected response. I used this discussion to talk about the perils of ambiguous wording in exam questions.

Many of the students in Teaching Shakespeare base their final projects on *Othello*. I suspect their choices are influenced by the small cast; the availability of recent feature films; and the teaching profession's increasing tendency to use literary texts to address issues of diversity, prejudice, and gender politics. The best of the projects exhibit a thoroughgoing familiarity with the play and use the text to achieve a particular objective. Here, for example, is a ten-minute segment of a class on 2.1 of *Othello*, which one of my students adapted from a lesson on rhetoric in the workbook *Discovering Shakespeare's Language* (Gibson and Field-Pickering 46):

Rhetoric today is usually termed repetitive, insincere, fake, yet in Shakespeare's days it was taught as the art of persuasion, one's ability to persuade another. Read over Iago's conversation with Roderigo (213–89). Does Iago make a convincing argument to Roderigo? How does he use rhetoric to persuade him or make his point? (Cite "proof," such as "Didst thou not see her paddle with the palm of his hand?" [255], stereotypes, such as "Her eye must be fed" [226], shrugging off Roderigo's statements, such as "Blessed fig's end!") What did he convince him to do? How?

For this, the third day of a twenty-day unit on *Othello* for seniors who had studied one or two Shakespeare plays in previous years, my student had chosen to skip lines 1-82 and 103-60 in her fifty-minute class on 2.1, focusing first on how Iago and Cassio differ in their treatment of women and then on Iago's exchange with Roderigo. She planned to follow the ten-minute rhetoric lesson with another five minutes on the comic gull as a character type and end with a homework assignment that involved journal writing. She posed these questions for the journal entry:

Have you ever convinced someone to do something you knew was wrong? How do you go about getting people to do what you want them to do? Is there anyone you can always count on to do whatever it is you ask? What role does this person play in you life?

Had this student, who happens to be a veteran teacher, chosen to discuss these topics in class, as another teacher might be tempted to do, she wouldn't have had time for the lesson on rhetoric that emerged from a close reading of the text. The journal questions (which seemed risky to me given her student population—a prison for males between the ages of fourteen and twenty-one years old), were designed to get unwilling writers to start writing about their own lives in the hope that the connections to the text would come later. *Othello*, she explained, would work well for readers who "are convinced that all of the novels and plays they are 'supposed' to read are written by and are about wealthy, old, white men." She hoped that her students would be drawn to Othello because "they feel as if they have something in common with him; they are both visible outsiders." I was particularly struck by her comment that "my students have made grave and irreversible mistakes and are suffering the consequences of those mistakes on a daily basis," which she juxtaposed with a quote from McDonald's "The Flaw in the Flaw":

[T]he theory of the flaw suggests that those who experience bad fortune get what they deserve, that suffering must be the result of some kind of weakness, that the great tragic figures shouldn't have been surprised

by and shouldn't resent their misery, that anybody who gets into big
trouble is probably a pervert who ought to be punished.   (8)

These students, she concluded, will see McDonald's point, for it is a painful
reflection of their own lives. Has she had the opportunity to try out these
teaching strategies? I hope so.

NOTE

[1]Citations to *Othello* are from Evans's *Riverside Shakespeare*.

Teaching Richard Burbage's Othello

Virginia Mason Vaughan

Teachers who want to make Shakespeare accessible to twenty-first-century students often use films to suggest the timelessness of his characters and their situations. It is tempting to root *Othello* in the here and now, and two recent screen adaptations do just that. Tim Blake Nelson's *O* reincarnates Othello as Odin, an outstanding black basketball player in an all-white prep school; Geoffrey Sax's *Othello* moves the tragedy to the London Metropolitan Police, where John Othello is promoted over his good friend Ben Jago. Both films highlight race as the tragedy's catalyst. These films not only probe the difficulties faced by a black male in a predominantly white society, they imply that Odin and John Othello react as they do because they are black. In the process they exploit the erotically charged spectacle of a black male body juxtaposed to the body of a white woman, a cultural phenomenon Celia R. Daileader calls "Othellophilia" (178). Consequently, the films' uses of Shakespeare's Othello, however well intentioned, reenforce racial stereotypes of the victimized, violent, and sexual black male that circulate in many other contemporary representations.

To move our students beyond the racial stereotypes embedded in contemporary popular culture, I suggest we offer historical perspectives. When we examine Shakespeare's tragedy within the conditions under which it has been performed, students can see that, in David Theo Goldberg's words (the students would phrase it differently), "race is a fluid, transforming, historically specific concept parasitic on theoretic and social discourses for the meaning it assumes at any given moment" (74). History shows that the racial significations we take from and ascribe to texts change as economic, social, and political conditions change. In the early modern period, in particular, concepts of racial difference were in a formative stage and were not as hardened as they would be in the nineteenth century. Our students need to understand that the way in which English playwrights imagined black Africanist figures was crucial for establishing a sense of English whiteness as normative. If they also examine the performance history of *Othello* in the eighteenth and nineteenth centuries, they will see how the slave trade and a burgeoning plantation economy influenced views of the play and its protagonist. In the process, they may also realize how their own interpretations are affected by contemporary notions of race.

When *Othello* is situated in its historical moment, its protagonist emerges as a blackface role, a part made for a skilled white impersonator. The white Shakespearean actor who impersonates Othello—like all actors—is pretending to be someone he is not, but to make the character convincing, he draws on his own ideas of what a black Moor would be like. Blackface performances, as Eric Lott has shown in his study of nineteenth-century minstrelsy, are necessarily unstable and contradictory; although the racial other is exploited for cultural capital, he is also paradoxically engaged and absorbed (29). On a more mundane level, a white student might think it cool to "act black," without recognizing the cultural forces at work in his or her notion of what acting black is. Students who look at the history of Othello on stage can learn how attitudes about what is white and what is black are formed, in part, through performance. They will recognize that Shakespeare's Othello was not the essential black hero but the product of a white imagination represented by English actors to a white audience.

Richard Burbage, the actor who performed all Shakespeare's major tragic roles, was a limner who knew something of paints. In 1613, the earl of Rutland paid him for painting an impresa, an emblem to carry into the lists, whose motto was written by Shakespeare (Chambers 308–09). It is likely that Burbage contrived the black makeup required to impersonate the Moor. An elegy written after Burbage's death in 1619 praised his performance of "the Greved Moore" (Shakespeare, *New Variorum Edition* 396), but this is the only knowledge we have indicating how the role of Othello was first enacted and how the audience responded. We can speculate, however, about what attitudes the audience members might have brought with them to the Globe.

In the latter decades of the sixteenth century, Londoners might have encountered black people, often as servants, entertainers, or seamen (Fryer 8). Literate Londoners might also have read European travelers' stories of their encounters with black Africans, which were available in Richard Eden and Richard Willes's compendium, *The History of Travayle in the West and East Indies, and Other Countreys* (1577), and in Richard Hakluyt's *Principall Navigations, Voiages, and Discoveries of the English Nation*, first published in 1589 and greatly expanded in a second edition of 1598-1600. In 1600, four

years before the composition of *Othello*, John Pory's translation of Leo Africanus's *History and Description of Africa* provided an ethnographic account
of northern and sub-Saharan Africa. Leo's claim, for example, that Moors are
known for jealousy provides an important clue about preconceptions that may
have helped shape Shakespeare's hero.[1] By the time *Othello* was first performed in 1604, English men and women may well through experience and
written accounts have been exposed to black-skinned people who were mark-
edly different from themselves (Vaughan and Vaughan 29). Although primary
texts such as Hakluyt and Leo are not currently available in textbook editions,
teachers can use photocopies of relevant passages or describe for the students
the kinds of materials that were accessible to Shakespeare and other dramatists. Selections from historical sources will also be featured in the Bedford
edition of *Othello* being prepared by Kim F. Hall.

Students should also be made aware of early modern theatrical conventions.
The first black Moor in a speaking role on the public stage was Muly Hamet,
the villainous Moor of George Peele's *The Battle of Alcazar*. Muly combines
the black-faced devils of the medieval morality tradition with sixteenth-century
geographic interest in the Moors of northern Africa. While the drama's other
Moors are figured white, Muly is depicted as the "negro Moore," distinguished
by his villainy as well as his color:

> The Negro *Muly Hamet* . . .
> Blacke in his looke, and bloudie in his deeds . . .
> Presents himself with naked sword in hand,
> Accompanied as now you may behold,
> With deuils coted in the shapes of men.
>   (Peele A2)

In a text more readily accessible to today's students than Peele's, Shakespeare's *Titus Andronicus* capitalizes on the same association between demonic behavior and black skin with Aaron, the villainous Moor. Aaron exults
in his evil designs: "Let fools do good and fair men call for grace, / Aaron will
have his soul black like his face" (3.1.205–06).[2] Unlike Peele, Shakespeare
introduces an erotic element into the black man's characterization by coupling
Aaron with the equally transgressive Tamora, white queen of the Goths.

The anonymous author of *Lust's Dominion* (c. 1600), sometimes attributed
to Thomas Dekker, imitated this motif with Eleazar, a black Moor who commits adultery with Spain's white queen. Like Aaron, Eleazar addresses the
audience and calls attention to his blackness and his villainy. The play's other
characters associate this blackness with the chromatic coding of the homiletic
tradition; Cardinal Mendoza describes Eleazar, for example, as "that feind; /
That damned *Moor*, that Devil, that Lucifer." The King of Portugal describes
him as a "Devil" and a "feind" (Dekker 149, 181).

Aaron and Eleazar both have speeches that call attention to the color of their complexion; both reiterate the common proverb that the Ethiop cannot be washed white. In the process of performance, their asides metadramatically remind the audience that their blackness is a disguise worn for performance. In these early plays blackness is adopted by the actor and used self-consciously for its power to signify evil.

That Burbage was remembered as the "grieved Moor" instead of the "devilish Moor" underscores what hundreds of critics have observed: Shakespeare took the tradition of the villainous Moor and turned it on its head, making his Moor the tragedy's heroic protagonist, the white ensign Iago the demonic villain. Without knowing what the theatrical tradition was before *Othello*, students can hardly appreciate the ways in which Shakespeare exploited that tradition and stretched its parameters.

Source study may seem rather old-fashioned, but it may help students understand Shakespeare's choices if they look at Giraldi Cinthio's original tale in the *Hecatommithi*. Many editions summarize this text, and a full translation is available in H. H. Furness's 1886 *New Variorium Edition* (available in paperback from Dover). Students will find that the changes Shakespeare made are not just for theatrical effect but have important implications for the characters. In Cinthio's original, for example, the Ensign tries to seduce Disdemona and fails, and this rebuff provides the motive for his villainous schemes. Once the Moor is convinced of his wife's infidelity, he pays the Ensign to kill the Corporal (the Cassio figure) and to help him murder Disdemona. They try to make her death look like an accident by bludgeoning her to death with a sand-filled stocking and pulling down the ceiling over the bed. When the truth eventually comes out, the Moor is exiled and killed by his wife's kinsmen. As the actor Hugh Quarshie argues, the biggest change in Shakespeare is the emphasis on Othello's blackness and the suggestion that Othello acts as he does simply because he is black (*Second Thoughts* 6–7). Shakespeare the dramatist thus catered to his audience's expectations that black Moors are passionate and easily made jealous.

Although Shakespeare's words leave little doubt about Othello's blackness and Desdemona's whiteness, students should see that the tragedy's color coding is nevertheless fluid. Edward Pechter notes of Iago's and Brabantio's remarks in the first three scenes, "The indiscriminate mixing of black and Moorish impressions serves to endow Othello with an unstable quality that adds to and may indeed be at the heart of his terrifying strangeness"(35). Underneath Brabantio's window Iago calls the Moor an "old black ram," and in the second scene, Brabantio refers to his "sooty bosom" and claims that he is a "thing" to be feared, not to be delighted in (1.2.70–71).[3] "Sooty" conveys connotations of filth as well as blackness; the *Oxford English Dictionary* defines *sooty* as "foul or dirty with soot; covered or smeared with soot." Soot is a covering applied to the surface, making the wearer black in appearance.

Othello refers to his own blackness during the temptation scene: "Haply for I am black" (3.3.267). When he's convinced of Desdemona's infidelity, he insists that "Her name, that was as fresh / As Dian's visage, is now begrimed and black / As mine own face" (3.3.389–91). *Begrimed*, like sooty, suggests an applied blackness. *The Oxford English Dictionary* defines it as "To blacken or soil with grime, or dirt which sinks into the surface and discolours it." During the play's final scene, Emilia describes Othello as "the blacker devil," a "filthy bargain," and "ignorant as dirt" (5.2.129, 153, 160). Soot, grime, and dirt all connote a dark coating that can be applied, then rubbed off, akin to the black makeup Burbage likely used. Like the homiletic tradition's association between blackness and the demonic, the imbrication of blackness with dirt conveys negative connotations, which may have contributed to the white audience's sense of its own superiority.

In addition, these terms generate, in John R. Ford's words, "metatheatrical moments, intended or not, that simultaneously create a character and deconstruct an actor's craft" (163). On her deathbed Desdemona cries that she fears Othello when his "eyes roll so" (5.2.38), a comment that suggests that Burbage's blackface highlighted the whites of his eyes. His Othello may not have been grotesque like the figures in nineteenth-century minstrel shows, but these admittedly sporadic cues in the text do call attention to the Moor's role as an impersonation, reminding the audience at crucial moments that the actor's blackness is a disguise.

Blackness is not the only cue to Othello's alterity, of course. In the 1622 Quarto, he compares himself to an Indian who "threw a pearl away / Richer than all his tribe" (5.2.345–46), a cultural comparison to East or West Indians who were ignorant of the value of a precious gem. In the First Folio, he uses the term "Iudean," which connotes Judas, the betrayer of Christ. Like the play's many references to the Turks, this reading sets up an opposition between heathen and Christian. Othello's accounts of "antres vast" (1.3.141) in the Senate scene and his description of the handkerchief given to his mother by an Egyptian (3.4.57–77) also suggest geographic otherness. The text thus provides a variety of terms used by and about Othello that demonstrates how complex English and European othering was in this period and, in particular, how categories of religion, color, and geographic origin could be superimposed on one another. Careful reading of the text can show our students that the monolithic conception of race that circulates in much contemporary discourse—so often oversimplified as black versus white—is also complicated by cultural, economic, and religious differences.

Laurence Olivier claimed that Othello was one of Shakespeare's most challenging roles and speculated that "Shakespeare and actor Richard Burbage got drunk together one night and Burbage said, 'I can play anything you write, anything at all.' And Shakespeare said, 'Right, I'll fix you, boy!' And then he wrote *Othello*" (Cottrell 337). Olivier felt that the role of Othello required too many emotional climaxes, each more difficult than the previous one. Quarshie, an experienced Shakespearean actor, sees the transition from the noble and dignified Moor of the Senate scene to the emotional wreck of the brothel scene as nearly unplayable. The shift comes in 3.3, commonly known as the temptation scene (3.3.90–482); in fewer than five hundred lines, Othello changes from being content as a happy newlywed to having a jealous and murderous rage. Quarshie thinks that, because this change happens so quickly, its success depends on the audience's expectations that the Moor is predisposed toward passionate revenge (*Second Thoughts* 7–8). The role's histrionic qualities, as Elise Marks argues—the way "Othello's tremendous passion overtakes and even overwhelms the actor who plays him, and 'swells' or 'surges' out into the bodies of those who watch him perform"—are simultaneously "unnerving and deeply pleasurable" (101).

Pleasure here comes from performance, from seeing the ways in which one imagines a passionate black man acted out. As when an audience breathes a satisfied sigh at a skilled female impersonator's taking off his wig to reveal his true identity—or feels delight at knowing a thin Eddie Murphy lurks inside the obese Nutty Professor—so the spectators at a blackface performance are most pleased when made aware of the difference between the actor and the role he plays. The history of *Othello* on stage is larded with references to this sort of pleasure. And it was the personation of grief—the passions of love and jealousy—that pleasured viewers the most. Spranger Barry, the most famous Othello of the eighteenth century, was effective because the audience "could observe the muscles stiffening, the veins distending, and the red blood boiling through his dark skin—a mighty flood of passion accumulating for several minutes—and at length bearing down its barriers, and sweeping onward in thunder, love, reason, mercy, all before it" (Bernard 28). James Quin, who performed Othello in the first half of the eighteenth century, was known for a bit of stage business in which he slowly took off his white glove and surprised the audience when he displayed the hand painted black underneath. This anecdote suggests that the spectators expected the actor's hands would be white. In another performance of Quin's, gloves drew the actress and critic Lena Ashwell's attention to the white actor's impersonation: "his face was very black—he wore black gloves and appeared to be black all over until he waved his arms about, and then where the gloves ended, he was very white, and that was exciting to watch" (Potter, *Othello* 30). The reminder of the actor's white skin told this viewer that she was watching great acting, not a real black man. Ashwell's recollection highlights how much the display of the Moor's black body is integral to the role and to the pleasurable response of white audiences.

Display is also subject to changing audience attitudes. It might be helpful for students to know that, during much of the play's acting history, Othello was a dark-complexioned white man, not what we would characterize as black. Beginning with Edmund Kean in 1814, nineteenth-century actors preferred to see the Moor as tawny, putting in practice Samuel Taylor Coleridge's opinion that "Othello must not be conceived as a negro, but a high and chivalrous

Moorish chief" (qtd. in Cowhig 17). A tanned Moor was clearly more acceptable to white audiences in the age of racial Darwinism.

Presumably Burbage's Othello was not tawny but black. A good way to understand the dynamics of a serious blackface impersonation akin to Burbage's is to examine Stuart Burge's 1965 film, *Othello*, which is notorious for Olivier's portrayal of a coal-black Moor. At first students find Olivier's over-the-top acting style dated and strange. But if the film is presented in the context of the history of performance, it is a brilliant object lesson on how race is constructed and disseminated. The most obvious features of the impersonation are physical: Olivier coated his body from head to toe with coal-black makeup, dyed his hands and lips with red, and wore a wig of matted curls. In preparation for the role, he used weights to develop his muscles and sought vocal training to lower his voice an octave. He copied his walk from Jamaicans he observed in London. His goal, he said, was "to lead the public towards an appreciation of acting—to watch acting for acting's sake" (qtd. in Cottrell 339).

Even more important than Olivier's adoption of these physical details is that his Othello vividly depicts white fantasies of the emotionally volatile and vengeful black man. As Robert Kee observed in his review of the performance, "Olivier's Othello is not exactly a representational Negro; he's a hybrid, though with a coal black face, someone who could only be the figment of a white man's imagination" (qtd. in Tynan 106). As this Moor succumbs to Iago's machinations, he loses the façade of civilization, rolls his eyes, and beats his arms as his natural primitive instincts take over. Students will likely see the Olivier Othello as racist—and no doubt it was. Our challenge is to help them bring that kind of recognition to racist elements of their own culture that are much less transparent.

Lest our twenty-first century students feel smug about their racial tolerance as opposed to the racism of centuries past, they should also realize that cultural expectations affect the ways Othello is presented today. The shift from white actors to actors of African heritage playing the role of Othello that began with Paul Robeson in the 1940s and continues in the present does not resolve the play's contradictions. Quarshie argues that "Othello is given lines to speak which might have been quite unremarkable for a white Elizabethan actor in black make-up, but which, particularly for a modern black actor, are problematic" (*Second Thoughts* 12). Oliver Parker's 1995 feature film with Laurence Fishburne in the title role uses jump cuts to make the Moor seem less credulous, but its display of the "athletic male body," in Francesca T. Royster's words, reinforces contemporary stereotypes. Royster observes, "Throughout the film, we see much of Fishburne's body either open shirted, shirtless, or nude." Fishburne's performance is characterized by a combination of physical power and reticence. "More often than not, Othello's responses to the characters around him are glares, grunts, or lapses into feverish sexual fantasy. . . . Fishburne's Othello is most evocative of a cultural figuration of the American black male in the 1990s" (" 'End of Race' " 66). The danger for us and for our students is the easy assumption that the actor is "real" and that the sexual violence he commits on screen is "the authentic and essential sign of his blackness" (Royster, " 'End of Race' " 64).

In her influential *Playing in the Dark* Toni Morrison wrote, "The fabrication of an Africanist persona is reflexive; an extraordinary meditation on the self; a powerful exploration of the fears and desires that reside in the writerly consciousness" (17). Seldom, however, do we treat Shakespeare's Othello as the Africanist persona he was for audiences not only in the early modern period but also in the four centuries since. Only when we see that Othello is not real—that he is not a valid portrayal of any black man who ever lived but the creation of actors like Burbage, Olivier, and Fishburne—can we begin to understand the "fears and desires" that have been superimposed on his persona, most often by white audiences, but in more recent history by actors and writers of color as well. The kinds of historical perspectives suggested here can help our students understand that when we imagine Othello, we are also imagining ourselves.

NOTES

[1]Sources that are particularly helpful in explaining the travel narratives' scope and impact are P. E. H. Hair's "Guinea," which surveys the West African material Hakluyt included; Richard Helgerson, who analyzes how the writers of travel compendia like Hakluyt and Eden contributed to England's sense of its nationhood; Jonathan Burton, who reexamines Leo Africanus's influence on Othello; and Oumelbanine Zhiri, who provides some extracts from Leo's account in Kamps and Singh.

[2]Citations to *Titus Andronicus* are from Bates's Arden 3 edition.

[3]Citations to *Othello* are from Honigmann's Arden 3 edition.

Teaching *Othello* through
Performance Choices

Miranda Johnson-Haddad

My approach to teaching Shakespeare's *Othello* was significantly affected by my experience as a Caucasian faculty member at Howard University, the nation's oldest historically black university. I have written elsewhere about how this teaching experience influenced my strategies for discussing the racist language in the play.[1] Recently I have found myself teaching *Othello* in the more ethnically diverse context of the University of California, Los Angeles, where I constantly seek to incorporate and expand on the insights I gained at Howard. At UCLA, I typically pair the text with performance studies, focusing on two stage productions at the Shakespeare Theatre in Washington, DC, both of which I was not only involved in but also reviewed. (Although I do use video clips from the many film versions available to discuss performance traditions, I increasingly find myself placing more emphasis on the choices that directors and actors have made in bringing the play to the stage.) Studying performance criticism and encouraging students to consider the text in the light of performance offer an effective means of approaching *Othello*. Performance criticism shows students how to analyze a play both intellectually (as critics) and subjectively (as playgoers). And this dual approach seems to me essential in teaching *Othello*, because our responses to this play—as readers, as critics, as playgoers—are complex, varied, culturally informed responses that are both cerebral and, often, highly visceral.

The two productions on which I focus in my classes were unusually thoughtful, provocative interpretations that confronted the race issues of the play. Studying these productions with my students has been illuminating for all concerned. The first production, in 1990, starred Avery Brooks as Othello and Andre Braugher as Iago; both are African American actors (Johnson-Haddad, "Shakespeare Theatre" [1991] 476–80). The second production, in 1997, starred Patrick Stewart, a Caucasian actor playing Othello as black (though not in makeup) amid an otherwise almost entirely African American cast playing Caucasians, in a production that the director Jude Kelly dubbed a "photonegative *Othello*" (Johnson-Haddad, "Shakespeare Theatre" [1998] 9; see also "Patrick Stewart"). In my classes, I distribute copies of my reviews of these productions (including an interview that I conducted with Patrick Stewart), and I discuss both the productions and the reviews in detail with my students. I also refer them to the Shakespeare Theatre Web site (www.ShakespeareDC. org), where they can read additional information about and see photos from each production.

We examine these two productions in the broader context of performance choices, one of the central ideas that I emphasize throughout my Shakespeare courses. I focus on the concepts of nontraditional as opposed to color-blind or gender-blind casting choices, using my own published definitions of these terms (Johnson-Haddad, "Shakespeare Theatre" [1991] 477 and "Shakespeare Performed" 101–02). I explain to the students the basic distinction between the two casting practices, which is that nontraditional casting places an actor of a race or gender not typically associated with a given character in that role to make a point. Color-blind or gender-blind casting, on the other hand, involves casting an actor of a race or gender not normally associated with a particular character in that role, but not with the intention of affecting playgoers' perceptions of the character, the play, the production, or anything else. In other words, we are meant to notice, observe, and mull over the implications of a nontraditional casting choice, but we are meant to ignore a color-blind or gender-blind one.

An instructive example of color-blind casting is a Shakespeare Theatre *Macbeth* from the late 1980s in which Banquo was played by an African American actor while his son, Fleance, was Caucasian. Gender-blind casting is trickier to identify (itself a fruitful topic for class discussion), but I have seen a production of *Macbeth* in which Banquo was female and only the pronouns were changed. (Is there something about the character of Banquo that lends itself to alternate casting?) A more nuanced example of gender-blind casting is a production of *The Winter's Tale* by the Washington Shakespeare Company in the early 1990s in which Camillo was played by a female actor; not only were the pronouns changed but also the name was changed, to Camilla. This comes close to gender-blind casting, although the name change hints at other possibilities.

Sometimes, of course, part of the exercise for playgoers is determining which casting choice is being used. I point this out to my classes and further suggest that whether we perceive a given choice as color- or gender-blind or as nontraditional may depend on many factors, including the perspective of the individual playgoer. For example, if a casting choice seems clearly intended to be color-blind, yet we are having trouble ignoring the actor's race, does the responsibility for this lie with us or with the director? Related questions to ask students might be whether a casting choice is nontraditional or color- or gender-blind and whether the plays resist certain casting choices. I have come to believe that truly color-blind casting is impossible in *Othello*. Given that race and race relations are central concerns of the play, it seems to me inevitable that playgoers will perceive any casting choice that involves race as nontraditional. I invite students to speculate about other nontraditional casting choices in *Othello* and to consider the implications of those choices. For example, we discuss the recent tendency in stage productions to cast an African American woman as Bianca and Jude Kelly's parallel choice in the "photo-negative" production to cast a Caucasian woman in the role and to have her play the character as Caucasian.

We also talk about the ways in which nontraditional or color-blind casting may backfire. Here I lapse into anecdotes. Anecdotalism unfortunately tends to be a complaint that some academics raise about performance criticism in general; nevertheless, I believe that anecdotalism holds a place both in performance criticism and in the classroom. Thus I tell my students about a Shakespeare Theatre production of *Troilus and Cressida* (1992) in which the Greek soldiers (Achilles, Patroclus, Ajax) were all played by African American actors and the Greek generals were all played by Caucasian actors. Although such nontraditional casting presented the audience with provocative images— specifically that of an older, racially empowered class of men sending a younger, racially disempowered class of men off to war—the Howard students who attended a performance with me did not take kindly to the fact that most of the characters whom the play presents as lazy, stubborn, or stupid were in this production African American (Johnson-Haddad, "Shakespeare Performed" 101–02). My UCLA students have been struck by my account of the Howard students' reaction, which has produced some excellent in-class discussions.

As I noted earlier, I use video clips when teaching *Othello* to emphasize the choices that are available to directors or actors. I have had consistent success with one exercise that compares three versions of act 4, scene 1 (Othello's seizure): Stuart Burge's 1965 film starring Laurence Olivier; the 1987 film of the Johannesburg, South Africa, production directed by Janet Suzman; and the 1995 film directed by Oliver Parker and starring Laurence Fishburne and Kenneth Branagh. I select this scene because I believe it represents that moment in the play when the potential for racist and stereotypical portrayal is most dangerously present. The scene also offers extraordinary performative opportunities, and challenges, for the actor playing Othello (and I point out to students the intriguing lack of stage directions). Using these three films as examples also allows for comparison among a Caucasian actor in blackface (Olivier), an African actor (John Kani), and an African American actor (Fishburne) playing Othello. The scene further provides Iago with extensive possibilities for revealing his racism to the audience or camera. In these versions, we see three different Iagos: Frank Finlay's understated and eroticized performance (in Burge); Richard Haddon Haines's portrayal of a virulently racist Iago (in Suzman); and Branagh's Iago as consummate actor (in Parker). Parker's version also enables us to see a production in which the director seems more than usually anxious about his Iago upstaging his Othello. Parker's choices have implications for how racism and performance intersect in productions of this play.[2]

I begin this exercise by showing the Olivier film, and I point out to students (which is necessary these days) that although Olivier's acting technique, on which he prided himself, may seem melodramatic and downright offensive to us today, we must understand it in its historical, theatrical, and even personal contexts as an individualized performance. Nevertheless, we also view the film in our historical, theatrical, and personal contexts, which affect our perceptions of the production and the play. A useful, although tangential, line of discussion is to ask students to consider the problems associated with a single performance being preserved statically, even iconically, on film and video and what the implications are of such preservation over time. Bearing all these considerations in mind, we can analyze the performances, the staging, and the editing choices involved for each production. We also note the differences between making an archival film of a stage version (as with Burge's and Suzman's productions) and making a movie of the play. Viewing the same scene presented three ways, with different emphases, interests the students and renders the act of criticism accessible. Ideally, analysis and discussion of this scene enable students to begin articulating their convictions about the play, the characters, and the performativity of the text.

This video exercise, like the discussions based on performance criticism described above, works well with both large and small classes. With smaller classes, the instructor may also have success with in-class performance exercises. (Even with larger classes, some of these exercises can be adapted for lectures or large-group discussions.) Possible performance exercises include the following:

> Iago's speeches in 1.1 contain many racist slurs and images. Perform this scene by speaking Iago's lines in a variety of ways: as deeply racist and offensive, lightly or comically (is this possible? why or why not?), or in other ways that may occur to you. Consider the reactions of the listeners, Brabantio and Roderigo. Discuss the implications for a black Iago delivering these lines.
>
> Perform 1.3 from different perspectives, for example, with the Senators in sympathy with Othello, then with them barely tolerating him but needing him for his military expertise. What messages can the characters convey through nonverbal business (gesture, blocking, body language, etc.)? How will the atmosphere of the Senate chamber affect Desdemona's entrance and her delivery of her lines?
>
> Silence or other nonverbal stage business can be used to subvert a seemingly racist text. Keeping this strategy in mind, select and stage a portion of one scene from *Othello*.

Additional large or small group discussions centering on performance may consider these topics:

> How can an actor's performance signal otherness or sameness, alien or native status? What is the role of accent, costume, gesture, lighting, blocking, and so forth?
>
> What is the nature of Othello's appeal to Desdemona? Is she attracted to him for his internal qualities? Or is she drawn by his otherness, his exoticism? How might performance convey the possibility of Desdemona's being attracted to Othello's exoticism, for example, in 1.3,

where Othello describes his travels, or in 3.4, where he explains the origins of the handkerchief. (The challenge tends to be that students often prove far too willing to blame the victim, Desdemona. A related exercise is to have one student read or recite Othello's lines while other students—playing Othello, Brabantio, Desdemona, and any other characters—mime without words the scenes recited.)

What are the connotations of the names Bianca and Barbary within the context of the play? What are the implications of these associations for casting Bianca?[23]

As I noted earlier, a performance-oriented approach to teaching any Shakespearean text frequently proves to be an anecdotal approach. This is especially true when the instructor focuses on live stage productions, which do not exist anymore, unlike productions that have been preserved, at least in a limited way, on film. When reviews of stage productions are available, students can read and discuss them. But ideally, instructors will also feel free to incorporate into classroom discussion descriptions of productions that they have seen but that haven't been reviewed by simply telling students about them. In such cases, anecdotalism (that is to say, memory) serves a valid pedagogical purpose. In a similar vein, I continue to search for ways to include my experience of teaching *Othello* at Howard University into any classroom context in which I may find myself. I am persuaded that the most effective way to achieve this integration is just to tell my students about the experience, and that includes describing my initial timidity—squeamishness, really—at teaching this play at Howard and my realization that I must overcome that timidity. I have considered how such telling arguably constitutes a performative act, one that can further enhance discussion about *Othello*, about performance, and about racism.

Othello, like *The Merchant of Venice*, can no longer be taught without reference to historical events of the last two hundred years, because we do not and cannot read it without reference to those events. At Howard, I was forced to confront the complex racism of the play as I had never been compelled to do before, and I learned that to approach this text gingerly may empower its racist elements in the wrong ways. But by using performance criticism in the classroom, I discovered a variety of methods for students and teachers alike to confront the unsettling elements of *Othello* head-on and to learn from the experience.

NOTES

[1]Throughout this essay I am indebted to Caroline McManus, with whom I coauthored an earlier version of this piece (Johnson-Haddad and McManus). My work on teaching *Othello* was profoundly influenced by a National Endowment for the

Humanities–Folger Institute workshop called Teaching Shakespeare through Performance in 1995–96, taught by Alan Dessen and Audrey Stanley, to both of whom I am also gratefully indebted.

[2]For those willing to spend an entire class period on this exercise, the 1990 production directed by Trevor Nunn and starring Willard White as Othello and Ian McKellen as Iago provides an interestingly low-key interpretation of this scene. And two recent contemporary revisions of the play—the 2001 version directed by Andrew Davies and Tim Blake Nelson's *O*—make for provocative viewing. Although both of these productions are adaptations, they present the seizure scene more obliquely than does the text.

[3]For additional exercises, discussion topics, and related research assignments, as well as a bibliography, see Johnson-Haddad and McManus.

"Ocular Proof":
Teaching *Othello* in Performance

Samuel Crowl

The past twenty-five years have seen a revolution in performance approaches to teaching Shakespeare. Many professors, following Miriam Gilbert's lead at Iowa, have turned their classrooms into rehearsal spaces where students spend more time on their feet speaking the text to one another than at their desks taking notes on imagery, characterization, theme, or historical context (see Gilbert). Others, spurred by the proliferation of study-abroad programs, whisked their students off to London and Stratford to taste Shakespeare in the flesh of live productions at the Royal National Theatre (RNT) and Royal Shakespeare Company (RSC). Still others, and perhaps the largest group, routinely incorporated film and television productions into their Shakespeare survey courses or have developed independent offerings in Shakespeare on film.

In all such instances, professors are trying to give their students varying ideas of how Shakespeare's texts were conceived originally as scripts for performance and of why those scripts have as much vitality for modern audiences (and modern media) as they did for those at the Theatre, Globe, and Blackfriars for whom they were first performed. *Othello*—particularly since our age has rightly made problematic the casting of a white actor in blackface for the title role—is no longer a staple of the Shakespearean repertory. Both the RSC and the RNT only have produced the play twice in the past twenty years. Great, or at least interesting, Hamlets seem to come along almost every year, whereas the compelling Othello tends to emerge only once a generation. In America the role has been claimed preeminently in the past fifty years only by Paul Robeson and James Earl Jones, and in England no performance has generated wide enthusiasm since Laurence Olivier's in 1964.

Fortunately we have two productions of *Othello* from the last decade of the twentieth century, made for television and film, which make for instructive contrasts when working with the play in the classroom. Trevor Nunn's television version grew out of his stage production for the RSC at the company's intimate black-box theater, The Other Place. The production had the formalist virtues associated with the RSC's approach to Shakespeare in the Peter Hall and Trevor Nunn eras and featured the American opera singer Willard White as Othello surrounded by a cast of RSC regulars. The production was small in scale, finely wrought in detail (particularly Ian McKellen's Iago), and harrowing in the physicality of the final confrontation between Othello and Desdemona. Nunn's treatment of the play, both on stage and television, had the quality of a black-and-white film in its basic color and costume design.

Oliver Parker's film, released just four years later, in 1995, was, by contrast, a romantic Technicolor epic inspired more by Franco Zeffirelli's ripe visual style than an aural exploration of the text's contrasting rhythms. Parker assembled an international cast of established film stars (the American Laurence Fishburne as Othello, the French Swiss Irène Jacob as Desdemona, and the British Kenneth Branagh as Iago) and employed a sweeping camera style and a lush film score in an attempt to refashion the text as an erotic thriller.

It is, of course, ideal if students can have the opportunity to see both productions in their entirety. But if such class time is not available to you, a series of clips can give them the flavor of each production and plenty of details to use in seeing how each creates its own approach to Shakespeare's text as it becomes a script for performance. Working with clips from the Senate scene (1.3), Iago's seduction and corruption of Othello (3.3), and the final catastrophe (5.2) will provide ample opportunity for students to grasp the range of options open to directors, actors, and designers when working with the same material. Obviously the instructor has many options in using such clips; one I prefer is to devote one two-hour class period to an investigation of these scenes from both Nunn's and Parker's productions. I assign three students to work with one of the three scenes in one of its versions, allowing an hour to a discussion of clips from each film or video. Thus in one two-hour period, eighteen students have been involved in leading the class in a discussion. In each group, I ask one student to be responsible for acting, another for direction, another for decor and music. Their responsibility is not to report on these areas but to use the superior care with which they have viewed the production and absorbed its details to ask good questions of the class and to lead the discussion in provocative directions.

The class can be structured to consider alternative versions of each scene back-to-back or to consider all the clips from one version first before moving on to the second production. This method allows students to develop strategies for reading Shakespeare in performance and to see how the same script can produce a variety of performance and production choices. It is this idea of choice, in my experience, that seems best to open up for them an expanding universe of Shakespearean possibilities as well as to create the understanding that choice, in any given production approach, also creates limitations.

The Senate scene in Nunn's production defines his approach to the play. The scene begins with the camera in tight on a green-felt-covered round table cluttered with maps, documents, a cigar box, and a brandy decanter and snifters. The only light comes from a hanging lamp suspended over the table. The Duke and First Senator are seated while they examine the dispatches still arriving from Cyprus. They are dressed in dark military uniforms suggestive of the Union army in the American Civil War. These details of set and costume tell us that we are in a war room rather than a political debating chamber; Nunn's production places us in a military world rather than a political or mercantile one. When Brabantio and Othello arrive, they too are immediately distinguished by their dress. Othello is in a magnificent military great coat loaded with silver buttons; Brabantio is dressed in a black morning coat—

civilian, not military, attire. His status is diminished—the lone citizen surrounded by officers responding to a military crisis—whereas Othello's is elevated by his presence in the familiar surroundings of a war council, not a stateroom or domestic parlor.

Brabantio's impact is further reduced by his behavior. The actor's (Clive Swift's) vocal tone is pleading instead of demanding. He defines his Brabantio by a large white handkerchief he uses repeatedly to wipe the tears and bluster away from his face. The Duke is initially solicitous but quickly becomes impatient with Brabantio's emotional appeals. When the Duke turns to Othello and invites him to tell his version of the courtship ("Say it, Othello" [1.3.127]), he settles into one of the green leather-backed chairs and lights a cigar: he's an eager and appreciative audience.[1] The camera focuses on Othello in medium close-up until he reaches "And sold to slavery" (1.3.138), when we are given a sympathetic reaction shot of the Duke and First Senator. Willard White presents a sincere, concerned straightforward Othello fully in control of himself and the situation.

Brabantio's power as a senator and outraged patriarch is vanquished by his own behavior and Othello's sure command. The ugly racism surreptitiously introduced by Iago in the opening scene and carried forward into the public sphere by Brabantio appears to have been routed here, trumped by Othello's military preeminence and by the threat the Turks pose. Students are quick to point out, however, that the scene ends not with Othello's triumphant exit but with Ian McKellen's Iago moving into the Duke's space to confide his private war plans for Cyprus. He sits at the officer's table and addresses the camera directly, furtively lifting a handful of cigars from the box as he confides that Othello "thinks men honest that but seem to be so" (1.3.400), thus defining himself in word and gesture. In this scene, Nunn's production establishes Othello (through White's formal bearing and sincere, straightforward delivery of "Her father lov'd me . . ." [1.3.128]) as the ultimate military insider rather than as Roderigo's "extravagant and wheeling stranger" (1.1.136). Similarly, the play's overt and covert racism is presented as lodged in the minds of Iago and Brabantio and not in the wider Venetian society as represented by the Duke and his fellow senators.

In 3.3—when the production has moved to Cyprus—students note that the set is now bathed in light. The sharp-eyed students see that the brandy decanter and snifters have given way to Desdemona's lemonade pitcher and tall glasses and that Nunn continues to use tables as the focus for the blocking of the action. Iago and Othello are seated at a rectangular camp table located in the equivalent of upstage left while Desdemona and Emilia have a small round wicker table downstage right as their base. By establishing these details, a teacher can allow students to see that the military and the domestic share the same space. Desdemona takes a drink to Othello and sits in his lap as she begins to lobby her husband on behalf of Cassio. Her girlish, loving intimacy includes a tender kiss. Her intrusion, interrupting Othello's attention to military matters, is noted by a reaction shot of McKellen's Iago and underlined by the disdainful glance he throws at Zoë Wannamaker's Emilia. Desdemona's playful passion and the production's conflation here of military and domestic space help trigger Iago's questions to Othello about Desdemona and Cassio. The camera repeatedly holds the men in a two shot as Iago's interrogation gathers momentum. Othello remains seated, shuffling military papers, trying to distract himself from Iago's irritating leading questions and gruff refusal to offer answers, while Iago first sits across from him, then rises to circle around behind him, and then eventually settles back down at Othello's side as his poison begins to work. As Iago's words begin to shake Othello's view of his wife and the world, Iago subtly begins to displace Desdemona as her husband's "fair warrior." By the time Desdemona returns to sit again in Othello's lap to try to bind his pounding head with her handkerchief, it is already too late; her napkin is "too little," for the medicine of her comfort has been already poisoned.

As with the Senate scene, Nunn's focus in 3.3 has been tight camera shots that rarely capture more than two actors in the frame. Nunn's attention has been on the script's language, on the intimacy of actors working in a confined space, and on small carefully selected details: the brandy, cigars, lemonade, a box of sweets brought to Desdemona by Cassio, the handkerchief, Emilia's pipe, and an ugly, vulgar kiss Iago gives to Emilia as reward for swiping the handkerchief. The effect is to create the atmosphere of a hot, cramped space where audience and actors are locked together in an intimate psychological and physical landscape with no room to escape the mounting tension. In the last long beat of the scene from 3.3.330 ("Look where he comes!") to line 480 ("I am your own for ever"), Iago effectively breaks down the last vestiges of Othello's defenses and turns him into a raging bull. Othello rips up the papers on the table where he and Iago have been working and then wipes the table clean. As he erupts, Iago is forced to defend himself with a chair as though he is now faced with controlling a wild, caged animal. All Othello's studied decorum and self-control disintegrate until Iago creates a new identity for him, sealed by a pact where Iago not only displaces Cassio ("Now art thou my lieutenant" [3.3.479]) but also Desdemona ("I am your own for ever" [3.3.480]).

In 5.2, Othello enters dressed, for the first time, in a white burnoose trimmed in brown, suggesting a return, in his tragic dislocation as husband and general, to his proud African roots. This conflicted move is reflected in his thoughts as well, since he sees his contemplated murder of Desdemona not as an act of jealous revenge (beneath his dignity) but as a means of protecting and defending other naive men: "Yet she must die, else she'll betray more men" (5.2.6). Nunn's production depicts Othello as a man infected by Iago's poison and imprisoned by his own deluded sense of himself as the defender of an adopted culture, which is reinforced by having the camera repeatedly capture Othello through the steel bars of the bed he shares with Desdemona.

The production, highlighted by Imogen Stubbs's playful, passionate, and insistent Desdemona and by Emilia's ambiguous sexual relationship with Iago and initially disdainful attitude toward Desdemona's girlish class presumptions, also seeks to emphasize the class and gender issues at work in the play as much as the more obvious racial ones. These ideas are powerfully captured in the vitality of Desdemona's resistance to Othello's physical threats and in Emilia's dawning realization of her husband's perfidy. Stubbs's Desdemona is not a passive victim but exhibits the same independent spirit in physically opposing Othello as she once demonstrated in loving him. Their battle is fierce and frightening in its intensity. When Othello finally subdues and then smothers Desdemona, first with his giant hand and then with a pillow, he does so in a frightful parody of sexual consummation. He straddles his wife as he smothers her; they enact the text's version of the ancient fellowship of sex and death so potent in the Western imagination. The production, by retaining both "O insupportable! O heavy hour! / Methinks it should be now a huge eclipse / Of sun and moon" (5.2.98–100) and "This look of thine will hurl my soul from heaven, / And fiends will snatch at it" (5.2.274–75), allows White's Othello to register the full impact of his destructive delusion. The last image we are given is of Othello and Desdemona alone together on the fatal wedding sheets with Iago standing at the foot of the bed staring silently at his handiwork.

Parker's 1995 film, by contrast, does not limit itself to enclosed rooms or confined spaces. As a film it seeks expanse and spectacle; it wants to translate Shakespeare's verbal images into visual ones. Film conventions allow Parker the freedom to open up Shakespeare's text by shooting on location and creating expensive, realistic studio sets; by employing a variety of camera devices (long shots, close-ups, zooms, etc.) and editing techniques (jump cuts, flashbacks, montage, etc.); by featuring a full film score; and by taking great liberties in translating the playscript into a screenplay.

The screenplay is what students first note about the opening of Parker's *Othello*, for the film begins not with the exchange between Iago and Roderigo but with a silent sequence (underlined by the film score's use of a mysterious mandolin melody) of gondolas passing one another as Desdemona crosses the Grand Canal heading to her wedding rendezvous with Othello. The film cuts from their embrace to the doge's palace, where the Senate is in a late-night session. The first words of the film are the Duke's, lifted from forty lines into 1.3: " 'Tis certain then for Cyprus" (43). The room is crowded; the actors playing the senators are dressed in clothes appropriate for the Italian Renaissance; the Duke is the most formally attired in blue and gold and speaks with a pronounced Italian accent. Brabantio has hastily dressed and is wearing an open-collared white shirt. Most interesting, he also speaks with a European accent, this time a French one. In fact, the actor playing the Duke (Gabriele Ferzetti) is Italian, and the actor playing Brabantio (Pierre Vaneck) is French. These details of costume and accent quickly allow my students to see that Parker's Venice is conceived as a mercantile rather than military state and that the jumble of accents (soon to be joined by those of Fishburne [American], Branagh [British], and Irène Jacob [Swiss French]) we hear in the Senate scene is meant to suggest the cosmopolitan flavor of the city. Fishburne's Othello, in age, dress, and bearing, is presented as an exotic outsider. He's young and virile, he's dressed in black and red with rings dangling from both ears, and his shaved head is marked with scars and tattoos. When he launches into "Her father lov'd me" (1.3.128), Parker's camera flashes back to Fishburne's Othello moving through Brabantio's garden as Desdemona greedily inclines her ear to hear his tales. Students come to see that such flashbacks or projections (of Cassio and Desdemona making love, for instance) are devices Parker repeatedly uses in treating many of Othello's longer speeches retained by the screenplay. For Parker, Othello's world is more visual than verbal, and one where texture frequently trumps text.

By contrast, Parker allows Branagh's Iago to appropriate the camera, to make it Branagh's intimate, to ensure that it is always attentive to Iago's text. We get, beginning with the end of 1.3, Iago's knowing conspiratorial soliloquies in tight close-up, often begun in profile so that Branagh can then draw us into Iago's cunning gutter imagination with just the slightest turn of his head to confide in us directly. Branagh delivers "I hate the Moor" (1.3.386) in an ugly whisper with each word given equal emphasis, and in the beats he takes between each word, Branagh makes us see Iago's pathological jealousy. For Parker's film, Iago is word, Othello image. Word and image unite as Iago shares his plot to destroy Othello and Desdemona directly with the camera and simultaneously toys with the black and white figures of a chess set.

Several key details from the film's treatment of 3.3 extend or repeat images and devices Parker initiated in the Senate scene. Iago and Othello are first discovered exercising with long sticks, Othello easily outmanning his opponent and sending him to the ground. The two men then move to the entrance to the armory, where Iago helps Othello towel off and casually begins to inquire about Cassio's relationship with Desdemona. As Iago's queries begin to sting and irritate, the camera follows the two men down several steps into the armory. We then get a shot of Othello through racks of muskets, pikes, and swords as he succumbs to suspicion. The film moves from the daylight world of military exercise, where Othello easily meets and parries Iago's thrusts, down into a murkier environment. Here verbal blows are substituted for physical ones, and Iago quickly gains the upper hand. Parker visually captures the way Shakespeare's text allows Iago to turn Othello's attention from the military to the domestic, from issues of martial defense to marital defensiveness. Again, Parker uses visual projections to cut away from Fishburne's expression of Othello's anxiety and agony and to present us with Othello's overheated imaginings of Desdemona's lasciviousness.

The same pattern persists in 5.2, where my students note that the screenplay cuts much of Othello's reaction to his fatal error, perhaps because Parker thinks that Shakespeare's language is both too arcane ("when we shall meet at compt" [5.2.273]) and hyperbolic ("roast me in sulphur! / Wash me in steep-down gulfs of liquid fire!" [5.2.279–80]) for a contemporary film audience. Students are also quick to note that the small dagger Othello uses to kill himself is slipped to him by Cassio, thus complicating Othello's relation to the Venetian world he dies defending. Some even recall that this is the dagger we saw Othello present to Cassio for serving as best man at his wedding in the film's opening montage. The film further reduces the text's concentration on Othello in its final moments by privileging Branagh's Iago even after the text has silenced him: "From this time forth I never will speak word" (5.2.304). Parker's camera cuts away from Othello's agony to follow Iago as he bolts from the bedchamber in a futile attempt to escape. When he is returned to look "on the tragic loading of this bed" (5.2.363), he is allowed to crawl up on it to wedge himself in between the bodies of Othello and Desdemona. Even the final shot of the film, which shows us two wrapped bodies being given a burial at sea, is ambiguous: are they the bodies of Othello and Desdemona? Othello and Iago? Desdemona and Emilia? Iago and Emilia? Parker's film loads both couples on that tragic bed.

Working with details from these scenes in the two productions allows students the opportunity to see how each takes a very different visual and interpretive approach to Shakespeare's text and to see what each seeks to illumine (and what to shade) about the play's tangled mixture of social, political, and psychological issues. These two productions also open up even larger issues about film and television Shakespeare. Is studio television, with its limited sets and floor-bound cameras, a medium more attentive to Shakespeare's text than film? Does television's private nature, the way it quietly has insinuated itself into our living rooms and provided in form and content a reflection of middle-class life and values, make it more congenial than film for representing the more domestic of Shakespeare's plays such as *Twelfth Night, The Merry Wives of Windsor,* and *Othello*? Is, conversely, film the only modern technological medium of performance that can properly capture the power and sweep of Shakespeare's dramatic imagination? Is film's grammar and rhetoric (the long shot, close-up, montage, jump cut, and zoom) more effective in translating Shakespeare's images into a dynamic performance narrative than television's more constricted and attenuated format? Finally, what do these two performances tell us about *Othello*? Is Shakespeare's tale ultimately a great reckoning in a little room or an epic clash of gender, race, and class sketched out against an archetypal landscape? Or does the text contain the possibilities of being realized by as many performance approaches as wit and imagination can conjure?

NOTE

[1]Citations to *Othello* are from Evans's *Riverside Shakespeare.*

Interpreting the Tragic Loading of the Bed in Cinematic Adaptations of *Othello*

Kathy M. Howlett

Teaching Shakespeare's *Othello* to students who were old enough to watch the O. J. Simpson trial unfold before a national television audience offers an opportunity for highlighting a significant interpretive crux of the play—the tragic loading of the bed. At the close of *Othello*, when Lodovico demands that Iago (and the audience) "Look on the tragic loading of this bed" (5.2.374), what is it that the audience sees? How are we meant to respond to the "object" on the bed that "poisons sight" yet must also "be hid" (375–76)?[1] The play's absence of stage directions in both the 1622 quarto and the 1623 folio generates multiple possibilities for performance and editorial practice. However, as students realize by viewing the endings of several film adaptations of the play, the performance of the final scene is never a citation of the text. The meaning of the "tragic loading of this bed" cannot be traced either to the independent authority of Lodovico as speaker or to the authority of the text. As W. B. Worthen observes, "Theatrical performance can never be 'historical' . . . as a means of recovering meanings inscribed in the text, because the theatre does not cite texts, it cites behavior" (132). Instead, lines from the play summon a context that determines the nature of the tragedy. As students view the films of *Othello*, they come to understand how practices of dramatic performance produce meaning "by deploying the text in recognizable genres of behavior" that give the text meaning as performance (127).

I frame my class discussion of Shakespeare's *Othello* with reference to the O. J. Simpson trial even as O. J. Simpson's narrative was framed in *Othello*'s contradictory and varied readings. Ironically, the play seemed to acquire agency and deploy meaning when recognizable behaviors in the Simpson case were associated with performative elements in Shakespeare's play. From Simpson's own avowal that he loved his wife "too much" (qtd. in Hodgdon, "Race-ing" 39) to the infamous Bronco chase and suicide threat, the story of America's fallen hero implicitly traced ideologies of race, gender, power, and sexuality in the early modern period as reflected in what journalists called "the case of the [late twentieth] century." In turn, critics such as Lisa Starks discover explicit connections between recent cinematic treatments of *Othello* and the O. J. Simpson trial. Such connections are inevitable, as Judith Buchanan observes: "Just as no contemporary production of *The Merchant of Venice* can duck the resonances of being played in a post-Holocaust world, so no contemporary production of *Othello* can be oblivious of how the interracial encounters in the play relate to those beyond its bounds" (190).

Yet even as the O. J. Simpson case stirred the nation to recognize itself in the mirror of Shakespeare's *Othello*, the public courtroom performance that illuminated a black man's oppression now made startlingly clear the elisions in Shakespeare's play. Despite the photos of Nicole Brown Simpson's bruised arms and blackened eye, the jurors were firm that this trial was about race and not about wife abuse and murder. As Barbara Hodgdon remarks, "Nicole Brown Simpson virtually disappeared from accounts of her own murder, replaced by the iconic and symbolic power of a national and local history whose touchstones were the lynched nigger and the 1991 Rodney King beating" ("Race-ing" 59). In the firestorm of commentary generated over racial slurs and innuendo, the murdered woman's story was heard only in the vulgarity of the prurient, lowbrow tabloids, where images of her battered face, however sensationalistic, could be ignored as nonevidentiary. That the cause of the battered wife should be championed in the tabloids reflects once again on the play, to the carnal and lowbrow Emilia's trumpeting charges before a disbelieving audience, who also ignores and silences her.

In *Othello* the issue of spousal abuse hovers uneasily between expression and erasure. In this respect, as Hodgdon observes, "Lodovico's 'Let it be hid' seems symptomatic of a refusal to address domestic violence shared by early modern and late twentieth-century cultures" ("Race-ing" 64; see also Bart and Moran). As a marker of a recent interpretive shift, critics have now begun to reassess the play's cinematic incarnations in the light of the problem of domestic violence. Whereas Hodgdon argues (pre–O. J.) that Orson Welles's film transfers *Othello* "to a transcendent realm that insulates the text from history and suspends issues of gender and race within an aesthetic vacuum" ("Kiss" 245), in the aftermath of the Simpson trial Carol Chillington Rutter describes Welles's *Othello* as "like a stalker film" in which "the love story is perverted" (254). Given the polarized responses to the Simpson trial, it should not be surprising that critical responses to cinematic adaptations of Shakespeare's *Othello* would become similarly vexed. As part of the students' investigations, therefore, I pose a version of the same (polarized) question to my class: Is this a play about miscegenation? race? or wife murder? Or are these issues somehow entangled in the play's representations?

I first ask the students to consider two important passages in *Othello* that provide clues about how we might read the final scene. I ask students not only to consider Lodovico's command to "Look on the tragic loading of this bed" as the central symbol for interpreting the tragedy but also to examine Emilia's call to be laid by her mistress's side (5.2.245). Who lies on the bed determines the nature of the tragedy as well as what must be hidden, and Emilia's articulated desire to be placed on that bed suggests alternative readings unexplored by the students in my classes and, as I point out, largely erased in performance. As Hodgdon observes, Emilia's suppressed voice is "another site for exploring the relations between women's speech and silence in *Othello*, one that aligns with recent studies citing women's unwillingness to file charges against spouses who have abused them or seek their arrest" ("Race-ing" 61).

While students examine the passages that provide textual evidence for the tragic loading of the bed, I offer them a truncated view of *Othello* in performance over the last several centuries to illuminate the entirely new direction that twentieth-century editors—and theatrical practice—would come to take. I explain that eighteenth-century audiences would have seen only Desdemona on the bed and that Othello's body would have fallen on the floor beside her. I also point out that the kiss that Othello desires to "die upon" was denied him in early performances because of the public outcry over miscegenation, particularly in nineteenth-century America. And, finally, Emilia's request to be laid by her mistress's side remained largely ignored over the course of three centuries. I refer students who wish to read more on the theatrical history of the play to James Siemon, Michael Neill, Philip C. McGuire, and Virginia Mason Vaughan. Their illuminating work on eighteenth- and nineteenth-century productions of the play demonstrates that Desdemona remains isolated on the bed, making this tragedy indisputably hers alone. For example, Vaughan reports that promptbooks for William Charles Macready's performance of *Othello* at the Theatre Royal, in Covent Garden (1837), record that the suicide of Othello "is usually blocked with the hero struggling to join Desdemona on the bed" but that he "staggers and falls" on the stage instead, albeit "close in front of the bed" (153). Similarly, Tommaso Salvini's Othello, performed in the 1870s and 1880s in New York and Boston, dies before reaching the bed, falling "backward, dying 'in strong convulsions of the body and legs. Quick curtain' " (Vaughan 169). Neill also notes that Victorian audiences would have been denied the "racial impropriety" of seeing both Othello and Desdemona on the bed and that performances would have cut the erotic suggestiveness of "To die upon a kiss," so that Desdemona might remain in "chaste isolation" ("Unproper Beds" 403–04).

I then direct the students' attention to the handout distributed to the class. In the first section, I photocopied lines from the 1622 Quarto and the 1623 Folio: "I kissed thee ere I killed thee. No way but this, / Killing myself, to die upon a kiss" (5.2.369–70). In the remaining space on the handout I typed the same passage, with stage directions, from some late-twentieth-century editions of the play. I leave a blank space on the sheet for the Bevington's *Complete Works*, which students use in class, and ask the students to fill in the blank with the editorial changes they find in their text. For some students this is their first encounter with early modern script, and they gingerly note that typesetting decisions yield differences in punctuation between the two passages and alter our reading of the lines ("no way but this"). The exercise also makes them keenly aware that the stage directions in brackets are not the "original Shakespeare" but subject to the cultural and historical conditions that temper our readings of the play.

Students observe that the folio and quarto are similarly silent on the issue of how the final scene might be interpreted, since where (and how) Othello dies is not specified in the minimal stage directions ("He dies" in the folio and "Dyes" in the quarto). In the prepared list of editorial changes, students note the similar changes in Arden 2, Riverside, New Cambridge, and Pelican, which require that Othello fall and die on the bed: "[Falls on the bed, and] dies." Students decide that the stage directions in these editions dictate an interpretation that focuses on the problem of mixed-race marriage in a world that wishes it to "be hid." However, they are somewhat taken aback by the specificity of the 1986 Signet edition and its graphic depiction of events: "[He falls over Desdemona and dies.]." Gone are Victorian notions of racial impropriety when Othello is made clearly, even exaggeratedly, visible on the bed. Some of the students interpret these stage directions as confirming the play's final moment of voyeuristic gratification in viewing the mixed-race coupling, even in death. Others see the "tragic loading" as the play's total erasure of Desdemona, who now disappears beneath Othello's dark form.

In the second part of the handout, I have similarly listed the folio and quarto versions of the passage that contain Emilia's request to "lay me by my mistress' side" (5.2.245), as well as the same passage in recent editions of the play. However, in striking contrast to the creative performative solutions for Othello's death devised by twentieth-century editors, Emilia's death receives no attention at all. (One notable exception, of course, is the edition we use in class, Bevington's *Complete Works*, which specifies, "Exit [with all but Othello and Emilia, who has been laid by Desdemona's side]," but since detecting the stage directions in our edition is part of the class exercise, not every student detects Bevington's editorial emendation nor recognizes its uniqueness until examined beside other editions of the play. When confronted with the problem of Emilia's request to lie by her mistress's side, students find that editors have been strangely silent. Given that Emilia's request appears both in the folio and quarto, one might argue that editorial emendation is superfluous. But theater practice tells us otherwise. For in the history of stage and film productions of *Othello*, Emilia lies gasping her final lines on the floor, not by Desdemona's side on the bed. Even some recent Shakespeare scholars argue that her request should be ignored. Neill assumes that the bed contains the bodies of Desdemona and Othello: "Lodovico's speech reduces the corpses to the condition of a single nameless 'object'—'the tragic loading of this bed.'" And although Neill acknowledges Emilia's request to be laid by her mistress's side, he dismisses this request as a symbolic usurpation of Othello's place on the bed ("Unproper Beds" 403). Perhaps, as I suggest to the class, this may be the very point the play is struggling to make—that to place Emilia's body with Desdemona's on the bed usurps that place we have accorded Othello and makes vivid that this is a tragedy about wife murder and not miscegenation—a story that has been hidden by the tacit agreement between editorial emendation and theatrical practice.

The first cinematic adaptation I show to my class is Dimitri Buchowetzki's silent *Othello*, a German film starring Emil Jannings as Othello. Jannings is recognizable to some of my students as Professor Rath from Joseph von Sternberg's *The Blue Angel* (1930). Werner Krauss, the film's Iago, as I point out to the class, would become famous for playing Jews, including the Shylock figure in the film *Der Kaufman von Venedig* (1925), and for his collaboration with the Nazi regime. The film's historical context (as a product of Weimar Germany and harbinger of Nazi power) not only explains the film's concentration on images of political power but also illuminates the film's stylizations, in that Janning's Othello's somnambular stagger and symbiotic relationship with Iago are reminiscent of Cesare in the expressionist film *The Cabinet of Doctor Caligari* (1920).

I find Buchowetzki's film useful in class discussions because it chronicles the legacy of Victorian productions that insist on Desdemona's angel-like purity, whereas Janning's brooding performance creates a menacing Othello that communicates the period's abhorrence of miscegenation. Even in the liberal 1920s in Berlin the discourse on protecting German culture from black barbarism begins to surface, largely in response to the influence of American music and dance. As Peter Jelavich explains:

> Rumors of the "black outrage" even affected the cabaret stage. In early 1922 the police banned two nude-show numbers involving black men with white women [and] instead prohibited the performance of a dance entitled "Erotik" by the Erna Offeney Ballet, because it involved a scene in which four black men forced a white woman to dance herself to death.
> (174–75)

Students are quick to comment on Othello's costume (his striped gown looking like a cross between a magician's robe and a clown suit), as well as Iago's appearance, whose large, expressive eyes, enormous earring, and ruffled black shirt give him a feminine softness. The tights Iago wears hug his round figure, and the camera continually focuses on his backside as he speaks to Othello, drawing the viewers' attention to the small ruffles that run down his spine to his fleshy buttocks. Even Iago's death seems strangely eroticized when we witness Iago's wide-eyed reaction to the enormous curved blade that Othello slowly removes from his scabbard. And, interestingly, in an adaptation that gives Desdemona all the purity of the Victorian angel of the house, the transfer of power from Othello to Cassio also acquires a degree of erotic suggestiveness absent between Desdemona and Othello.

As Hodgdon, Stephen Buhler, and others have pointed out, Buchowetzki's *Othello* deprivileges the tragic loading of the bed and replaces the spectacle of Desdemona's body with the reconciliation of Othello and Cassio. In this film it is Othello, not Lodovico, who tells Iago to "Look on the tragic loading of this bed," where Desdemona lies alone but out of frame. It is Iago who is stabbed and dies, not Emilia, whose meek and girlish femininity would scarcely dare to challenge Othello's place on the bed. And, in the final scene where Othello joins Desdemona on the bed, the power of the image is diminished by its framing through a Moorish archway and the long shot from which we barely perceive Othello's huddled form embracing the lower half of Desdemona's body, in a gesture that resembles religious adoration. Any hint of the fascination of desire is obscured or deleted in Buchowetzki's film, for even the kiss that Othello desires to "die upon" is blocked from our view by the back of Othello's head. However, the diminished significance of the tragic loading of the bed and the omission of Emilia's death open up new avenues for class discussion and make apparent how a particular political and cultural moment can shape a performance. If the end of this film contemplates the successful transfer of power rather than the tragic loading of the bed, it also reveals how Weimar culture expressed political anxieties as gender anxieties.

The next film I show is Welles's *Othello*, a production that Michael Anderegg argues occludes the issue of race, or at the very least "destabilizes the seemingly straightforward dichotomies—white/black; Venice/Cyprus; male/female; human/monstrous—that govern Shakespeare's text" (102). Yet even as the question of Othello's race seems embarrassingly absent in this film, the issue of perspective—or what we actually see as the tragic loading of the bed—is made crucial. In this film Lodovico never utters his final lines about the bed, and Othello has the final word. Although Emilia is killed by her husband, she dies outside the room where Desdemona lies. Nor does Desdemona stay on the bed after she is killed, but her body manages to roll off it. As Welles's Othello lifts Desdemona's body before the assembly of Venetians who gaze down from a casement in the domed ceiling, the couple falls backward out of frame and into the darkness of cinematic space. Our view, finally, is that of the Venetians above, distant and removed from a tragedy we can barely discern.

Perspective is everything, as Welles would agree. For the film buffs in class, Welles's *Othello* generates keen discussion about how to interpret this final scene. Has Welles, they ask, managed to negate the interpretative crux of the play by denying our vision of it? Critics, however, are adept at maneuvering around this problem. Peter Donaldson finds in the film's final, dizzying, rotating point-of-view shot a "visual analogy between the marriage bed and the prison" (118). Similarly, Virginia Vaughan argues that Emilia's absence from the bedchamber does not prevent the film from being centrally concerned with "husbands who murder their wives in an effort to contain them" (214). And although critics such as Hodgdon, Donaldson, and Jack Jorgens contend that Welles's film places the viewer in "the distant world of legends and dreams" (Jorgens 192) and not in a historical place and time, my own work on Welles's *Othello* argues that Welles's artistic imagination was inspired by the art of the quattrocentro Venetian Vittore Carpaccio ("Voyeuristic Pleasures").

If Welles's film threatens to negate the historical moment of its inspiration and creation, the John Dexter and Stuart Burge *Othello* places the viewer squarely in the turbulent 1960s of its making. Laurence Oliver's performance has been called a racist fantasy on the one hand and praised for its social realism on the other. His performance alone makes the film worthy of inclusion in this group of cinematic interpretations of the play, but it also is a useful example in displaying how the tragic loading of the bed conjures the horrors of miscegenation. Timothy Murray has been particularly energetic in reducing the film to the single moment when Olivier's black makeup rubs off on the white face of the dead Desdemona (Maggie Smith). Murray puzzles over why "the director chose, for whatever practical or conceptual reasons, not to edit this dirty still out of the film" and argues that "Othello's darkened strains read as material traces of nothing less than the Eurocentric horror of miscegenation, a horror often glossed by critical overinvestment in the humanist theme of the enigma of moral darkness" (109). Indeed, my classes usually express some outrage over this *Othello*, not simply because of the "dirty still" that remains in the final cut of the film but because of Olivier's performance. Murray credits Olivier's performance with doing "more to maintain the cultural ideology of negritude, which inscribes resistance in the web of colonial fantasy, than to expose it to any sustained performance of retrospective critique" (111). However, if Murray finds in this film a "colonial fantasy," Jorgens discovers "a real social and political context," albeit "sketched in a sparse theatrical style" (192). Yet the theatrical style Jorgens praises raises hoots of nervous laughter from my students. For example, Jorgens praises the way Othello reaches out to the body of the dead Desdemona and then withdraws "his hand in shock at the coldness of her flesh"; the way "he embraces her corpse and speaks in a small wavering voice of unutterable sorrow"; and the way, with "titanic fury and agony," Othello "creates with his arms cascades of liquid fire pouring over his head and wails with West Indian inflection, 'Desdemon's daid! Daid!' " (204).

Anthony Davies explains that our discomfort with Olivier's performance has more to do with the clash of aesthetics than with any racist fantasy. The way the camera selectively focuses on Olivier's Othello leads Davies to conclude that "While one is captivated—and held so—by Olivier's performance, the uneasiness produced by the aesthetic clash of cinematic centrifugality with theatrical centripetality is never far below the surface" ("Filming *Othello*" 200). I ask my students whether some of the interpretative problems they perceive with the film are because it's a filmed stage production. Does the contrast between Olivier's polished black body and Smith's pale Desdemona, although effective in the theater, seem exaggerated to the point of parody under the scrutiny of the camera's gaze? Similarly, although Emilia's request to be laid by her mistress's side visibly moves her male auditors, they inexplicably turn and leave her lying on the floor. Gestures that might be barely perceived in the theater assume great significance on film and illuminate the problem of privileging Emilia's speech but not her dying request.

However, the film's final moments present an unusual twist to the problem of the tragic loading of the bed. For after Lodovico tells his auditors to look on the bed, he then turns to Iago and charges, "This is thy work" (5.2.375). Still gazing down on the kneeling Iago, Lodovico pauses, then loudly proclaims, "The object poisons sight" (375). At Lodovico's command to "[l]et it be hid" (376), two guards lift the screaming Iago and carry him away. In this film's interpretation of the final scene, Iago's villainy is the poison that must be hid, and it is the racist himself who must be driven from the stage. As the lights dim and the actors leave the stage, the camera dollies back to reveal an illuminated bed and the black and white bodies on it. No longer admonished by Lodovico that this image poisons sight, the audience now freely gazes on the mixed-race pair as the play's tragic centerpiece. But even this final moment invites contradictory readings: the image of Olivier's exaggerated blackness embracing the whiteness of Smith's robes can be interpreted as racist fantasy or realistic political critique.

Oliver Parker's *Othello* presents the students with a number of contemporary actors recognizable from other films and a film stylization (thriller) with which they are familiar. Unlike Janning's stylized, expressionistic acting; Welles's understated, almost abstract realization of the role; or Olivier's overblown theatricality, Lawrence Fishburne offers us our first naturalistic presentation of Othello. Even more significant, Fishburne is the first African American actor cast in a general-release film version of Shakespeare's *Othello*. But what do the students make of this Othello? Their opinions range as widely as those of the critics. Buhler complains that Parker's film operates in popular racist stereotypes and fetishizes Fishburne's Othello as a "black aggressor" (27), whereas Samuel Crowl finds Fishburne "radiates a natural authority and nobility" ("Checkmate" 96). For Rutter, Fishburne is "dangerously violent from the beginning" (255); in contrast, Hodgdon finds Fishburne's Othello "a powerfully controlled, self-possessed figure, radiating a quiet, reserved dignity from a magnificent physical presence" ("Race-ing" 65).

Since Fishburne's representation of Othello is beset with contradictory readings, asking students how to interpret the final catastrophe will yield similar debate. In this film, not only Othello, Desdemona, and Emilia but also the wounded Iago end up on the bed. I ask the students whether the final image of the bed has been invested with the same imaginative evocation of masochistic longing that we see in Welles's *Othello*. Or is this scene, as Starks argues, an erotic spectacle, as in the O. J. Simpson trial, that fixates our view on "not only Fishburne's body but also the bed itself, the site of his sexuality" (69)? Certainly Iago's inclusion on the bed complicates our understanding of the tragedy in numerous ways. Does his inclusion indicate that the "white man's story has prevailed" (Buhler 29)? Or does it raise the specter "of the perversely racialized, misogynistic imaginary that, in the wake of the O. J. Simpson trial, split one nation in two" (Hodgdon, "Race-ing" 73)? Is Iago "clinging like a needy child to his dead general's leg," which has been "fetishized as a point of fascination by the intradiegetic attentiveness (voyeuristic and physical)" (Buchanan 184)? Or is this final gesture the "homoerotic bonding of Iago and Othello" (Starks 74) of a "gay man who loves Othello but cannot admit it and so destroys him and his wife" (Burt 241)? The students' (and critics') fascination with Iago is understandable, given how the director allows him the illusion of control as he plays with the boundaries between viewer and the fiction on the screen.

Although this film is the only film version of the play to honor Emilia's request to lie by her mistress's side, the critics remain strangely silent on its significance. Admittedly, the film undercuts the speech even as it privileges Emilia's request, for as soon as the wounded Emilia utters, "Oh lay me by my mistress's side," the camera cuts to Iago's flight from the room to the scene where the dying Roderigo points an accusatory finger at the hunted man. The scene then returns to Emilia, already lying on the bed, who utters her "willow, willow" speech to Desdemona's corpse in a quiet and private moment unattended by Lodovico and his men (5.2.257). Perhaps the de-emphasis on Emilia's speech in this scene accounts for why some critics erase her from the scene altogether, as when Buhler describes how Lodovico drags Iago to the bed "upon which the bodies of Othello and Desdemona lie" (29) and details how Iago crawls up on the bed but never mentions that Emilia also lies there. Kenneth Rothwell is one of the few critics to acknowledge Emilia's inclusion on the bed, arguing she is present as one of the "bodies of Iago's victims" (237).

However, the inclusion of three bodies on the bed, not two, precludes a simple explanation of what the tragedy on the bed might be. Anna Patrick's portrayal of Emilia also complicates our understanding of her relevance in the final scene. For although Patrick imparts to Emilia a loftier stature (better spoken, more elegant in gesture) than we have seen in other film Emilias, her Emilia is also more degraded. My students are struck by Iago's sexual assault on Emilia earlier in the film, when she offers her sleeping husband the stolen handkerchief in a scene that makes the viewer complicit in Emilia's abuse and Iago's sexual perversity (sniffing the handkerchief as he apparently sodomizes Emilia on their bed). Some students argue that Emilia's inclusion on the bed in the final scene is the logical extension of this earlier scene with Iago, much as Desdemona's death on the bed is the result of Othello's voyeuristic fantasies of Cassio and Desdemona in bed. Such a line of reasoning moves students to see the tragic loading in terms more of psychological and sexual forces than of racial fascination.

The overwhelming power of the visual image in the final scene of *Othello* persuades me that adaptations such as Tim Blake Nelson's *O* can be useful in illuminating the play's markers that Shakespeare's language, the conventions of Renaissance drama, and editorial practice can obscure or confuse. Even more significant, this film merges the two points of fascination with which I began this exercise—Shakespeare's play and the O. J. Simpson trial. The film's titular hero, Odin, or O, is a black athlete in an elite prep school who dates blond Dessie. According to Nelson, an American prep school "was the ideal setting for a retelling of Shakespeare's tale of race, jealousy, and violence." Yet far from suggesting the complexities of Venetian society, the setting conjures up comparisons with the rarefied world of professional sports in the United States and with the hero worship that troubled the Simpson case. Even more to the point, Nelson clarifies his reading of the play as it pertains to his adaptation: "To me, *Othello* is first about love and jealousy, third about race" (260). Yet in a production that claims to be about love, the ending contemplates the isolation of the black athlete as the film's emblematic centerpiece.

Students note that this film recalls theatrical conventions from a previous century when Desdemona lies alone on the bed. Yet given its contemporary stylization, Dessie's death is frighteningly brutal and explicit, without the glamour or sentimentality we see in Parker's film. She is strangled in the glaring light of her dorm room and across her narrow iron bed as Odin kneels above her. Emily's death is also shockingly violent and even more abrupt. In a confrontation with Hugo, Emily angrily retorts that "Hugo gave the scarf to Michael" every time Hugo frantically shouts, "Tell the truth, Emily!" Suddenly, Hugo turns and shoots her in the stomach. Emily falls backward onto the floor with the force of the blast, never uttering another word, the silence reminding us of the fragility of this moment in the play and of what is lost in this adaptation.

However, Odin is given plenty to say. As he slowly walks out of the room in full realization of how Hugo has "played" him, he waves a gun demanding that the frightened students who have scattered at his approach "sit down and shut the fuck up. Now somebody here knows the truth. Somebody needs to tell the goddamn truth." And the truth he tells is the story of his life as a black man. He sarcastically tells those assembled around him that when "all of you are sitting around talking about the nigger who lost it back in high school, you make sure you tell 'em the truth," that "I ain't no different than any of you all. . . . My mom's ain't no crack head, I wasn't no gang-banger." Odin insists, "I loved that girl," but he wants his auditors to know that "it wasn't a drug dealer that fucked me, it was this white, prep-schooler." Yet the world "where I'm from," Odin tells the students, made him "do this," as he turns the gun on himself. In this adaptation, *Othello*'s "honorable murderer" is reconstituted as the white liberal conscience that masks Iago's cynicism and as the specter of the angry, black, urban male embracing his death fantasy in one last desperate action. Odin's death in freeze-frame allows the viewer to contemplate this moment as the film's emblematic centerpiece, its tragic loading of the bed. The tableau's elongation of time is melodramatic and reverses the viewer's experience of the deaths of the female characters. After the gun blast, there is only silence, until Odin falls backward, with outstretched arms, as Desdemona's aria from Verdi's *Otello* slowly swells to drown out the sounds of the cries and sirens. In the wordless emotions of the image, Odin's death articulates the experience of his oppression. But do the limits of the film's aesthetic make invisible the sphere of sexuality? As the silent forms of Dessie and Emilia are removed from the building in body bags, the question of woman's marginality and near silence hovers uneasily over a film that eradicates the narrative function of its female characters.

Nelson calls his film "an American version of Shakespeare's tragic tale" and, in the theatrical trailer, continually refers to "Shakespeare's version" as if to remind us that there can never be a reconstruction or a derivation of the play, only a contemporary understanding of the material difference of early modern textuality. Adaptations of *Othello* such as *O* are not intended as an expression of the play itself but arise, as Worthen argues, "at the interface where texts and performances, language and bodies, engage, represent, resist one another" (136). Perhaps, some might say, this film has only beautified itself in Shakespeare's feathers. But in tracing how our texts, films, and the critics who discuss them renegotiate the tragic loading of the bed, students learn to interpret for themselves whether Shakespeare's drama can ever be an idealized and unified repository of value and meaning. Viewing this specific scene from several films offers a salient way to test the interpretative boundaries and skills of the students, who are aided in their discovery of the play's ambiguities by reflecting on our culture's unsolved and troubled history of race relations and domestic violence.

NOTE

[1]Citations to *Othello* are from Bevington's *Complete Works*.

Teaching *Othello* with Works by Elizabeth Cary and Aphra Behn

Lisa Gim

Teaching *Othello* comparatively with two early modern texts that confront similar issues—Elizabeth Cary's *The Tragedy of Mariam, the Fair Queen of Jewry* and Aphra Behn's *Oroonoko*—opens discussion of this play in many directions that are particularly appealing to students. These works share a number of similarities, including themes about love, race, jealousy, and the fatal effects of male possessiveness on women in marriage. They also share a focus on gender roles in relation to power, interracial love relationships, and the effects of racism. All three texts depict husbands who kill their strong, virtuous wives and thus raise the question of how to think about such an act in relation not only to the works' particular themes but also to seventeenth-century cultural contexts.

Reading Shakespeare's, Cary's, and Behn's works comparatively has improved my students' final-paper topics. Instead of producing only single-character studies and close readings, many of my students' essays now include comparisons, address broader issues, and are attuned to the cultural milieu that produced these texts and their authors. Recent papers have examined female resistance and obedience; marriage and fidelity; social pressure and interracial marriage; and chastity, the female body, and the limits of the female self.

Comparative Rationale

These three texts treat shared gender issues in a number of ways. Both Shake-speare's and Cary's works explore the parameters of female power. As virtuous and strong women, Desdemona and Mariam struggle to balance conjugal obe-dience with assertiveness: each dares through her marriage to defy not only her parent but also her husband. Like Desdemona and Emilia in *Othello* (3.4, 4.2, 4.3), the female characters in *Mariam* repeatedly discuss their status as women and wives (1.1–6, 2.1, 2.3, 3.1, 3.3, 4.3, 4.4, and 4.8).[1] Mariam's first conflict—which is between her sense of duty to her husband and her desire to repudiate him (Beilin, *Redeeming*; Miller), a man who had seized the throne through the murders of her grandfather and brother and secured his power by his marriage to her—centers on her personal integrity. Issues of female auton-omy are further explored in Salome's extensive soliloquy (1.4.1–64), which cri-tiques the lack of legitimate control women have over their lives, love, and bodies. The commodification of female bodies is a constant motif in both plays, seen in the position of women from different social classes: Desdemona, Bianca, Mariam, Salome, Doris, and the slave Graphina. Mariam's execution by her husband for suspected adultery, so she "shall not live fair fiend to cozen more" (4.4.55)—an obvious parallel to Desdemona's murder by Othello, "else she'll betray more men" (5.2.6)—provides the final emphasis on gender con-flict, which is the main issue in Cary's play, as it is in *Othello*.

In *Othello* and *Oroonoko*, and to a lesser extent in *Mariam*, gender conflicts are set in relief with reference to race: racial prejudice and its destructive effects clearly lead the male protagonists to murder their virtuous wives. In *Othello*, what is at first a strong interracial marriage between Othello and Desdemona that transcends cultural opposition is destroyed by Iago's mix of misogyny and racism, which enlists Othello's insecurity, jealousy, and distrust of female nature (Adelman, "Iago's Alter Ego"; Snow; Newman, "'Wash'"). *Mariam* explores racism in Mariam's identification of herself as purely Jewish and Herod and Salome as descendants of Esau (Weller and Ferguson 38). Her designation of their "mongrel race" of "parti-Jew and parti-Edomite" (1.3.25–32) feeds both Salome's hatred of her sister-in-law and Herod's mi-sogyny. Explicit discussions about Mariam's racialization are dealt with also in the context of Herod describing his wife as "fair" and too beautiful to punish and in Salome's retort that Mariam is "sable," adulterous, and deserves death (4.74.162). In *Oroonoko*, the narrative's thematic and plot focus is squarely on race and racialization in the protagonist's enslavement and his struggles to reunite with Imoinda and win their freedom. When the slaves' rebellion fails, Oroonoko's killing of his pregnant wife to spare her and their unborn child further suffering becomes more complex to interpret than the spousal murder in *Othello*; Imoinda dies "Smiling with Joy she shou'd dye by so noble a Hand" (*Oroonoko* 61).

Teaching Experiences

I have taught *Othello* with *Mariam* and *Oroonoko* in a variety of courses, including a special senior seminar on early modern English literature, a seventeenth-century class, a Shakespeare class, and a world drama class. Students were exclusively English majors in the first two and a mix of majors and nonmajors in the last two.

In the senior seminar on early modern English texts, we compared *Mariam* and *Othello* to examine gender constructions and conflicts. One session focused on the moments in *Othello* and in *Mariam* when the husband in each play becomes convinced that his wife is unfaithful. We examined the language of each husband and what it revealed about him and the period's ideologies of masculine control and female obedience. A subsequent debate centered on whether female victimization or wifely self-assertion and resistance characterized the texts' heroines. Questions posed included, How do Desdemona's final words compare to Mariam's final speech? Is Desdemona's "I, myself" (5.2.129) an expression of her integrity and autonomy, or is it an obedient expression of selfless, dutiful virtue? Why does Mariam stubbornly maintain her fidelity and innocence to Herod but also blame herself for her "improvident" lack of "humility" (4.8.29–38)? A related issue arose when we read *Oroonoko* with Shakespeare's and Cary's plays in a seventeenth-century class: How do we view Imoinda's killing by her husband and her compliance? As an assertion or a victimization? How do we compare this with the wives' deaths in *Othello* and *Mariam*? How active are these wives in resisting their murders? Such comparative connections and perspectives excited the classes' interest beyond critical reading of the individual texts and led to group research projects organized so that students could explore the parameters of seventeenth-century women's roles.

Further study not only enabled students to compare the power and resistance of female characters (Fischer; Ferguson, "Running On" and "Spectre"; Gajowski; Kennedy) but also raised some broader issues. We spent an additional class assessing *Othello* and *Mariam* in relation to gendered authorship. Although their dramatic genres are distinct—the public play as opposed to the private closet drama—the plays debate similar issues, which students can discuss. Moreover, background readings and group research projects about the conditions of women's writing and the intellectual significance of genres like the closet drama (Findlay, Hodgson-Wright, and Williams; Gutierrez; Straznicky) worked to complicate for students such oversimplified categories as male and female with respect to authorship and modes of early modern writing. In the seventeenth-century class, adding *Oroonoko* as an early novella broadened the generic as well as the gender scope of our study. We used *Oroonoko* also to address more extensively the construction of race as well as gender in seventeenth-century literature. The following background readings proved useful: on perceptions of marriage, women, race, and alienness (Belsey; Brown; Callaghan, "Re-reading"; Ferguson, "Juggling"; Gallagher; K. Hall, *Things* and "Beauty"; Hall and Kennedy; Hendricks and Parker; Hodgdon, "Kiss"; Loomba, *Shakespeare, Race*; J. MacDonald, *Women*; Newman, " 'Wash' ") and on the social and cultural climates for writers of these periods (Beilin, *Redeeming Eve*; Lewalski; Todd, *Critical Fortunes* 3–43; Vaughan). In addition, the following critical editions of the texts proved extremely valuable: for cultural-context editions of *Othello*, see Honigmann's edition; for *Othello* and *Mariam*, see Shakespeare (ed. Carroll); for *Mariam*, see Cary (ed. Weller) and Ferguson and Cary (ed. Hodgson-Wright); for *Oroonoko*, see Behn (ed. Lipking) and Behn (ed. Gallagher). Close-reading exercises studying parallel passages and their speakers, as well as the authors' presentation of gender issues, have encouraged my students to become more engaged with larger questions about early modern authorship and collaboration and with the study of how culture affects literary creation.

In a lower-level world drama survey aimed at a mix of majors and non-majors, reading *Mariam* and *Othello* comparatively helped motivate the class to grapple with the unfamiliar diction of the seventeenth century and to comprehend some of the cultural issues concerning gender in this period. During their comparison of Cary's Mariam and Shakespeare's Desdemona, students theorized about the futility of female virtue in the light of patriarchal culture's perception of women as inherently flawed and as objectified property. This observation became a key motif that the students refined and tested as they read plays from subsequent literary periods and other cultures, including Henrik Ibsen's *A Doll House*, Bertolt Brecht's *The Good Woman of Setzuan*, and Caryl Churchill's *Top Girls*. It intrigued nonmajors that Shakespeare and Cary were interested in topics that touched their own lives over three centuries later—female sexuality and its control by men, racial prejudice and its destructive results, the complexities of love and hate.

Questions for Comparative Discussion

The following groups of questions address not only gender issues but also more comprehensive themes and motifs that have proved useful in exploring *Othello* in relation to *The Tragedy of Mariam* and *Oroonoko*. Each cluster includes multiple, interrelated comparative questions, many more than might be used in a single class but that may be easily tailored to suit a variety of different course settings and audiences.

1. What motivates the antagonists in these three works? What reasons does Iago claim for his desire to destroy Othello? What motivates Salome's hatred for Mariam, a passion that causes not only Mariam's death but also her brother Herod's destruction? Why is Byam so determined to destroy Oroonoko?

2. How do these texts present the marriages and relationships between

husbands and wives? How does Shakespeare present the issue of race in Desdemona and Othello's relationship—both in regard to their feelings for each other and from the viewpoints of outsiders? Why does Othello believe Iago over Desdemona? What perspective does this play suggest about relationships between the sexes versus same-sex relationships? What kind of love does Herod have for Mariam? Why does Herod love, distrust, order the death of, and then idolize Mariam? How does Cary portray love in *The Tragedy of Mariam*? Is there any love in this play that we may see as admirable or ideal? How does the portrayal of marital love and jealousy compare with that in Shakespeare's *Othello*? What kinds of love are depicted in *Oroonoko*? What characterizes the love relationship between Oroonoko and Imoinda?

3. In all three works, each wife offers a perspective on her death. Compare and evaluate Desdemona's exchange with Othello and her final dying words with Mariam's final speech and with Imoinda's comments before her death. What are the parameters of each woman's autonomy? Why do Desdemona and Mariam take responsibility for their deaths? In *Oroonoko*, Behn describes graphically and at length the death of Imoinda by her husband's hand. How does Imoinda's situation compare with that of the other wives? How do we interpret Oroonoko's killing of his pregnant wife? How does Behn as narrator interpret it? What does the fate of these wives suggest about the parameters of female autonomy and female resistance in seventeenth-century English society?

4. What messages concerning race do these works communicate? Consider both the hero and victimized-outsider aspects of Othello in relation to his place in Venetian society. Compare the portrayal of this marriage in *Othello* with the marriage and racial tensions in Cary's *Mariam*. What does Mariam's description of Salome and her brother as "parti-Jew, parti-Edomite" signify? How does Mariam view her racial status in relation to Herod's and Salome's? How do Salome and Alexandra view it? What perspectives does Herod provide on his marriage to Mariam before and after her death? What advice does the chorus offer? Consider also the marriage between the racial and social unequals Pheroras and the slave, Graphina. Evaluate the attraction that Behn confesses for Oroonoko in her novella. What does this suggest about the cultural mores of Behn's time in relation to race and place (England and Surinam)? About the social and thematic emphases concerning race that Behn wants to communicate to her readers? (Note that although Behn's novel evokes sympathy toward Oroonoko and critiques slavery, her description of him as noble stresses Oroonoko's likeness to a Western man rather than an African man. Later, Behn emphasizes this further by choosing to call him by the Roman name given to him, "Caesar" (37), and by calling Imoinda "Clemene" (38) for much of the novella.) What does Behn's emphasis on the westernizing of Oroonoko's name and nature imply about cultural attitudes toward race in this period? How does this emphasis sentimentalize *Oroonoko*'s characters and story? Does it complement or contradict Behn's critique of

slavery? Compare the story's ending and the insertion of Behn's character into the story with slave narratives and historical accounts of slavery by observers given in Lipking's Norton critical edition text of *Oroonoko*.

5. Evaluate the perspectives that Shakespeare's *Othello* and Cary's *Tragedy of Mariam* offer on the relationships between men and women. How do these relationships compare with those in *Oroonoko*? How does Behn as female narrator and protagonist treat and regard Oroonoko? Imoinda? Analyze her narration in three particular incidents: during the trip to the Indian village; during the slave rebellion that Oroonoko leads; and during Oroonoko's capture, torture, and execution. What might her accounts suggest to us about Behn's attitudes toward gender and race? What implied comparisons does she draw between herself and Oroonoko? Between herself and Imoinda? What do her comparisons suggest about cultural mores of Behn's time and the positions that she and Oroonoko share as outsiders—as a woman and a black slave—relative to patriarchal culture? Where might this place Imoinda? What sorts of views do the works present on relationships between men?

6. How would you characterize these women—Mariam, Alexandra, Salome, Doris, and Graphina—and their interrelationships in Cary's play? Compare and contrast their female roles and the play's portrayal of their sex. What motivates Salome's hatred of Mariam? How does Mariam regard Salome? How do we interpret Salome's contradiction of Herod's description of Mariam as "fair" by insisting her sister-in-law was "sable"? How do these women and their interrelationships compare with Desdemona and Emilia's in *Othello*? Consider also Bianca's role in Shakespeare's play. Evaluate the women in *Oroonoko*. What different roles do women play in the final slave rebellion? Consider Behn's absence from Oroonoko's death scene, the active role taken by Imoinda, and the saving of Byam's life by his Indian mistress. How does Behn as narrator ultimately evaluate her own role in the story of Oroonoko?

7. How, in the end, do we view Mariam, her resistance, and her death? Compare her role with Desdemona's and Imoinda's (and even to Behn's herself as female narrator and possible heroine in *Oroonoko*). To what extent is each woman powerless? To what extent does each woman choose her fate? How do we evaluate comparatively the death of each wife by her husband and its significance? How do the wives' deaths compare with Othello's self-punishing suicide, Herod's grief and self-punishing remorse, and Oroonoko's failed suicide and subsequent silence during his execution by the white slaveholders?

8. How does each work frame the issue of female power and autonomy in its society? What overall conclusions can you draw from these works' perspectives concerning women's roles in the seventeenth century?

The following questions are assignments devised for group projects:

9. Despite the thematic similarities shared by *Othello*, *The Tragedy of Mariam*, and *Oroonoko*, each work is distinct from the others in its genre as staged

play, closet drama, or novella. Evaluate the differences in these genres and in how they model the works' emphases, characters, and viewpoints. (Students consult writings by Gutierrez; Ferguson, "Transmuting Othello"; Straznicky; Vaughan.)

10. Discuss the contrasting circumstances of these works' authors and creations. (Students consult writings by Beilin, *Redeeming Eve*; Chibka; Duffy; Fischer; Goreau; Lewalski; Mendelson; Spengemann.) What role, if any, does the author's gender play in the works' perspectives on gender? (Students also may read writings by Belsey; Erickson, *Patriarchal Structures*; Ferguson, "Room" and "Juggling"; Gallagher; K. Hall, "Beauty"; Kemp; Pearson; Rose; Sussman; Todd, *Critical Fortunes*.)

NOTE

¹Citations to *Othello* and *Mariam* are from Othello *and* The Tragedy of Mariam (ed. Carroll). Citations to *Oroonoko* are from Lipking's edition.

Tales of a Fateful Handkerchief:
Verdi, Vogel, Cinthio, and Shakespeare
Present *Othello*

Sheila T. Cavanagh

When the curtain opens on Verdi's famous nineteenth-century opera *Otello*, the audience members do not see Roderigo and Iago deep in conversation. They also do not witness Brabantio pleading for the Senate to punish his newly revealed son-in-law, nor do they hear Desdemona affirming her love for Othello while begging permission to accompany him on his military mission to Cyprus. In short, viewers of the opera do not see or hear any of the text that fills Shakespeare's first act of *Othello*. Apparently encouraged to omit these opening scenes by his librettist, Arrigo Boito (Huscher 14), Verdi begins *Otello* with a powerful storm, as the people of Cyprus anxiously await the arrival of their new leader. In this version, the Othello and Desdemona characters have already married without incident, Brabantio becomes one of the many characters lost in the conversion from play to opera, and the audience's important first vision of Othello fixes him as a powerful figure in the martial world with a beloved spouse at his side.

Shakespeare's source text, a tale from Cinthio's (Giambattista Giraldi) sixteenth-century *Hecatommithi*, also differs greatly from the famous drama it inspired. In Cinthio, only the doomed wife, Disdemona, is named; the other characters are known by labels, such as the Moor, the Ensign, and the Corporal. While readers of this text find some familiar details from *Othello*, Cinthio's story frequently offers information about characters' motivation and responses, which are absent in the later drama. In Clare Carroll's terms, a "comparison of Cinthio's tale to *Othello* shows how a melodrama was transformed into a tragedy" (Cinthio 216). The connection between the story and the play is clear, but the two narratives vary considerably.

Like *Otello*, the 1994 play *Desdemona: A Play about a Handkerchief*, by the Pulitzer Prize–winning dramatist Paula Vogel, omits large sections of Shakespeare's text. Written in the tradition of Tom Stoppard's 1967 *Rosencrantz and Guildenstern are Dead*, Vogel's *Desdemona* focuses exclusively on events that purportedly take place behind the scenes during *Othello*. Losing even more characters than the opera in the process, *Desdemona* offers an alternate view of Shakespeare's drama that contradicts many traditional presuppositions about the early modern *Othello*. Placed in conjunction with Verdi's and Cinthio's work, however, *Desdemona* provides audiences with a perspective on Shakespeare's play that draws attention to portions of the drama that students often overlook. Paula Vogel's *Othello* is not Verdi's, Verdi's is not Shakespeare's, and Cinthio's narrative differs from each of its successors;

nevertheless, when the four narratives are read together, they create an insightful dialogue for students of Shakespeare's text.[1]

In this essay, I explore some of the ways that these disparate renditions of the same story can help illuminate aspects of Shakespeare's *Othello* for undergraduates. All three additional narratives are currently in print and can be incorporated fairly simply into a syllabus. The Cinthio and Vogel texts are relatively short, so they do not greatly increase the reading load for a class. Portions of the opera can be introduced either through film or audio clips or by providing segments of the translated libretto for specific classroom assignments. Juxtaposing these narratives can facilitate a variety of discussions, including the theoretical implications of literary adaptation. Here, however, I focus on ways that introducing students to these texts can challenge their preconceptions about *Othello* and can encourage them to consider how Shakespeare frequently appears to have deliberately countered reader expectations and narrative desires at key moments.

The excision of *Othello*'s act 1 from the libretto of *Otello* leaves the audience with a Desdemona very different from the one presented by Shakespeare, since without Brabantio's impassioned pleas to the senate, many of the seeming contradictions surrounding Desdemona's character are lost. The sorrowful father's cries that Desdemona "is abused, stol'n from me, and corrupted / By spells and medicines bought of mountebanks" (1.3.62–63), combined with his assurances that his daughter is "[a] maiden never bold; / Of spirit so still and quiet that her motion / Blushed at herself" (1.3.96–98), suggest a quiet and demure Desdemona who could not possibly have succumbed to Othello's wooing without the aid of magic.[2] Shakespeare, of course, calls that characterization into question soon after Brabantio's speech to the senate, when the young woman not only publicly affirms her love for Othello but also boldly asks leave to accompany him into the martial realm of Cyprus: "[t]hat I did love the Moor to live with him, / My downright violence and storm of fortunes / May trumpet to the world. . . . Let me go with him" (1.3.249–51, 260). Without these scenes, the operatic Desdemona does not raise the same questions for an audience that astute readers and viewers of Shakespeare's drama might ask. There is, for example, less room for Verdi's Desdemona to be presented as scheming—or to be portrayed as sexually knowledgeable—a characterization that has become popular in modern productions. When the opera follows the confines of the libretto, it is more likely to present a stereotypically virginal Desdemona whose innocence is unassailable and whose status as Othello's victim is never questioned, a Desdemona who matches the representation offered in many traditional productions of *Othello*, which skirt over such contradictions as those raised above.

From this familiar perspective, Vogel's Desdemona is almost unrecognizable. Far from fashioning a sexually naive heroine, Vogel presents a bawdy, foul-mouthed, promiscuous Desdemona who spends her days turning tricks in Bianca's brothel. Taking advantage of the considerable time that Desdemona is absent from the stage in *Othello*, Vogel offers a wildly adulterous character, who ironically appears to be sleeping with almost every man on Cyprus, except for Michael Cassio. This Desdemona uses chicken blood to counterfeit a virgin's stain on her wedding sheets and laughs uproariously with Bianca over the fantasy that Othello might himself someday visit this house of ill repute: "Oh, Bianca, what a thought. Do you think he'd come? I'd die for sure—and wouldn't he be mad if he'd paid for what he got for free at home?" (248). Vogel does not completely erase the more traditional Desdemona, however. Instead, Vogel gives Emilia a speech wherein she tells Bianca about the youth of Othello's bride: "We all of us servants in her father's house talked on end about Miss Desdemona. For a time, she wanted to be a saint, yes? A nun with the sisters of mercy. At age twelve she was washing the courtyard stones for penance, with us wiping up behind her" (244). In this rendition, Desdemona was a great challenge to Brabantio "until her father finally saw sense and sent her to the convent to be bred out of her boredom" (244). Desdemona's efforts to be saintly as a youth were a passing fancy, and Emilia presumes that the adult Desdemona's turn as a sexual renegade will also become boring for her. Accordingly, she warns Bianca not to expect her association with Desdemona to last: "she's gullin' you, as sure as 'tis she's gullin' that ass of a husband who's so taken with her; but let me tell you, you'll go the way like all the other fancies she's had in Venice" (244). As these few excerpts indicate, Vogel's Desdemona bears little resemblance to conventional theatrical and operatic portrayals.

Such divergent representations encourage students to return to Shakespeare's play in order to better understand their source. Without close reading, students often assume that the play only presents a fairly angelic young bride. By placing Desdemona's portrayal in another context, however, students are more likely to realize that Shakespeare's representation is more complex than they generally imagine. Although Vogel's version exaggerates questions about Desdemona raised in Shakespeare, her amplification can lead to valuable class discussion. That Desdemona is offstage for much of Shakespeare's *Othello* provides Vogel with the space she needs to construct her counternarrative. Although her portrayal occasionally verges toward the farcical—when the young wife and Bianca dissolve into laughing fits over their bawdy jokes about horse pricks and chamber pots, for example (247)—the play also amplifies questions about Desdemona that more typical stage portrayals tend to suppress. Verdi and Vogel offer what can be seen as polarized representations of Othello's doomed wife.[3] At the same time, however, each characterization can also be understood to exaggerate qualities displayed by Shakespeare's Desdemona. In most individual performances of *Othello*, the director and actors must choose whether to present Desdemona's repeated, impassioned pleas on behalf of Cassio as the misguided efforts of a naive young bride or to use them to plant seeds of doubt about Desdemona. As we know, both Verdi's and Shakespeare's Othello character display understandable frustration or irritation while Desdemona insists that he make peace with Cassio. In Shake-speare's version, Desdemona continues to prod Othello even when he re-peatedly tries to avoid the suit (3.3.45–85). The parallel interchange in *Otello* is even more poignant, since Desdemona's pleas on Cassio's behalf are inter-woven with Otello's increasingly insistent cries that Desdemona produce the missing handkerchief (Verdi and Boito 68–71). In both cases, however, Des-demona and Othello remain at cross purposes, leaving the audience unclear about Desdemona's motivation. These questions can easily be lost in the en-suing tragedy, however. Thus, reading them in the context of Verdi and Vogel reminds students that hints of both the "good" Desdemona and the "bad" Desdemona can be found in Shakespeare's text. As Iago reminds Othello about the purportedly honest young bride, "She did deceive her father, mar-rying you; / And when she seemed to shake and fear your looks, / She loved them most" (3.3.206–08). Although the true Desdemona can never be located, these widely different portrayals offer students a glimpse at the range of ways she can be interpreted and can encourage them to appreciate the nuances in Shakespeare's characterization.

Similar insights can be gained into the complexity of other figures in the drama when they are approached from this multitextual perspective. Vogel's play only contains three characters—Desdemona, Emilia, and Bianca—and Verdi's opera omits many figures entirely, so both of these adaptations focus on select scenes and individuals. Cinthio's version also contains only a handful of characters. Emilia appears in all three texts, however, giving students al-ternative views of Iago's unwittingly or willingly complicit wife and enabling them to examine her various levels of involvement with her treacherous husband.

Shakespeare's Emilia does not provide explicit information about the extent of her understanding of Iago's villainy, although she professes ignorance: "What he will do with it / Heaven knows, not I; / I nothing but to please his fantasy" (3.3.296–98). Emilia's language is more confusing than revelatory in this scene. Despite terming Iago "wayward" and acknowledging to herself that Desdemona is extremely attached to the token (298), Emilia determines to pass the handkerchief or its copy along to Iago. She briefly questions her husband about it but readily leaves when he refuses to answer (3.3.298–319). This short interaction gives minimal information about Emilia's feelings to-ward her husband or her rationale for helping him. In Shakespeare's play, of course, Emilia eventually dies for her involvement in this scheme (5.2.244). In the meantime, however, she proffers additional ambiguous information about her role in the tragedy. When Othello angrily demands the handkerchief from his frightened and perplexed wife, Emilia observes the interaction with-out intervening. As soon as Othello leaves, however, Emilia lashes out against men, in a tirade that raises further questions about her relationship with Iago. Here she counsels Desdemona that Othello's rage is inevitable, given his gen-der, but she offers no indication that she knows anything about the missing handkerchief: "'Tis not a year or two shows us a man. / They are all but stomachs, and we all but food; / They eat us hungerly, and when they are full / They belch us" (3.4.100–03). For students who desire clarity, Emilia's speeches are likely to prove inadequate.

Cinthio, Verdi, and Vogel, on the other hand, offer at least partial explanations for some of the issues Shakespeare leaves undecided. In *Otello*, Emilia does not give the handkerchief to Iago willingly. In fact, her husband wrenches it from her hand in an abusive scene: "You resist in vain when I command!" (Verdi and Boito 57). The interchange ends when Iago snatches the handkerchief from his resistant wife; the duo then joins with Desdemona and Otello as they each sing about the drama in their lives (58–59). Thus, although Verdi and Boito do not present an Emilia who intervenes to keep the final tragedy from occurring, they offer a character who does not willingly participate in Iago's treachery.

Cinthio offers a similar scenario. Emilia, who is first mentioned in this account as "a fair and honest young woman" (220), is terrified to reveal what she knows, although she balks at personal participation: "The Ensign's wife, who knew everything (for her husband had wished to use her as an instrument in causing the Lady's death, but she had never been willing to consent), did not dare, for fear of her husband, to tell her anything" (226). Cinthio's Emilia, therefore, acts from a mixture of goodwill and cowardice.

Vogel's Emilia succumbs to Iago's trickery. In this version, Iago, who does not appear onstage, is presented as having persuaded his wife that he needed the handkerchief for a joke. When Emilia, in a fit of foreboding, admits to Desdemona that she gave the item to her husband, she insists that she thought she was joining Iago in a prank: "It was to be a joke, you see; my husband put me up to it, as a lark, he said, just to see" (253). The women quickly realize that their fate will be anything but funny; still, Emilia insists that she doesn't know "what [her husband] thinks" (253) or what has been planned. Vogel's Emilia, who has earlier acknowledged considerable disappointment in her sexual relationship with Iago (252), only slowly comes to realize the implications of her complicity with a husband she doesn't really know or understand. She also expresses remorse and tries to protect Desdemona. Her efforts, of course, come too late, although the play ends before Othello enters the bedchamber with murder in his heart. Once again, therefore, Cinthio, Verdi, and Vogel counter the ambiguous characterizations found in Shakespeare's drama, giving students the opportunity to discuss the different theatrical rationales for providing closure or for presenting uncertainty and to find passages to support their impressions. The text, of course, generally prompts them to refine their opinions.

For those students who demand clear explanations, there may be no more pressing matter in *Othello* than the question of Iago's intentions. He offers several dubious motivations for his behavior in the play, claiming that he resents Cassio's promotion (1.1.19–34), indicating that he believes that Othello has slept with Emilia (1.3.379–83), and implying that he desires either Desdemona or Othello for himself (2.1.281–82, 3.3.461–67). Shakespeare's text undermines attempts to attribute a definitive motive both through the number of reasons offered and by Iago's pronouncement at the end of the play that he will offer no further information: "Demand me nothing. What you know, you know. / From this time forth I never will speak word" (5.2.308–09). Accordingly, audiences of Shakespeare's play receive no unequivocal explanation for Iago's actions, just as they are left without the satisfaction of witnessing Iago's punishment, since Shakespeare leaves Iago alive at the end of the play.

Cinthio, in contrast, gives the audience the opportunity to see Iago die. Although this tale offers little explanation for Iago's treachery, apart from his characterization as having "the most scoundrelly nature in the world" (220), it portrays Iago as continuing his evil after the death of Othello—who was slain by Disdemona's relatives (230). This time, Iago does not escape punishment; he is "tortured so fiercely that his inner organs were ruptured" (230). This ending can spark useful discussions, since it gives students the opportunity to discuss why Iago is left alive at the end of Shakespeare's *Othello* and why it is not uncommon for this conclusion to be altered in productions and adaptations of the play.

Vogel's *Desdemona* includes no male characters in the play and ends without presenting *Othello*'s tragic denouement; it thus leaves many of these issues unaddressed. The libretto of *Otello*, however—enhanced in some productions—offers a more specific accounting of Iago's rationale and of the fate that awaits him. In one of *Otello*'s most powerful scenes, Iago offers a detailed explanation for his treachery: "I am that daemon, and I am dragged along by mine, the inexorable God in whom I believe. I believe in a cruel God who created me in his image and who in fury I name" (Verdi and Boito 46). In this powerful account, Iago includes nothing about any of the other characters. Unlike Shakespeare's Iago, who places some blame on his victims, the operatic villain claims only that he acts at the behest of a cruel God. This pronouncement, which presents Iago as evil personified, occasionally fuels an ending that appears neither in Shakespeare's play nor in Verdi's libretto but that can be seen in some productions of the opera, namely, Otello's murder of Iago before his own suicide. In these renditions, the audience receives the satisfaction that they are denied by most productions: seeing Iago die can offer a view of justice being served that his arrest alone does not provide.

As this discussion of *Othello* and three related texts suggests, students, critics, and audience members grapple repeatedly with questions arising from the complex characterizations of many Shakespearean figures. Although this short sixteenth-century tale, classic nineteenth-century opera, and bawdy twentieth-century reconceptualization may initially appear to have little in common, a closer look at some of the issues they confront indicates that each struggles creatively with interpretive questions left unclear in Shakespeare. Some of the questions they attempt to answer or at least to consider receive contradictory or ambiguous presentations in Shakespeare; at other times, they present an interpretive model that exaggerates one piece of Shakespeare's evidence while suppressing the original contradictions. Verdi, Vogel, and Cinthio are three of many Shakespearean adaptations that can offer us fresh eyes with which to return to *Othello* and present students with new, thought-provoking analyses of the drama's characters.

NOTES

[1] I am grateful to the Shakespeare Society of Eastern India for the opportunity to present an earlier version of this essay at the 2002 World Shakespeare Congress in Kolkata. Their feedback and gracious hospitality are much appreciated.

[2] Citations to *Othello* are from Carroll's edition.

[3] Cinthio's Disdemona falls somewhere between these two representations.

Paper, Linen, Sheets:
Dinesen's "The Blank Page" and
Desdemona's Handkerchief

Janelle Jenstad

With the goal of having students arrive at an understanding of the instability and interrelationship of textiles and texts in *Othello*, I take a comparative approach in my final class on the play, a one-hour lecture and discussion on the handkerchief, sheets, and Desdemona's body.[1] Isak Dinesen's short story "The Blank Page" conveniently takes linen wedding sheets as its subject and is framed by a discussion of storytelling and the role of the observer-hearer-reader in making meaning. Dinesen challenges readers to think about their responses to an ambiguously blank page and opens up discussion about the ways in which Desdemona, her handkerchief, and her sheets are intersecting sites of conflicting inscriptions and interpretations. This lecture and discussion would be useful to teachers looking for a way to structure a lecture on the handkerchief, to introduce some basic critical notions of textuality and interpretation, or to compare Shakespeare with modern texts.

A rich and energetic body of criticism links the contested texts of handkerchief, wedding sheets, and Desdemona's body.[2] Lynda E. Boose establishes the parallel between the strawberry spots of the handkerchief and the stains of hymenal blood on wedding sheets ("Othello's Handkerchief" 363). Drawing on Boose's work, Edward A. Snow argues that the handkerchief is "visual proof of Desdemona's adultery largely because it subconsciously evokes for Othello the blood-stained sheets of the wedding-bed and his wife's loss of virginity there" (390). Peter Stallybrass similarly argues that the handkerchief is "metonymically associated with the operations of the body, is metaphorically substituted for the body's apertures ["noses, ears, and lips" (4.1.40) in particular], and its transference from hand to hand comes to imply . . . the secret passage of 'an essence that's not seen' [4.1.16]" (139). Valerie Wayne sees the handkerchief as the woman's text, "the historical antidote to the blank page of Desdemona's body where Othello inscribed 'whore' " (173). More recently, Susan Frye offers a reading of the way *Othello* and *Cymbeline* "disrupt women's historic relation" to textiles: stage "textiles mark and then signify the contested female body, which can be possessed entirely by men and, thus reduced, may be disposed of violently" (215, 221).

We all bring recent scholarly work into the classroom every time we rehearse its conclusions, but there is merit in having students arrive at these conclusions through guided discussion. Some students will encounter these critics later for their research projects, but it is usually unrealistic to expect undergraduates to read five critical essays and ultimately more harmful than helpful to assign just one. However, they will be able to read "The Blank

Page," which is short enough to make available in a course pack or as a handout.

Before this class, the students and I have spent four hours discussing genre, Othello's position as a racialized other in war and in peace, Iago's reconstruction of reality through language, and the relation between women's voices and their chastity. We have also discussed various contradictions and ambiguities in the text, such as the dual time scheme and the consummation or nonconsummation of Othello's marriage to Desdemona. I deliberately avoid mentioning the handkerchief; it has by now become the central absence in our understanding of the play. The students have been anticipating this discussion, however, because the "Facts, Contexts, and Study Questions" section for *Othello* in their course pack includes the following questions and exercises: "Where did Othello's handkerchief come from? What does it look like? For what reason(s) is Othello so upset that Desdemona has lost it? Chart the movement of the handkerchief from one character to another." I also ask students to trace the motifs of evidence and proof.

We begin with a simple exercise. I ask where Othello obtains the handkerchief. One student gives the account from 3.4.53–73: "That handkerchief / Did an Egyptian to my mother give"(53–54).[3] After a moment, usually without prompting, someone will disagree and give the account from 5.2.223–24: "It was a handkerchief, an antique token / My father gave my mother." I ask the class which answer is right and let the discussion run for a minute or two while I take note of who invokes which arguments. Someone always suggests that Othello's testimony is less reliable in 5.2 than in 3.4 because he is crazed by jealousy. Another student will counter that Othello's account of the handkerchief in 3.4 seems like a bogeyman story calculated to frighten Desdemona. When I intervene, it is to make the point that what we are really discussing is not the contradiction but rather our own reasons for accepting some evidence while rejecting other evidence. In short, we need to talk about the role of the interpreter in ascribing significance. *Othello* foregrounds the problem of interpreting conflicting evidence. If we have not done so already, we look briefly at 1.3.1–46 with its conflicting messages about the Turkish fleet, noting that the Duke chooses to believe what accords with his own expectations and preconceptions about Turkish military strategy.

Another set of questions leads into the next key point. When does the handkerchief make its first appearance in the play? Having made a scene-by-scene summary for the play,[4] all the students are able to answer that it appears relatively late. For what reason is Iago so pleased at having the handkerchief in his possession? Because he recognizes its potential as evidence: "Trifles light as air / Are to the jealous confirmations strong / As *proofs* of holy writ" (3.3.326–28; my emphasis). When is the next occurrence of the word *proof*? In Othello's insistence, only about forty lines later, that Iago "*prove* my love a whore. / Be sure of it. Give me the ocular *proof*" (3.3.364–65; my emphasis). Here, the word appears in two case forms within two lines (an example of traduction).[5] We have already discussed the ways that Othello's language begins to sound like that of Iago as the two men move toward their "sacred vow" at the end of this long scene (3.3.464); thus it is not difficult for students to see the fatal connection between Iago's determination to invoke the handkerchief as evidence and Othello's jealous predisposition to see that evidence as the confirmation of what he fears. Having demanded "ocular proof" from *Iago*, Othello immediately transfers the burden of proof to *Desdemona*, who has to produce the handkerchief to prove that it has not been lost.[6]

That the handkerchief is charged with unusual significance is clear enough from the repetition of the word *handkerchief* throughout 3.4 and 4.1, culminating in Othello's fragmented speech before he "falls down in a trance" (4.1.41, stage direction; editorial conflation of folio and quarto stage directions). However, it is hard for students to understand why a mere handkerchief, whatever its origins, should be so significant. They tend to share Iago's view of the handkerchief as a trifle "light as air," but not his conviction that it can function as "holy writ," and they are mystified by Othello's claim that a husband's love might be predicated on his wife's not losing or giving this trifle away. I find it useful to point out the number of times Othello deploys the impersonal pronoun "it" throughout his first story of the handkerchief's origins (3.4.53–83). While the grammatical referent is clear ("[t]hat handkerchief" in the first line [3.4.53]), it is easy, as we move further from the referent, to imagine that Othello is talking about something else.

Numerous passages establish the metonymic connection between handkerchief, wedding sheets, and Desdemona's body. I present this statement as a thesis to the class, remind them that a metonym stands in for something to which it is closely related, and then work through the evidence supporting the thesis that sheets and handkerchief stand in for Desdemona. A triangle on the chalkboard—with sheets, handkerchief, and Desdemona at the three points—helps map out the three equations we need to make. I start with the handkerchief and Desdemona. As creators, menders, and copyists of textiles, women are already implicitly linked to textiles. Evidence of this link includes Cassio's asking Bianca to "[t]ake me this work out" (3.4.175) and praise for Desdemona's being "so delicate with her needle" (4.1.179–80). Iago, ostensibly downplaying its importance but returning persistently to the lost handkerchief, rhetorically juxtaposes and thus links the handkerchief explicitly to Desdemona's supposedly lost honor: "Her honour is an essence that's not seen. / They have it very oft that have it not. / But for the handkerchief—" (4.1.16–18; see also 4.1.168–70).

Establishing this metonymic relation helps make sense of Othello's obsessive focus on the handkerchief, especially when he finally tells Desdemona the reason for his passion: "[t]hat handkerchief / Which I so loved and gave thee, thou gav'st to Cassio" (5.2.50–51). That he "saw [his] handkerchief in's [Cassio's] hand" (5.2.67) is all the evidence Othello needs to condemn Des-

demona. Given the handkerchief's function as metonymic signifier of Desdemona's honor, the mere fact of its circulation is proof enough, especially
since the "metonymic chain" of popular patriarchal discourse suggests, as Gail
Kern Paster argues, that "a woman who leaves her house is a woman who
talks is a woman who drinks is a woman who leaks. Any point in the linkage
may imply or abridge the rest" (51). In our discussion of gender, we have
already applied this patriarchal logic both to Desdemona's pleas on Cassio's
behalf and to Emilia's confession in 5.2 and noted how in both cases mere
talking turns a woman's "virtue into pitch" because of what it implies about
her chastity (2.3.334).

We still characterize promiscuity today in terms of geographic movement.
When students read *Troilus and Cressida*, they often comment that Helen
"really gets around." Likewise, the handkerchief gets around, passing alter-
nately from man to woman and woman to man in a sequence—but not a
chain—of exchanges: Othello to Desdemona, who drops it accidentally; Emilia
to Iago, who drops it deliberately and secretly in Cassio's chamber; Cassio to
Bianca; and Bianca back to Cassio (and in performance, Bianca often drops
the handkerchief at Cassio's feet).

As the handkerchief circulates, its meaning changes with each exchange.
One could argue that between Othello and Desdemona it is a sign of his love,
between Emilia and Iago a sign of her obedience, between Cassio and Bianca
a sign of his power over her. Part of the point here is that the handkerchief
is a blank page whose meaning changes (or accumulates new meanings) with
context and reader.[7] But it is also possible to see a devaluing of the love token
as it circulates, from signifier of fidelity to signifier of infidelity. Bianca draws
the same conclusion about the handkerchief that Othello is meant to ("[t]his
is some minx's token" [4.1.147]), its very circulation suggesting to her—as to
Othello—the promiscuity of the woman it represents.

Freighted with symbolism, the handkerchief is an important stage property,
required at least three times in the play (3.3.290–333, 3.4.174–96, and
4.1.141–62).[8] To get students thinking about its materiality, I ask what sort of
handkerchief they would supply for a contemporary performance of *Othello*.
The deliberately naive question of Harry Berger, Jr., "is it as big as a flag or
as small as a facial tissue?" ("Impertinent Trifling" 235), pushes us to consider
the sheets and can also raise questions about the masculinity or femininity of
the handkerchief (and therefore its ownership). Most students will assume
that the handkerchief has to have visible red spots. I historicize the handkerchief by showing them pictures of Renaissance textiles. Frye's essay conveniently reproduces a black-and-white photograph of a sampler from 1598 (225),
which clearly shows two distinct strawberry patterns, one worked in red and
green and the other in blackwork (224). I then point out to students the
mismatch between the exotic Egyptian origins of the handkerchief (in Othello's first account) and the domestic Englishness of its strawberry design. As

a text, it is anything but stable. Depending on who is writing its meaning, it is love token; fertility symbol; magic fetish; warning; and, in Iago's words, Desdemona's honor (or supposed lack thereof).

Two equations (handkerchief=Desdemona and sheets=handkerchief) would necessarily imply the third: that the sheets are a metonym for Desdemona. Othello's apostrophe to his absent wife, whom he addresses as "Strumpet" (5.1.35), links the handkerchief and the sheets verbally through the word "spotted": "Thy bed, lust-stained, shall with lust's blood be spotted" (5.1.37). Iago has, of course, described the handkerchief as "[s]potted with strawberries" (3.3.440), a passage students will usually invoke—if they have not done so already—if asked to explain how 5.1.37 links handkerchief and sheets. Thus we have arrived, through a process of discovery, at something like Frye's conclusion that "in *Othello* . . . women tend to become the cloth rather than its producers and consumers" (221).

My next question is, for what reason does Desdemona tell Emilia to put "my wedding sheets" on the bed at 4.2.107–08?[9] The Dinesen story now becomes useful because it relates a custom that, although not part of my students' normal cultural practices, is nevertheless crucial to our understanding of Desdemona's request. "The Blank Page," narrated by an "old coffee-brown, black-veiled woman" (99)—an "Egyptian charmer" of sorts whose stories and identity have merged with those of her mother and grandmother—tells of a convent that makes linen wedding sheets for the royal family of Portugal and is rewarded by being allowed to keep "that central piece of the snow-white sheet which bore witness to the honor of a royal bride" (103). The story explains how, on the morning after a royal wedding, the wedding sheet was publicly displayed by the "Chamberlain or High Steward" (102)—a man, one might note—who "would solemnly proclaim: *Virginem eam tenemus*—'we declare her to have been a virgin.' Such a sheet was never afterwards washed or again lain on" (102-03). The blood-stained linen is framed and hung in the convent's gallery, where "[w]ithin the faded markings of the canvases people of some imagination and sensibility may read all the signs of the zodiac. . . . Or they may there find pictures from their own world of ideas" (103). Among the framed pieces of fabric and hymenal blood is a pure-white square. The narrator's goal is not to explain the story of the white square but to suggest that this square provokes the deepest thought and profoundest silence from viewers. At some later point, usually to expand their thinking about the text of Desdemona's sheets, I will have the students brainstorm about the reasons for which this particular page is blank. Students' responses include the possibilities that the young woman died before marriage, that she became a nun, that she never married and instead died an old maid, that she was not a virgin at her marriage, or that the marriage was never consummated.

Armed with this story, students are able to speculate that Desdemona's wedding sheets are spotted with the hymenal blood that proves she was a virgin on her wedding night. If wedding sheets are not normally reused—

except as winding sheets, as Desdemona hints in her request to be shrouded "[i]n one of these same sheets" (4.3.24)—her request marks a noteworthy divergence from cultural practice. Another possibility, if one accepts the shorter of the time schemes that seem to operate in *Othello*, is that the marriage has not yet been consummated and the sheets are still blank. We might find limited support for this second possibility in Othello's statement, "When I have plucked thy rose / I cannot give it vital growth again. / It needs must wither. I'll smell thee on the tree" (5.2.13–15), and also in his reluctance to make Desdemona bleed (5.2.3).

If the marriage has not been consummated, Desdemona's virginity—and therefore her marital chastity—can still be tested. In entertaining this possibility, I am careful not to overdetermine Othello's tragedy; indeed, this is a point where I can productively foreground my own subjectivity as a reader of the blank texts of the sheets, thereby using myself as an example of the very phenomenon we have been discussing all along. I tend to want to see Desdemona as a text written by men and as a woman whose voice is suppressed and overwritten by the script that Iago imposes on her until "I myself" is effectively the "[n]obody" of her dying words (5.2.133). The hymenal blood on the linen is a woman's text in "The Blank Page." It is oddly satisfying to me to think that Othello's ultimate mistake might lie in not allowing Desdemona's body to attest to her faith.

However, I stress that the sheets remain a blank to us, for, unlike the handkerchief's strawberry spots, their text (embroidery or blood or nothing) is not clarified, nor does it have to be in performance.[10] As for Desdemona, she both is and is not a blank page. Othello will not "scar that whiter skin of hers than snow, / And smooth as monumental alabaster" (5.2.4–5). (It is helpful to point out that in Shakespeare's source material, the *Hecatommithi*, the wife's skull is broken and her body crushed by fallen rafters. Shakespeare's deviations from his sources invite us to ask about the effect of such changes.) Desdemona's body may remain literally unblemished, but it has been metaphorically scarred and inscribed with the word *whore*, a text dictated by Iago. In 4.2, Othello senses *whore* is the wrong text to write on her body: "Was this fair paper, this most goodly book, / Made to write 'whore' upon?" (4.2.73–74). Desdemona, who says "whore" even as she says that she "cannot say 'whore,' " speaks the text written on her and understands the word to be performative: "It does abhor me now I speak the word" (4.2.165–66). We are left with the question of her virginity unresolved, looking at the blank page of Desdemona and wondering what to read therein.

In her story, Dinesen calls linen a "page" (104) and the mixture of blood and semen "the rarest ink of all" (100), which has prepared students to accept that the handkerchief and sheets are texts. Careful work on the metonymic relation between women and linens will lead students to the conclusion that Desdemona is a text. Dinesen's story also prepares them to interrogate the relation between the viewer and the page. There are various ways to forward discussion from here. What does the text of Desdemona mean to Othello? to Iago? to us? To what extent do men control the reading of the textiles in the play? Why is it that Othello can read the text of the handkerchief but not the sheets? One could even ask how the Venetians read—and write—Othello himself. A valuable exercise might be to ask students to debate the different views of the handkerchief offered by Wayne and by Frye: is it the woman's text (Wayne) or a woman's textile co-opted and controlled by men (Frye)?

"The Blank Page" allows me to introduce the idea of textual indeterminacy—and the importance of the observer-hearer-reader in determining meaning—without having to invoke theoretical terms that students may not yet have encountered. We talk about different modes of writing, the multiplicity of texts in the play, and the ramifications of reading those texts from different biases about the play and its characters. This discussion can also be a good opportunity to deploy a basic theoretical vocabulary in such a way that context demystifies the terms. Without any critical fanfare (which would be inappropriate for students who have not yet taken or, in the case of nonmajors, will never take a critical-theory course), I am able to introduce the words *signifier* and *slippage*, for example. The theoretical investment of the discussion can be increased or decreased according to the needs and background of the particular group of students.

NOTES

[1] I have tried to give a sense of the various directions this lecture has taken over the last five years and might take in the immediate future; teachers wishing to adapt this approach may need to be selective for a fifty-minute class.

[2] In addition to the critics cited here, see Carol Thomas Neely (esp. *Broken Nuptials* 128–31); Karen Newman, " 'Wash' "; and Harry Berger, Jr., "Impertinent Trifling."

[3] Citations to *Othello* are from Greenblatt's *Norton Shakespeare*.

[4] The scene-by-scene summary—one page consisting of one catchy phrase for each scene—is an exercise I require students to undertake for each play.

[5] I like to introduce rhetorical terms throughout the course to give students ways of talking about how the language works. A student-friendly glossary is Katie Wales's "An A to Z of Rhetorical Terms."

[6] The question, does Othello ever have ocular proof, usually directs the discussion to 4.1.

[7] What the handkerchief means in each exchange is, of course, debatable. One can have a profitable discussion about the changing signification of the handkerchief as it passes between hands. The key point to make is that the meanings of labile signifiers depend on context and interpretation.

[8] Another useful exercise is to have students think about the times when the handkerchief is in view of the playgoers. Does Desdemona observe the implicit stage direction in "she reserves it evermore about her / To kiss and talk to" (3.3.299–300)? When does Iago hide it in 3.3? Does Bianca give the handkerchief to Cassio or drop it? If she drops it, who picks it up and when?

⁹The phrasing of a question is important. Generally, I find that "why" questions intimidate students; they are unsure if they are meant to be addressing authorial intention, the imperatives of staging, or character motivation. "For what reason(s)" and "what is the effect of" are better phrases for eliciting discussion of text and character.

¹⁰Like the handkerchief, the sheets have to be materially realized in performance, and one could make an unambiguous statement in modern performance by painting the sheet. One production of *Troilus and Cressida* had Pandarus (Bernard Hopkins) enter with a blood-stained sheet and unfurl it mischievously at "How now, how now, how go maidenheads?" (4.2.25), thus clarifying Cressida's sexual history. *Othello* does not invite such clarification. In any case, all the implied stage directions suggest that Desdemona remains on the bed throughout the scene, thus at least partly hiding the sheets with her body so that we cannot read them.

Finding *Othello*'s African Roots through Djanet Sears's *Harlem Duet*

Joyce Green MacDonald

In the fourteen years that I have been teaching *Othello* to undergraduates at the University of Kentucky, I've repeatedly found that the first impulse of my students—especially those new to the play or to Renaissance studies generally—is to formulate the play's conflicts around Desdemona instead of around Othello. Aided by the contextual materials they've turned up in their research projects and in various assigned readings—for the last three years, from Russ McDonald's exemplary *Bedford Companion to Shakespeare*—they've had no trouble getting the rules about gender and patriarchy that Desdemona violates when she runs away with the man she loves. In the most recent set of classroom discussions, students characterized Brabantio's declaration to Iago and Roderigo that his respectable "house is not a grange" (1.1.106) as snooty and snobbish; they were quick to see Desdemona as a romantic rebel against the arbitrary strictures of class and social authority neatly expressed in her father's annoyed reprimand.[1]

And yet, in the same scene, the house-proud Brabantio has no trouble listening to and apparently believing Iago's characterizations of his daughter's sexual behavior with the Moor—grossly inappropriate public remarks that, if overheard, would surely heighten his fears about what the neighbors will think. I have thus suggested to my students that although it is temptingly easy to mock Brabantio's pompous patriarchal respectability, he may actually be more deeply motivated by a fear that Iago senses and expertly manipulates: fear of the consequences of his daughter's sexual misbehavior, which is a fear that his bloodline will be racially erased by Othello's. My suggestion implies that Brabantio is more fragile and frightened than authoritarian, that Iago's disreputable talk gives shape to a preexisting set of specifically racial as well as sexual fears, and that Brabantio's sense of his own fatherhood is constituted in race as well as gender.

However, when I try to argue these points from performance—that racial notions circulate in the play before Othello ever makes an appearance and are as much as, if not more of, a determining ground for relationships and characters in the play as are Brabantio's beliefs about gender hierarchies—I encounter some handicaps. The *Othello* directed by Jonathan Miller is virtually useless to me in making a case about the text's racial unconscious: casting Anthony Hopkins as Othello obviously cuts off most opportunities for visualizing the clear racial difference Brabantio believes in and recoils from in disgust, and Bob Hoskins's brilliantly jovial and malevolent Iago so completely overshadows Hopkins's Moor that it preempts the rest. I find myself mesmerized by Laurence Olivier's Othello (see Burge), but its emotional extravagance makes many of my students uncomfortable. Students perhaps under-standably tend to experience the makeup as more of a distraction than an invitation to consider questions of racial performance and identity. More stu-dents are familiar with Oliver Parker's 1995 film of the play, but in many respects it seems to substitute its own racist clichés for what I've called the play's racial unconscious: the widening eyes of Irène Jacob's Desdemona as Laurence Fishburne's Othello unbuckles his pants, the jungle-drum sound-track accompanying the scene of their first lovemaking, the intercutting of their wedding-night scene with that of the anonymous couple doing the nasty in the wagon above Iago's and Roderigo's heads. Here, contemporary racial fears and fantasies are on full display but lack any demonstration of how the Shakespearean text might have participated in, or even anticipated, their formation.

This year, as I continued to think about how to reassert the links between race and gender and sexuality in my students' responses to *Othello*, I decided to use a contemporary adaptation of the play, the African Canadian playwright Djanet Sears's *Harlem Duet*. I had been reading Sears out of my own scholarly interests in Shakespearean adaptation and in the representation of racial iden-tity in Shakespearean productions; one morning, I had the brainstorm of bringing a brief section of it to class as an illustration of research I would be asking them to do for their major project in the class. Over the past three or four years, I've tried to strengthen the research component of my students' work in the Shakespeare survey course, where most of my *Othello* teaching takes place. This year, I wrote my research expectations more formally into course requirements by asking students to complete, in addition to a short research project earlier in the semester, a longer research paper on an ad-aptation of a Shakespeare play. For convenience's sake, I asked students to find their adapted texts from "Editions and Adaptations of Shakespeare," a valuable subcollection contained in the vast *Literature Online* project main-tained on the Web by Chadwyck-Healey (available by subscription only); sev-eral plays on our syllabus appeared, in their adapted versions, in this subcol-lection. But I set up an in-class discussion of what an adaptation is and of the kinds of relations an adaptation might bear to its Shakespearean original around a passage from Sears's play, which as a whole directly addresses the challenge raised by *Othello*'s opening scene. *Harlem Duet* asserts that ideas about gender and sexuality in the play are connected to, rather than distinct from, ideas about race and skin color.

Sears's play is a contemporary reworking of *Othello*, set in Harlem in three historical periods. Instead of being merely a modernized version, Sears's *Har-lem Duet* forcibly dislocates a strictly patriarchal reading of Shakespeare's play by telling its story from the perspective of the black women who are its main characters and who, I have argued elsewhere, haunt the memory of *Othello*: Othello's absent mother, the Egyptian "charmer" who enchanted the strawberry-embroidered handkerchief (3.4.57), Desdemona's mother's maid

"Barbary" (4.3.26) ("Black Ram" 193–94). The primal scene of Sears's black feminist citation of Shakespeare's tragedy is not Othello's murder of Desdemona and his subsequent suicide but the hero's moment of transit from his placement in black culture to his embrace of his white wife. Sears repeatedly imagines this scene as a moment of traumatic emotional violence against the women who loved Othello first, before he met Desdemona. In the second of *Harlem Duet*'s historical settings, Harlem in 1928, Othello's displaced black partner is driven to madness and cuts him with a razor after he reveals to her that he's fallen in love with a white woman:

> Deadly deadly straw little berries it's so beautiful you kissed my fingers you pressed this cloth into my palm buried it there an antique token our ancient all these tiny red dots on a sheet of white my fingernails are white three hairs on my head are white the whites of my eyes are white too the palms of my hands and my feet are white you're all I'd ever and you my my I hate Sssshh. (305)

In Sears's third, contemporary scene, the heroine Billie remembers how devastating it was even to imagine she saw her Othello on the subway with his new white lover: "I had to renew my prescription" (296). For the Edenic rapture of the romance between Shakespeare's Othello and Desdemona—"and when I love thee not, / Chaos is come again" (3.3.91–92)—Sears substitutes a black urban pastoral: "I love that I can see the Apollo from our—from my balcony" (300), Billie tells her Othello. "Black is beautiful . . . So beautiful. This Harlem sanctuary . . . here. This respite . . . like an ocean in the middle of a desert" (313).

My students' visceral identification with Desdemona suggests to me the extent to which professors of literature have succeeded in gendering the Renaissance. As I worked with *Harlem Duet* as the subject for our adaptation discussion, I began realizing that my students' readiness to recognize gendered differences in Renaissance England might make it an ideal text with which to begin a more detailed study of how gender voices race in *Othello*. Their sympathies for Desdemona's defiance of paternal control have sometimes morphed, in both discussion and written work, into contempt for Othello. Some students see Othello's murder of Desdemona as the exercise of an extreme version of Brabantio's patriarchalism. This startling connection between Brabantio and Othello stems partly from students' impulse to normalize and simplify *Othello*'s truly painful moral complexities and partly from their difficulty in imagining Othello in the racial, cultural, and religious contexts Shakespeare establishes for him.

Let me backtrack a little to touch on the circumstances of teaching Shakespeare courses at the University of Kentucky, a midsize state university (about 34,000 students, undergraduate and graduate combined). Since our Shakespeare survey can satisfy requirements for students in several different majors in arts and sciences and for several colleges of the university, it attracts a widely heterogeneous population: English majors, theater majors, students with an interest in Tudor history or religion, future secondary school teachers, and a surprisingly (at least, to me) high percentage of students who have never studied Renaissance literature at all. My inexperienced students, many of whom register for the course because they believe that studying Shakespeare will add intellectual value to their college educations, frequently prove to be among my most imaginative and responsive. But this lack of a common preparation for the course can also result in some pedagogical difficulties. Students' depth or accuracy of knowledge about Renaissance culture can be very uneven. Every year, for example, I have students who have difficulty evaluating the quality of evidence in the Shakespeare authorship debates. Every year there are students who cannot acknowledge the historical distinctions between the evangelical Protestant faiths they may have been brought up in and the state of Elizabethan Protestantism. And every time I've taught *Othello* in the last four or five years, I've had a few students who remain skeptical about the extent or even existence of Elizabethans' beliefs about Africa and Africans, no matter how hard I work to present illustrating material. I've heard too many classroom anecdotes from far-flung friends and colleagues to assume that my Shakespeare students' resistance to knowledge about race in the Renaissance is uncommon or peculiar. I think the sources of students' doubt are linked to their presuppositions about what the Renaissance was really like, presuppositions that can be hard to erode.

As I reread *Harlem Duet*, I recognized how neatly it addresses many of my issues in teaching *Othello*. For one thing, its reconsideration of Shakespeare's tragic interracial love in the light of the histories of African-descended people in Canada and the United States offers my students a more familiar setting in recounting its racial histories than Renaissance England does. Sears's play simultaneously recognizes and ameliorates the difficulties of establishing historical distance between Shakespeare's Cyprus and Venice and today as it retells its central story in three North American time frames.

But if Sears offers a way around the problem of addressing Renaissance racial attitudes, her treatment of gender difference engages another issue head-on: *Harlem Duet* refuses to let itself be read as Desdemona's story. It insists that gender has a race and that this double identity operates differently for its white and black female subjects, as well as for its men. Sears reproduces *Othello* as an indictment of the psychological power of a white imaginary, a power to which her three Othellos succumb as they choose Desdemona over their black lovers. The third, contemporary Othello, an academic, is unexpectedly appointed to lead a student semester in Cyprus over Chris Yago, the white colleague who had hoped to land the job, and now "a whole bunch" of his white department members "are challenging affirmative action" (299). Although Othello recognizes that racism has led his colleagues to assume that any black person is less qualified for the appointment than a white man, he still believes the court case is "a good thing. . . . Injustice against Blacks can't be cured by injustice against Whites" (299). After having left Billie, his wife, for Mona, Othello returns to the apartment he shared with her to pack his things, and the couple ends up making love for the last time. Their time together is interrupted by Mona's arrival in the building's vestibule, where she speaks to Othello on the intercom. He tells her he hasn't finished packing yet, but when Mona refuses to answer, his "demeanor changes" and he scrambles into his clothes: "Mone? Mona? I'm coming, OK? I'll be right . . . Just wait there one second, OK? OK?" (301).

In Sears's version of *Othello*'s events, it is Billie who puts a spell on the handkerchief Othello received from his female ancestors on his father's side, a handkerchief that possesses a significance different from the erotic one Shakespeare assigns it:

> It is fixed in the emotions of all your ancestors. The one who laid the foundation for the road in Herndon, Virginia, and was lashed for laziness as he stopped to wipe the sweat from his brow with this kerchief. Or, your great great grandmother, who covered her face with it, and then covered it with her hands as she rocked and silently wailed, when told that her girl child, barely thirteen, would be sent 'cross the state for breeding purposes. Or the one who leapt for joy on hearing of the Emancipation Proclamation, fifteen years late, mind you, only to watch it fall in slow motion from his hand and onto the ground when told that the only job he could now get, was the same one he'd done for free all those years, and now he's forced to take it, for not enough money to buy the food to fill even one man's belly. And more . . . so much more. What I add to this already fully endowed cloth, will cause you such . . . Wretchedness.   (306)

Out of her sense of betrayal, Billie adds new poison to the cloth and gives it back to him before ending the play in a psychiatric ward. (Sears's treatment of the handkerchief doesn't entirely overwrite Shakespeare's. Another aspect of her play retains his conviction of the operation of its erotic magic in a highly comic way.)

As I noted, I brought in only a short selection of *Harlem Duet*, from the disjointed speech about the strawberry-embroidered handkerchief. In class, we used it to talk about ways of adapting, adopting, and remaking Shakespearean meanings; here, a woman speaks about the handkerchief's power after killing her husband, and the frenzy of her dislocated speech contrasts usefully with the sorrowful dignity of the information Shakespeare's Othello provides about it. Students found the passage from Sears to be a useful way of getting to Othello's shock and rage about the handkerchief's loss, but they were also struck by how the passage's reversal of roles—a woman's madness substituting for a man's—seemed to make the scene read differently. It struck

them as somehow more seemly for a woman to do violence out of love than
for a man; it was easier for them to see her crime—and potentially Othello's
as well—as a crime of passion rather than of malice. Sears's character calls
the handkerchief "our ancient," and *ancient* is an alternative term used in the
play for Iago's rank of ensign. Students had noticed the unusual term in reading, and to hear Sears's character use it again both emphasizes the deep-rooted
love she shares with her Othello and points back to Iago. The passage, brief
as it is, led students to hear Othello's account with fresh ears.

Intrigued by the results of my spontaneous experiment with Sears's version
of Shakespeare, I am already planning a fuller comparative look at *Harlem
Duet* and *Othello* for my next section of the Shakespeare survey. I will concentrate on Sears's appropriation of the handkerchief motif as a means for me
not only to clarify what adapting Shakespeare means but also to complicate
and challenge my students' response to Desdemona's situation. Billie's characterization of the nature of the magic in the web of Sears's handkerchief—
that it is a token of racial, rather than romantic, fidelity—stands in stark contrast to the story Shakespeare's Othello tells about the handkerchief, adding
new gravity to an account students have sometimes found superstitious and
hard to believe. Indeed, in my classrooms, I think the power Othello assigns
to the handkerchief may pose a major roadblock between students and their
grasp of the character; it seems irrational, especially when set against Brabantio's very legible assumptions about his right to arrange his daughter's marital
fate. This is precisely the point about the story of the handkerchief—that it
confirms Othello's existence as a character who truly originates from outside
Venice's social order.

Harlem Duet has been useful to me as a way of suggesting to my students
how race registers in *Othello*, and I plan to make more use of its resources
in the future. I don't, however, pretend to have fully addressed the issues
Sears's play raises independent of its origins in *Othello*. Beginning with Shakespeare, Sears ultimately mounts a distinct rearrangement of the *Othello* materials. Her play insists on the power of black love as the foundation of black
community and sees that foundation under a continual racial assault that tends
to operate through sexual means. For Sears, Desdemona is an almost archetypal figure of the destruction of black unions. Her Civil War Othello is
lynched after returning to the scene of his enslavement to help the daughter
of his former master: "She needs me. She respects me. Looks up to me, even.
. . . When I'm with her I feel like . . . a man" (302). We later see his slave wife
cradling her dead husband:

> Once upon a time there was a man who wanted to find a magic spell in
> order to become White. After much research and investigation, he came
> across an ancient ritual from the caverns of knowledge of a psychic. "The
> only way to become White," the psychic said, "was to enter the White-
> ness."   (310)

The question I have here is whether placing the blame for chaos on Desdemona, on black men's supposedly irresistible attraction to white women or on their ignorance of the meaning of their own blackness, results in a reading as partial and as flawed as one that places the entire burden of the play's pain at Othello's door. But that question must grow out of a consideration of the special relation between text and adaptation, a relation that only partially retains direct lines of descent and perhaps more centrally sets out to reframe questions and posit new answers. The process of reframing—formulating new questions, shifting perspectives, unfixing textual certainties—strikes me as pedagogically useful. I want my students to see Shakespeare's Othello as he is; and to do that, sometimes it might be valuable to see him as someone other than Shakespeare's. Sears's alternative *Othello*, with its foregrounded insistence on the links between the ways white women, black women, and black men see themselves and one another, has the potential of helping students see Othello more completely in the Shakespearean text.

NOTE

[1]Citations to *Othello* are from Evans's *Riverside Shakespeare*.

NOTES ON CONTRIBUTORS

Emily C. Bartels is associate professor of English at Rutgers University, where she won the Faculty of Arts and Sciences Award for Distinguished Contributions to Undergraduate Education. She is also associate director of the Bread Loaf School of English (Middlebury College). Her book *Spectacles of Strangeness: Imperialism, Alienation, and Marlowe* (1993) won the Roma Gill Prize for the best work on Marlowe. She has edited a collection of essays on Marlowe and published articles on *Othello* and early modern representations of the Moor, the subject of her current book project.

Douglas Bruster, associate professor of English at the University of Texas, Austin, published *Drama and the Market in the Age of Shakespeare* (1992), *Quoting Shakespeare* (2000), and *Shakespeare and the Question of Culture* (2003). He is textual editor of *The Changeling* for the "Collected Works of Thomas Middleton" (forthcoming).

Sheila T. Cavanagh, Masse-Martin/NEH Distinguished Teaching Professor at Emory University, is the author of *Cherished Torment: The Emotional Geography of Lady Mary Wroth's* Urania (2001), *Wanton Eyes and Chaste Desires: Female Sexuality in* The Faerie Queene (1994), and articles on Renaissance literature and pedagogy. She is the director of the Emory Women Writers Resource Project, a Web site devoted to women's writing from the sixteenth to the twentieth century.

Samuel Crowl, Trustee Professor of English at Ohio University, has published *Shakespeare Observed: Studies in Performance on Stage and Screen* (1992), *Shakespeare at the Cineplex: The Kenneth Branagh Era* (2003) and written articles, essays, and reviews on Shakespeare in performance. He has twice been selected a University Professor—Ohio University's top teaching honor.

Peter Erickson is the author of *Patriarchal Structures in Shakespeare's Drama* (1985) and *Rewriting Shakespeare, Rewriting Ourselves* (1991) and coeditor of *Shakespeare's "Rough Magic": Renaissance Essays in Honor of C. L. Barber* (1985) and *Early Modern Visual Culture: Representation, Race, and Empire in Renaissance England* (2000).

Lisa Gim, associate professor of English at Fitchburg State College, has published articles on Queen Elizabeth I, early modern women writers, Shakespeare, and George Puttenham. She is currently revising her book manuscript, "(Re)presenting Regina: Literary Representations of Queen Elizabeth I by Women Writers of the Sixteenth and Seventeenth Centuries."

Jean E. Howard, William Ransford professor of English at Columbia University, is the author of *The Stage and Social Struggle in Early Modern England* (1994) and, with Phyllis Rackin, *Engendering a Nation: A Feminist Account of Shakespeare's English Histories* (1997). She is coeditor of *The Norton Shakespeare* (1997). She is currently completing "Theater of a City," a study of early modern London comedy.

Kathy M. Howlett, associate professor of English and codirector of cinema studies at Northeastern University, is the author of *Framing Shakespeare on Film* (2000). She has published articles on Shakespeare, film, Aphra Behn, and the rise of the novel.

Maurice Hunt, Research Professor of English and head of the English department at Baylor University, is the author of *Shakespeare's Romance of the Word* (1990), *Shakespeare's Labored Art* (1995), *Shakespeare's Religious Allusiveness: Its Play and Tolerance* (2004), and articles on Shakespeare, John Webster, Francis Beaumont and John Fletcher, Edmund Spenser, and John Milton. He has edited three books, including *Approaches to Teaching Shakespeare's* The Tempest *and Other Late Romances* (1992) and *Approaches to Teaching Shakespeare's* Romeo and Juliet (2000).

Janelle Jenstad, assistant professor of English at the University of Victoria, has published essays in journals such as *Early Modern Literary Studies, Shakespeare Bulletin: A Journal of Performance Criticism and Scholarship, Elizabethan Theatre*, and the *Journal of Medieval and Early Modern Studies*. Her research interests include merchants, goldsmiths, usury, gold, and money in early modern culture and theater; Shakespeare in performance; and Shakespeare in Canada.

Miranda Johnson-Haddad is a visiting lecturer of English at the University of California, Los Angeles. She has published articles on Dante, Ariosto, Shakespeare, and Spenser, as well as theater reviews in *Shakespeare Quarterly* and *Shakespeare Bulletin: A Journal of Performance Criticism and Scholarship*. She was performance editor, with Alan Dessen, of *Shakespeare Quarterly*.

Cynthia Lewis, Charles A. Dana Professor of English at Davidson College, has published *Particular Saints: Shakespeare's Four Antonios, Their Contexts, and Their Plays* (1997) and articles in publications such as *Shakespeare Quarterly, Studies in English Literature: 1500–1900, Renaissance Drama*, and *Comparative Drama*. She is currently working on a study of epistemology in Shakespeare's *Love's Labor's Lost*.

Joyce Green MacDonald, associate professor of English at the University of Kentucky, is the author of *Women and Race in Early Modern Texts* (2002), as well as several articles on Renaissance and Restoration drama and performance. She edited *Race, Ethnicity, and Power in the Renaissance* (1996). Her current projects include articles on New World postcolonial Shakespeares and on Derek Walcott's *A Branch of the Blue Nile* and *Antony and Cleopatra*.

Cynthia Marshall, professor of English at Rhodes College, is the author of *Last Things and Last Plays: Shakespearean Eschatology* (1991), *The Shattering of the Self: Violence, Subjectivity, and Early Modern Texts* (2002), and numerous articles on Shakespeare's plays. She is editor of *Shakespeare in Production: As You Like It* (2004). Her research interests focus on critical theory, performance studies, and early modern literature, especially drama.

Michael Neill, professor of English at the University of Auckland, is the author of *Issues of Death: Mortality and Identity in English Renaissance Tragedy* (1997) and *Putting History to the Question: Power, Politics, and Society in English Renaissance Drama* (2000). His edition of *Othello* is forthcoming from Oxford University Press.

Nicholas F. Radel, professor of English at Furman University, published *The Puritan Origins of American Sex* and articles on Shakespeare and Renaissance drama in journals such as *Shakespeare Quarterly* and *Renaissance Drama*. His research and teaching interests include sexuality studies, early modern drama, and modern drama. A current book-length study involves sodomy and silence in early modern England.

Francesca T. Royster, associate professor of English at DePaul University, has published *Becoming Cleopatra: The Shifting Image of an Icon* (2003), as well as essays in *Shakespeare Quarterly* and in edited volumes focused on race in early modern English writing. Her book project, titled "Staging Disobedience," considers the intersections of animality and race in performance and the ways that such configurations of danger have been marketed in theater, film, and musical performances.

Martha Tuck Rozett, professor of English at State University of New York, Albany, is the author of *The Doctrine of Election and the Emergence of Elizabethan Tragedy* (1984), *Talking Back to Shakespeare* (1994), *Constructing a World: Shakespeare's England and the New Historical Fiction* (2003), and articles and reviews in *Shakespeare Quarterly* and *Shakespeare Bulletin*. Her research and teaching interests include Shakespeare's plays in performance, Shakespeare pedagogy, historical fiction, and genre theory.

Geraldo U. de Sousa, associate professor of English at the University of Kansas, is the author of *Shakespeare's Cross-Cultural Encounters* (2002) and numerous articles on Renaissance drama and culture. He is the editor of *Mediterranean Studies*, the interdisciplinary journal of the Mediterranean Studies Association.

Virginia Mason Vaughan, professor of English at Clark University, is author of *Othello: A Contextual History* (1994), coauthor of *Shakespeare's Caliban: A Cultural History*, and coeditor of Othello: *New Perspectives* and *The Tempest* (Arden 3). Her publications reflect an interest in race and other modes of alterity in early modern texts, especially Shakespeare's. Her most recent book is *Performing Blackness on English Stages, 1500–1800*.

Michael Warren, professor emeritus of English literature at the University of California, Santa Cruz, has published *The Division of the Kingdoms* (1983) with Gary Taylor; *The Complete* King Lear *1608–1623* and *The Parallel* King Lear *1608–1623* (1989); *Shakespeare: Life, Language and Linguistics, Textual Studies, and the Canon: An Annotated Bibliography of Shakespeare Studies 1623–2000* (2002); and articles on the texts of plays of Shakespeare and his contemporaries.

SURVEY PARTICIPANTS

The following Shakespeare instructors generously responded to the survey on teaching *Othello* that preceded preparation of this volume. Without the invaluable information and insights they provided, the book would not have been possible.

Emily C. Bartels, *Rutgers University, New Brunswick*
Alanna K. Brown, *Montana State University*
Douglas Bruster, *University of Texas, Austin*
Sheila T. Cavanagh, *Emory University*
Lisbeth Chapin, *University of Denver*
Stephen Cohen, *University of South Alabama*
Michael J. Collins, *Georgetown University*
Herbert R. Coursen, *University of Maine, Augusta*
Samuel Crowl, *Ohio University*
Christy Desmet, *University of Georgia*
Janet Field-Pickering, *Folger Shakespeare Library*
Margaret Gardiner, *University of Virginia*
Lisa Gim, *Fitchburg State College*
Gerald Harp, *Kenyon College*
R. Chris Hassel, Jr., *Vanderbilt University*
Lisa Hopkins, *Sheffield Hallam University, United Kingdom*
Jean E. Howard, *Columbia University*
Kathy M. Howlett, *Northeastern University*
Sujata Iyengar, *University of Georgia*
Janelle Jenstad, *University of Victoria*
Debra Johanyak, *University of Akron, Wayne College*
Miranda Johnson-Haddad, *University of California, Los Angeles*
Joan Hutton Landis, *Curtis Institute of Music*
John L. LePage, *Malaspina University-College*
Cynthia Lewis, *Davidson College*
George Evans Light, *Mississippi State University*
Joyce Green MacDonald, *University of Kentucky*
Bindu Malieckal, *Saint Anselm College*
Cynthia Marshall, *Rhodes College*
Sharon Meltzer, *Richard C. Daley College*
Paul Menzer, *University of North Texas*
Naomi J. Miller, *University of Arizona*
Michael Neill, *University of Auckland*
Edward Pechter, *Concordia University*
Nicholas F. Radel, *Furman University*
Robert H. Ray, *Baylor University*
Albert Rolls, *Holt, Rinehart, and Winston, Inc.*
Francesca T. Royster, *DePaul University*
Martha Tuck Rozett, *State University of New York, Albany*

Michael Shurgot, *South Puget Sound Community College*
Geraldo U. de Sousa, *University of Kansas*
Lisa S. Starks, *University of South Florida, Saint Petersburg*
Eric Sterling, *Auburn University, Montgomery*
Frances Teague, *University of Georgia*
Humphrey Tonkin, *University of Hartford*
Virginia Mason Vaughan, *Clark University*
Bente Videbaek, *State University of New York, Stony Brook*
Michael Warren, *University of California, Santa Cruz*
George Walton Williams, *Duke University*

WORKS CITED

Books, Articles, Other Sources

Adamson, Jane. Othello *as Tragedy: Some Problems of Judgment and Feeling.* Cambridge: Cambridge UP, 1980.

Adelman, Janet. *The Common Liar: An Essay on* Antony and Cleopatra. New Haven: Yale UP, 1973.

———. "Her Father's Blood: Race, Conversion, and Nation in *The Merchant of Venice.*" *Representations* 81 (2003): 4–30.

———. "Iago's Alter Ego: Race as Projection in *Othello.*" *Shakespeare Quarterly* 48 (1997): 125–44.

———. *Suffocating Mothers: Fantasies of Maternal Origin in Shakespeare's Plays,* Hamlet *to* The Tempest. New York: Routledge, 1992.

Adler, Doris. "The Rhetoric of *Black* and *White* in *Othello.*" *Shakespeare Quarterly* 25 (1974): 248–57.

Aiken, Susan Hardy. *Isak Dinesen and the Engendering of Narrative.* Chicago: U of Chicago P, 1990.

Alexander, Catherine M. S., and Stanley Wells, eds. *Shakespeare and Race.* Cambridge: Cambridge UP, 2000.

Anderegg, Michael. *Orson Welles, Shakespeare, and Popular Culture.* New York: Columbia UP, 1999.

Anderson, Linda. *A Kind of Wild Justice: Revenge in Shakespeare's Comedies.* Newark: U of Delaware P, 1987.

Andreas, James R. "The Curse of Cush: Othello's Jewish Ancestry." Kolin 169–87.

———. "The Neutering of *Romeo and Juliet.*" *Ideological Approaches to Shakespeare: The Practice of Theory.* Ed. Robert P. Merrix and Nicholas Ranson. Lewiston: Mellen, 1992. 229–42.

———. "Othello's African American Progeny." *South Atlantic Review* 57.4 (1992): 39–57.

———. "Rewriting Race through Literature: Teaching Shakespeare's African Plays." *Shakespeare Yearbook* 12 (2001): 215–36.

———. "Shakespeare and the Invention of Humanism: Bloom on Race and Ethnicity." *Harold Bloom's Shakespeare.* Ed. Christy Desmet and Robert Sawyer. New York: Palgrave, 2002. 181–97.

———. "Signifyin' on Shakespeare: African American Appropriations of *Othello* and *The Tempest*: A Prospectus." E-mail to Peter Erickson. 5 Sept. 2001.

———. "Signifyin' on *The Tempest* in Gloria Naylor's *Mama Day.*" *Shakespeare and Appropriation.* Ed. Christy Desmet and Robert Sawyer. London: Routledge, 1999. 103–18.

———. "Silencing the Vulgar and Voicing the Other Shakespeare." *Nebraska English Journal* 35 (1990): 74–88.

————. "Writing Down, Speaking Up, Acting Out, and Clowning Around in the Shakespeare Classroom." Salomone and Davis 25–32.

Andrews, Kenneth. *Elizabethan Privateering*. Cambridge: Cambridge UP, 1964.

————. *Trade, Plunder, and Settlement: Maritime Enterprise and the Genesis of the British Empire, 1480–1630*. Cambridge: Cambridge UP, 1984.

Auden, W. H. "The Joker in the Pack." *"The Dyer's Hand" and Other Essays*. New York: Random, 1962. 246–72.

Bachelard, Gaston. *The Poetics of Space*. Trans. Maria Jolas. New York: Orion, 1964.

Bacon, Francis. *New Atlantis*. London: Newcomb, 1659.

————. "Of Revenge." *Essays*. 1597. World's Classics. London: Oxford UP, 1902. 18–19.

Bart, Pauline B., and Eileen Geil Moran, eds. *Violence against Women: The Bloody Footprints*. Newbury Park: Sage, 1993.

Bartels, Emily C. "Making More of the Moor: Aaron, Othello, and Renaissance Refashionings of Race." *Shakespeare Quarterly* 41 (1990): 433–54.

————. "Strategies of Submission: Desdemona, the Duchess, and the Assertion of Desire." *Studies in English Literature: 1500–1900* 36 (1996): 417–33.

Barthelemy, Anthony Gerard. *Black Face, Maligned Race: The Representation of Blacks in English Drama from Shakespeare to Southerne*. Baton Rouge: Louisiana State UP, 1987.

————, ed. *Critical Essays on Shakespeare's* Othello. New York: Hall, 1994.

————. "Ethiops Washed White: Moors of the Non-Villainous Type." Barthelemy, *Critical Essays* 91–103.

Bate, Jonathan, and Russell Jackson, eds. *The Oxford Illustrated History of Shakespeare on Stage*. Oxford: Oxford UP, 2001.

————. *Shakespeare: An Illustrated Stage History*. Oxford: Oxford UP, 1996.

Beckerman, Bernard. *Shakespeare at the Globe, 1599–1609*. New York: Macmillan, 1962.

"Begrimed." *The Oxford English Dictionary*. 2nd ed. 1989.

Behn, Aphra. *Oroonoko; or, The Royal Slave*. Ed. Catherine Gallagher. Boston: Bedford–St. Martin's, 2000.

————. *Oroonoko*. Ed. Joanna Lipking. New York: Norton, 1997.

Beilin, Elaine. "Elizabeth Cary and *The Tragedie of Mariam* and History." *A Companion to Early Modern Women's Writing*. Ed. Anita Pacheco. Oxford: Blackwell, 2002. 136–49.

————. *Redeeming Eve: Women Writers of the English Renaissance*. Princeton: Princeton UP, 1987.

Bell, Derrick. "Police Brutality: Portent of Disaster and Discomforting Divergence." *Police Brutality: An Anthology*. Ed. Jill Nelson. New York: Norton, 2001. 88–102.

Belsey, Catherine. *The Subject of Tragedy: Identity and Difference in Renaissance Drama*. London: Methuen, 1985.

Berger, Harry, Jr. "Acts of Silence, Acts of Speech: How to Do Things with Othello and Desdemona." *Renaissance Drama* ns 33 (2004): 3–35.

——. *Fictions of the Pose: Rembrandt against the Italian Renaissance*. Stanford: Stanford UP, 2000.

——. "Impertinent Trifling: Desdemona's Handkerchief." *Shakespeare Quarterly* 47 (1996): 235–50.

——. "Three's a Company: The Spectre of Contaminated Intimacy in *Othello*." *Shakespearean International Yearbook* 4 (2004): 235–63.

Bernard, John. *Retrospections of the Stage*. Vol. 1. London: Colburn, 1830.

Berry, Herbert. *Shakespeare's Playhouses*. AMS Studies in the Renaissance 19. New York: AMS, 1987.

Berry, Philippa. *Shakespeare's Feminine Endings: Disfiguring Death in the Tragedies*. New York: Routledge, 1999.

Bland, Sheila Rose. "How I Would Direct *Othello*." *Othello: New Essays by Black Writers*. Ed. Mythili Kaul. Washington: Howard UP, 1997. 29–41.

Bloom, Harold. *The Anxiety of Influence: A Theory of Poetry*. Oxford: Oxford UP, 1973.

Boose, Lynda E. " 'The Getting of a Lawful Race': Racial Discourse in Early Modern England and the Unrepresentable Black Woman." Hendricks and Parker 35–54.

——. "Othello's Handkerchief: The 'Recognizance and Pledge of Love.' " *English Literary Renaissance* 5 (1975): 360–74.

Bowers, Fredson. *Elizabethan Revenge Tragedy, 1587–1642*. Princeton: Princeton UP, 1966.

——. "Hamlet as Minister and Scourge." *"Hamlet as Minister and Scourge" and Other Studies in Shakespeare and Milton*. Charlottesville: UP of Virginia, 1989. 90–101.

Bradley, A. C. *Shakespearean Tragedy: Lectures on* Hamlet, Othello, King Lear, Macbeth. London: Macmillan, 1904.

Bray, Alan. "Homosexuality and the Signs of Male Friendship in Elizabethan England." *Queering the Renaissance*. Ed. Jonathan Goldberg. Durham: Duke UP, 1994. 40–61.

——. *Homosexuality in Renaissance England*. London: Gay Men's, 1982.

Breitenberg, Mark. *Anxious Masculinity in Early Modern England*. Cambridge: Cambridge UP, 1996.

Brenner, Robert. *Merchants and Revolution: Commercial Change, Political Conflict, and London's Overseas Traders, 1550–1653*. Princeton: Princeton UP, 1993.

Brode, Douglas. *Shakespeare in the Movies: From the Silent Era to* Shakespeare in Love. New York: Oxford UP, 2000.

Brown, Laura. "The Romance of Empire: *Oroonoko* and the Trade in Slaves." *The New Eighteenth Century: Theory, Politics, English Literature*. Ed. Felicity Nussbaum and Brown. New York: Methuen, 1987. 41–61.

Brownstein, Oscar Lee, and Darlene M. Daubert. *Analytical Sourcebook of Concepts in Dramatic Theory*. Westport: Greenwood, 1981.

Bryden, Ronald. "A Moor for the Seventies." *Observer Review* 12 Sept. 1971: 26.

——. "Olivier's Moor." *New Statesman* 1 May 1964: 696.

Buchanan, Judith. "Virgin and Ape, Venetian and Infidel: Labellings of Otherness in

Oliver Parker's *Othello." Shakespeare, Film, Fin de Siècle*. Ed. Mark Thornton Burnett and Ramona Wray. Basingstoke, Eng.: Macmillan, 2000. 179–202.

Buhler, Stephen M. "Ocular Proof: Three Versions of *Othello." Shakespeare in the Cinema: Ocular Proof*. Albany: State U of New York P, 2002. 11–31.

Bullough, Geoffrey, ed. *Major Tragedies*: Hamlet, Othello, King Lear, Macbeth. London: Routledge, 1973. Vol. 7 of *Narrative and Dramatic Sources of Shakespeare*.

Bulman, J. C., and H. R. Coursen, eds. *Shakespeare on Television: An Anthology of Essays and Reviews*. Hanover: UP of New England, 1988.

Burt, Richard. "The Love That Dare Not Speak Shakespeare's Name: New Shakesqueer Cinema." *Shakespeare, the Movie: Popularizing the Plays on Film, TV, and Video*. Ed. Lynda E. Boose and Burt. London: Routledge, 1997. 240–68.

Burton, Jonathan. " 'A Most Wily Bird': Leo Africanus, *Othello*, and the Trafficking in Difference." Loomba and Orkin 43–63.

Calderwood, James L. *The Properties of* Othello. Amherst: U of Massachusetts P, 1989.

Callaghan, Dympna, ed. *A Feminist Companion to Shakespeare*. Oxford: Blackwell, 2000.

———. "Looking Well to Linens: Women and Cultural Production in *Othello* and Shakespeare's England." Howard and Shershow 53–81.

———. " 'Othello Was a White Man': Properties of Race on Shakespeare's Stage." Hawkes 192–215.

———. "Re-reading Elizabeth Cary's *The Tragedie of Mariam, Faire Queene of Jewry*." Hendricks and Parker 163–77.

Campbell, Lily B. "Theories of Revenge in Renaissance England." *Modern Philology* 28 (1931): 281–96.

"The Captious Critic." *Illustrated Sporting and Dramatic News* 7 June 1930: 640.

Carlin, Murray. *Not Now, Sweet Desdemona*. Nairobi: Oxford UP, 1969.

Carroll, Noël. *Theorizing the Moving Image*. Cambridge: Cambridge UP, 1996.

Cartelli, Thomas. *Repositioning Shakespeare: National Formations, Postcolonial Appropriations*. London: Routledge, 1999.

Cartmell, Deborah. *Interpreting Shakespeare on Screen*. New York: St. Martin's, 2000.

Cary, Elizabeth. *The Tragedy of Mariam*. Othello *and* The Tragedy of Mariam. Ed. Clare Carroll. Longman Cultural Ed. New York: Longman, 2003. 142–212.

———. *The Tragedy of Mariam, the Fair Queen of Jewry*. Ed. Stephanie Hodgson-Wright. Toronto: U of Toronto P, 2000.

———. The Tragedy of Mariam, the Fair Queen of Jewry, *with the* Lady Falkland, Her Life. Ed. Barry Weller and Margaret W. Ferguson. Berkeley: U of California P, 1994.

Chambers, E. K. *The Elizabethan Stage*. Vol. 2. Oxford: Clarendon, 1923.

Chapman, George. *The Revenge of Bussy D'Ambois. The Plays of George Chapman: The Tragedies (A Critical Edition)*. Ed. Allan Holaday, G. Blakemore Evans, and Thomas L. Berger. Cambridge: Brewer, 1987. 423–522.

Chibka, Robert L. " 'Oh! Do Not Fear a Woman's Invention': Truth, Falsehood, and Fiction in Aphra Behn's *Oroonoko*." *Texas Studies in Literature and Language* 30 (1988): 510–37.

Christenbury, Leila. "Problems with *Othello* in the High School Classroom." Salomone and Davis 182–90.

Cinthio (Giambattista Giraldi). *Gli Hecatommithi*. Third Decade, Story 7. Trans. Geoffrey Bullough. Bullough 241–52.

———. *Gli Hecatommithi*. Third Decade, Story 7. Trans. Geoffrey Bullough. Othello *and* The Tragedy of Miriam. Ed. Clare Carroll. Longman Cultural Ed. New York: Longman, 2003. 215–30.

Clark, Austin. "Orenthal and Othello." Program note for *Othello*. Talawa Theatre Co. The Drill Hill, London. 1997. N. pag.

Clayton, Thomas, Susan Brock, and Vicente Forés, eds. *Shakespeare and the Mediterranean: The Selected Proceedings of the International Shakespeare Association World Congress, Valencia, 2001*. Newark: U of Delaware P, 2004.

Cleaver, Eldridge. *Soul on Ice*. New York: McGraw, 1968.

Cliff, Michelle. *No Telephone to Heaven*. New York: Dutton, 1987.

Coghill, Nevill. *Shakespeare's Professional Skills*. Cambridge: Cambridge UP, 1964.

Cohen, Walter. "The Undiscovered Country: Shakespeare and Mercantile Geography." Howard and Shershow 128–58.

Coleridge, Samuel Taylor. *Coleridge's Shakespeare Criticism*. Ed. T. M. Raysor. 2 vols. London: Dent, 1960.

Colie, Rosalie L. *The Resources of Kind: Genre-Theory in the Renaissance*. Ed. Barbara K. Lewalski. Berkeley: U of California P, 1973.

Colley, Linda. *Captives*. New York: Pantheon, 2002.

Cook, Ann Jennalie. *The Privileged Playgoers of Shakespeare's London, 1576–1642*. Princeton: Princeton UP, 1981.

Cottrell, John. *Laurence Olivier*. Englewood Cliffs: Prentice, 1975.

Coursen, H. R. *Watching Shakespeare on Television*. Rutherford: Fairleigh Dickinson UP, 1993.

Cowhig, Ruth. "Blacks in English Renaissance Drama and the Role of Shakespeare's Othello." *The Black Presence in English Literature*. Ed. David Dabydeen. Manchester: Manchester UP, 1985. 1–25.

Crewe, Jonathan. "Out of the Matrix: Shakespeare and Race-Writing." *Yale Journal of Criticism* 8.2 (1995): 13–29.

Crowl, Samuel. "Checkmate: Parker's *Othello*." Crowl, *Cineplex* 91–104.

———. *Shakespeare at the Cineplex: The Kenneth Branagh Era*. Athens: Ohio UP, 2003.

———. *Shakespeare Observed: Studies in Performance on Stage and Screen*. Athens: Ohio UP, 1992.

Daileader, Celia R. "Casting Black Actors: Beyond Othellophilia." Alexander and Wells 177–202.

———. *Racism, Misogyny, and the* Othello *Myth: Inter-racial Couples from Shakespeare to Spike Lee*. Cambridge: Cambridge UP, 2005.

D'Amico, Jack. *The Moor in English Renaissance Drama*. Tampa: U of South Florida P, 1991.

Danson, Lawrence. *Shakespeare's Dramatic Genres*. Oxford: Oxford UP, 2000.

David, Richard. *Shakespeare in the Theatre*. Cambridge: Cambridge UP, 1978.

Davies, Anthony. "Filming *Othello*." Davies and Wells 196–210.

———. *Filming Shakespeare's Plays: The Adaptations of Laurence Olivier, Orson Welles, Peter Brook, and Akira Kurosawa*. Cambridge: Cambridge UP, 1988.

Davies, Anthony, and Stanley Wells, eds. *Shakespeare and the Moving Image: The Plays on Film and Television*. Cambridge: Cambridge UP, 1994.

Davis, James E., and Ronald E. Salomone. *Teaching Shakespeare Today: Practical Approaches and Productive Strategies*. Urbana: NCTE, 1993.

Dekker, Thomas. *Lust's Dominion*. *The Dramatic Works of Thomas Dekker*. Ed. Fredson Bowers. Vol. 4. Cambridge: Cambridge UP, 1961. 115–230.

Dessen, Alan C. *Elizabethan Stage Conventions and Modern Interpreters*. Cambridge: Cambridge UP, 1984.

———. *Recovering Shakespeare's Theatrical Vocabulary*. Cambridge: Cambridge UP, 1995.

Devisse, Jean. *The Image of the Black in Western Art*. Trans. William Granger Ryan. Vol. 2 of *From the Early Christian Era to the "Age of Discovery."* Gen. ed. Ladislas Bugner. New York: Morrow, 1979.

Diamond, Elin. Introduction. *Performance and Cultural Politics*. Ed. Diamond. New York: Routledge, 1996. 1–12.

Dinesen, Isak [Karen Blixen]. "The Blank Page." *Last Tales*. New York: Vintage, 1975. 99–105.

Dollimore, Jonathan. *Sexual Dissidence: Augustine to Wilde, Freud to Foucault*. Oxford: Oxford UP, 1991.

Donaldson, Peter S. *Shakespearean Films / Shakespearean Directors*. Media and Popular Culture: A Series of Critical Books. Boston: Hyman, 1990.

Donker, Marjorie, and George M. Muldrow. *Dictionary of Literary-Rhetorical Conventions of the English Renaissance*. Westport: Greenwood, 1982.

Dowling, Maurice. *Othello Travestie*. London: Duncombe, 1834.

Duberman, Martin Bauml. *Paul Robeson*. New York: Knopf, 1989.

Dubrow, Heather. *Genre*. London: Methuen, 1982.

Duffy, Maureen. *The Passionate Shepherdess: Aphra Behn: 1640–89*. London: Cape, 1977.

Dutton, Richard, and Jean E. Howard, eds. *A Companion to Shakespeare's Works*. Vol. 1. Oxford: Blackwell, 2003.

Earle, T. F., and K. J. P. Lowe, eds. *Black Africans in Renaissance Europe*. Cambridge: Cambridge UP, 2005.

Edwards, Christopher. "Noble Ethic." *Spectator* 29 Sept. 1984: 34.

Ellison, Ralph. *Invisible Man*. New York: Random, 1952.

Else, Gerald F. *Aristotle's Poetics: The Argument*. Cambridge: Harvard UP, 1967.

Erickson, Peter. "Contextualizing *Othello* in Reed and Phillips." *Upstart Crow: A Shakespeare Journal* 17 (1997): 101–07.

———. " 'God for Harry, England, and Saint George': British National Identity and the Emergence of White Self-Fashioning." Erickson and Hulse 315–45.

―――. "Images of White Identity in *Othello*." Kolin 133–45.

―――. "Multiculturalism and the Problem of Liberalism." *Reconstruction* [Cambridge, MA] 2.1 (1992): 97–101.

―――. "On the Origins of American Feminist Shakespeare Criticism." *Women's Studies* 26 (1997): 1–26.

―――. *Patriarchal Structures in Shakespeare's Drama*. Berkeley: U of California P, 1985.

―――. "Representations of Blacks and Blackness in the Renaissance." *Criticism* 35 (1993): 499–526.

―――. "Representations of Race in Renaissance Art." *Upstart Crow: A Shakespeare Journal* 18 (1998): 2–9.

―――. Rev. of *English Ethnicity and Race in Early Modern Drama*, by Mary Floyd-Wilson. *Renaissance Quarterly* 57 (2004): 734–35.

―――. *Rewriting Shakespeare, Rewriting Ourselves*. Berkeley: U of California P, 1991.

―――. "The Two Renaissances and Shakespeare's Canonical Position." *Kenyon Review* ns 14.2 (1992): 56–70.

Erickson, Peter, and Clark Hulse, eds. *Early Modern Visual Culture: Representation, Race, and Empire in Renaissance England*. Philadelphia: U of Pennsylvania P, 2000.

Evans, G. Blakemore. "Shakespeare's Text." *The Riverside Shakespeare*. By William Shakespeare. 1st ed. Boston: Houghton, 1974. 55–70. Rpt. in Shakespeare, *Riverside* 27–41.

Evans, K. W. "The Racial Factor in *Othello*." *Shakespeare Studies* 5 (1969): 124–40.

Everett, Barbara. *Young Hamlet: Essays on Shakespeare's Tragedies*. Oxford: Clarendon, 1989.

Ferguson, Margaret. "Juggling the Categories of Race, Class, and Gender: Aphra Behn's *Oroonoko*." Hendricks and Parker 209–24. Rpt. of *Women's Studies* 19 (1991): 159–81.

―――. "A Room Not Their Own: Renaissance Women as Readers and Writers." *The Comparative Perspective on Literature*. Ed. Clayton Koelb and Susan Noakes. Ithaca: Cornell UP, 1988. 93–116.

―――. "Running On with Almost Public Voice: The Case of 'E. C.' " *Tradition and the Talents of Women*. Ed. Florence Howe. Urbana: U of Illinois P, 1991. 37–67.

―――. "The Spectre of Resistance: *The Tragedy of Mariam* (1613)." *Staging the Renaissance: Representations of Elizabethan and Jacobean Drama*. Ed. David Scott Kastan and Peter Stallybrass. London: Routledge, 1991. 235–50.

―――. "Transmuting Othello: Aphra Behn's *Oroonoko*." Novy, *Cross-Cultural Performances* 15–49.

Findlay, Alison, Stephanie Hodgson-Wright, and Gweno Williams. " 'The Play Is Ready to Be Acted': Women and Dramatic Production 1550–1670." *Women's Writing: The Elizabethan to the Victorian Period* 6.1 (1999): 129–48.

Fischer, Sandra K. "Elizabeth Cary and Tyranny, Domestic and Religious." *Silent but for the Word*. Ed. Margaret P. Hannay. Kent: Kent State UP, 1985. 225–37.

Fischlin, Daniel, and Mark Fortier, eds. *Adaptations of Shakespeare: A Critical Anthology of Plays from the Seventeenth Century to the Present*. London: Routledge, 2000.

Floyd-Wilson, Mary. *English Ethnicity and Race in Early Modern Drama*. Cambridge: Cambridge UP, 2003.

Foakes, R. A. "Hamlet's Neglect of Revenge." Hamlet: *New Critical Essays*. Ed. Arthur F. Kinney. New York: Routledge, 2002. 85–99.

Ford, John R. " 'Words and Performances': Roderigo and the Mixed Dramaturgy of Race and Gender in *Othello*." Kolin 147–67.

Fowler, Alastair. *Kinds of Literature: An Introduction to the Theory of Genre and Modes*. Cambridge: Harvard UP, 1982.

Freud, Sigmund. "Creative Writers and Daydreaming." Freud, *Works* 9: 141–53.

———. "Some Neurotic Mechanisms in Jealousy, Paranoia, and Homosexuality." Freud, *Works* 18: 221–32.

———. "Some Psychical Consequences of the Anatomical Distinction between the Sexes." Freud, *Works* 19: 248–58.

———. *Standard Edition of the Complete Psychological Works of Sigmund Freud*. Ed. James Strachey. London: Hogarth, 1964.

Frye, Susan. "Staging Women's Relations to Textiles in Shakespeare's *Othello* and *Cymbeline*." Erickson and Hulse 215–50.

Fryer, Peter. *Staying Power: The History of Black People in Britain*. London: Pluto, 1984.

Gajowski, Evelyn. "The Female Perspective in *Othello*." Vaughan and Cartwright 97–114.

Gallagher, Catherine. "Oroonoko's Blackness." *Aphra Behn Studies*. Ed. Janet Todd. Cambridge: Cambridge UP, 1996. 235–58.

Garber, Marjorie. "Character Assassination: Shakespeare, Anita Hill, and JFK." *Media Spectacles*. Ed. Jan Matlock and Rebecca Walkowitz. New York: Routledge, 1993. 23–39.

Garner, S[hirley] N[elson]. "Shakespeare's Desdemona." *Shakespeare Studies* 9 (1976): 233–52.

Garner, Shirley Nelson, and Madelon Sprengnether, eds. *Shakespearean Tragedy and Gender*. Bloomington: Indiana UP, 1996.

Gay, Peter. *Weimar Culture: The Insider as Outsider*. New York: Harper, 1968.

Gibson, Rex, and Janet Field-Pickering. *Discovering Shakespeare's Language: 150 Stimulating Activity Sheets for Student Work*. New York: Cambridge UP, 1998.

Gilbert, Miriam. "Teaching Shakespeare through Performance." *Shakespeare Quarterly* 35 (1984): 602–08.

Godwyn, Morgan. *The Negro's and Indians Advocate*. London: J. D., 1680.

Goldberg, David Theo. *Racist Culture: Philosophy and the Politics of Meaning*. Oxford: Blackwell, 1993.

Goldberg, Jonathan. "The Print of Goodness." *The Culture of Capital: Property, Cities, and Knowledge in Early Modern England*. Ed. Henry S. Turner. New York: Routledge, 2002. 231–54.

Golden, Thelma, ed. *Black Male: Representations of Masculinity in Contemporary American Art.* New York: Whitney Museum of Art, 1995.

Goreau, Angeline. *Reconstructing Aphra: A Social Biography of Aphra Behn.* New York: Dial, 1980.

Granville-Barker, Harley. *Prefaces to Shakespeare.* Vol. 2. 1947. Princeton: Princeton UP, 1978.

Green, Juana. "The Sempster's Wares: Merchandising and Marrying in *The Fair Maid of the Exchange* (1607)." *Renaissance Quarterly* 53 (2000): 1084–118.

Greenblatt, Stephen. "The Dream of the Master Text." Shakespeare, *Norton* 65–76.

———. *Renaissance Self-Fashioning: From More to Shakespeare.* Chicago: U of Chicago P, 1980.

Greene, Gayle. " 'This That You Call Love': Sexual and Social Tragedy in *Othello.*" *Journal of Women's Studies in Literature* 1 (1979): 16–32.

Greg, W. W. *The Editorial Problem in Shakespeare: A Survey of the Foundations of the Text.* 3rd ed. Oxford: Clarendon, 1954.

———. *The Shakespeare First Folio: Its Bibliographical and Textual History.* Oxford: Clarendon, 1955.

Griffin, John Howard. *Black like Me.* Boston: Houghton, 1961.

Gubar, Susan. " 'The Blank Page' and the Issues of Female Creativity." *Writing and Sexual Difference.* Ed. Elizabeth Abel. Chicago: U of Chicago P, 1982. 73–93.

Gurr, Andrew. *Playgoing in Shakespeare's London.* Cambridge: Cambridge UP, 1987.

———. *The Shakespearean Stage 1574–1642.* 3rd ed. Cambridge: Cambridge UP, 1992.

Gurr, Andrew, and Mariko Ichikawa. *Staging in Shakespeare's Theatres.* Oxford Shakespeare Topics. Oxford: Oxford UP, 2000.

Gurr, Andrew, with John Orrell. *Rebuilding Shakespeare's Globe.* New York: Routledge, 1989.

Gutierrez, Nancy A. "Valuing *Mariam*: Genre Study and Feminist Analysis." *Tulsa Studies in Women's Literature* 10 (1991): 233–51.

Hadfield, Andrew, ed. *A Routledge Literary Sourcebook on William Shakespeare's Othello.* London: Routledge, 2003.

Hair, P. E. H. "Guinea." *The Hakluyt Handbook.* Ed. D. B. Guinn. Vol. 1. London: Hakluyt Soc., 1974. 197–207.

Hakluyt, Richard. *The Principal Navigations, Voyages, Traffiques and Discoveries of the English Nation.* Ed. Walter Raleigh. Vol. 7. Glasgow: MacLehose, 1903–05.

Hall, Kim F. "Beauty and the Beast of Whiteness: Teaching Race and Gender." *Shakespeare Quarterly* 47 (1996): 461–75.

———. "Culinary Spaces, Colonial Spaces: The Gendering of Sugar in the Seventeenth Century." *Feminist Readings of Early Modern Culture: Emerging Subjects.* Ed. Valerie Traub, M. Lindsay Kaplan, and Dympna Callaghan. Cambridge: Cambridge UP, 1996. 168–90.

———. "*Othello* and the Problem of Blackness." Dutton and Howard 357–74.

———. " 'These Bastard Signs of Fair': Literary Whiteness in Shakespeare's Sonnets." Loomba and Orkin 64–83.

————. *Things of Darkness: Economies of Race and Gender in Early Modern England.* Ithaca: Cornell UP, 1995.

————. " 'Troubling Doubles': Apes, Africans, and Blackface in Mr. Moore's Revels." *Race, Ethnicity, and Power in the Renaissance.* Ed. Joyce Green MacDonald. Madison: Fairleigh Dickinson UP, 1997. 120–44.

Hall, Kim, and Gwynne Kennedy. "Early Modern Women Writing Race." *Teaching Tudor and Stuart Women Writers.* Ed. Susanne Woods and Margaret P. Hannay. New York: MLA, 2000. 235–39.

Hall, Stuart. "Creolization, Diaspora, and Hybridity in the Context of Globalization." *Créolité and Creolization.* Ed. Okwui Enwezor et al. Ostfildern-Ruit, Ger.: Cantz, 2003. 185–98.

Hallett, Charles A., and Elaine S. Hallett. *The Revenger's Madness: A Study of Revenge Tragedy Motifs.* Lincoln: U of Nebraska P, 1980.

Hanmer, Thomas, ed. *The Works of Shakespeare.* Oxford, 1744.

Harewood, David. Interview with Andrew G. Marshall. "My Mother Thought Shakespeare Sent Me Mad." *Independent* 12 May 1998: 14.

Hawes, Jane. *An Examination of Verdi's* Otello *and Its Faithfulness to Shakespeare.* Studies in the History and Interpretation of Music 46. Lewiston: Mellen, 1994.

Hawkes, Terence, ed. *Alternative Shakespeares.* Vol. 2. London: Routledge, 1996.

Heilman, Robert B. *Magic in the Web: Action and Language in* Othello. Lexington: U of Kentucky P, 1956.

Helgerson, Richard. *Forms of Nationhood: The Elizabethan Writing of England.* Chicago: U of Chicago P, 1992.

Hendricks, Margo. "Civility, Barbarism, and Aphra Behn's *The Widow Ranter.*" Hendricks and Parker 225–39.

————, ed. "Forum: Race and the Study of Shakespeare." *Shakespeare Studies* 26 (1998): 19–79.

Hendricks, Margo, and Patricia Parker, eds. *Women, "Race," and Writing in the Early Modern Period.* London: Routledge, 1994.

Hinman, Charlton. *The Printing and Proofreading of the First Folio of Shakespeare.* 2 vols. Oxford: Clarendon, 1963.

Hodgdon, Barbara. "Kiss Me Deadly; or, The Des/Demonized Spectacle." Vaughan and Cartwright 214–55.

————. "Race-ing *Othello,* Re-engendering White-Out." *The Shakespeare Trade: Performances and Appropriations.* Philadelphia: U of Pennsylvania P, 1998. 39–73.

Honigmann, E. A. J. *Shakespeare: Seven Tragedies.* London: Macmillan, 1976.

————. "Shakespeare's Revised Plays: *King Lear* and *Othello.*" *Library* 6th ns 4 (1982): 142–73.

————. *The Stability of Shakespeare's Text.* London: Arnold, 1965.

————. *The Texts of* Othello *and Shakespearian Revision.* London: Routledge, 1996.

House, Humphrey. *Aristotle's* Poetics: *A Course of Eight Lectures.* Rev., with pref., Colin Hardie. London: Hart-Davis, 1956.

Howard, Jean E. "An English Lass amid the Moors: Gender, Race, Sexuality, and

National Identity in Heywood's *The Fair Maid of the West*." Hendricks and Parker 101–17.

———. "Gender on the Periphery." Clayton, Brock, and Forés 344–62.

Howard, Jean E., and Scott Cutler Shershow, eds. *Marxist Shakespeare*. London: Routledge, 2001.

Howard, Tony. "Shakespeare's Cinematic Offshoots." Jackson 295–313.

Howlett, Kathy M. *Framing Shakespeare on Film*. Athens: Ohio UP, 2000.

———. "The Voyeuristic Pleasures of Perversion: Orson Welles's *Othello*." Howlett, *Framing* 52–91.

Hunt, Maurice. "Predestination and the Heresy of Merit in *Othello*." *Comparative Drama* 30 (1996): 346–76.

———. *Shakespeare's Religious Allusiveness: Its Play and Tolerance*. Aldershot, Eng.: Ashgate, 2004.

———. "The Three Seasons of Mankind: Age, Nature, and Art in *The Winter's Tale*." *Iowa State Journal of Research* 58 (1984): 299–309.

Hunter, G. K. "Othello and Colour Prejudice." *Proceedings of the British Academy* 53 (1967): 139–63.

Huscher, Phillip. "Giuseppe Verdi: *Otello*." Verdi and Boito 12–16.

Hutson, Lorna. *The Usurer's Daughter: Male Friendship and Fictions of Women in Sixteenth-Century England*. London: Routledge, 1994.

Hyman, Stanley Edgar. *Iago: Some Approaches to the Illusion of His Motivation*. New York: Atheneum, 1970.

Iyengar, Sujata. "White Faces, Blackface: The Production of 'Race' in *Othello*." Kolin 103–31.

Izon, John. *Sir Thomas Stucley c. 1525–1578: Traitor Extraordinary*. London: Melrose, 1956.

Jackson, Russell, ed. *The Cambridge Companion to Shakespeare on Film*. Cambridge: Cambridge UP, 2000.

Jelavich, Peter. *Berlin Cabaret*. Cambridge: Harvard UP, 1993.

Johnson-Haddad, Miranda. "Patrick Stewart." *Shakespeare Bulletin* 16.2 (1998): 11–12.

———. "Shakespeare Performed: The Shakespeare Theatre, 1992–93." *Shakespeare Quarterly* 45 (1994): 98–108.

———. "The Shakespeare Theatre at the Folger, 1990–91." *Shakespeare Quarterly* 42 (1991): 472–84.

———. "The Shakespeare Theatre *Othello*." *Shakespeare Bulletin* 16.2 (1998): 9–11.

Johnson-Haddad, Miranda, and Caroline McManus. "Moors, Jews, and the Performance of Cultural Identity: Teaching *Othello* and *The Merchant of Venice* in the Diverse Urban Classroom." *Teaching Shakespeare through Performance*. Ed. Tom Gandy. NEH–Folger Inst. Workshop, 1996. Mar. 19 2005 <http://www.tamut.edu/english/folgerhp/folgerhp.html/>. Path: Individual and Group Projects.

Jones, Eldred Durosimi. *Othello's Countrymen: The African in English Renaissance Drama*. London: Oxford UP, 1965.

Jones, Ernest. "The Case of Louis Bonaparte." *Miscellaneous Essays*. Vol. 1 of *Essays in Applied Psycho-Analysis*. London: Hogarth, 1951. 39–54.

——. *Years of Maturity 1901–1919*. Vol. 2 of *The Life and Work of Sigmund Freud*. New York: Basic, 1955.

Jonson, Ben. *Works*. Ed. C. H. Herford, Percy Simpson, and Evelyn Simpson. 11 vols. Oxford: Oxford-Clarendon, 1925–52.

Jordan, Winthrop. *White over Black: American Attitudes toward the Negro, 1550–1812*. Chapel Hill: U of North Carolina P, 1968.

Jorgens, Jack J. *Shakespeare on Film*. Bloomington: Indiana UP, 1977.

Kahn, Coppélia. *Man's Estate: Masculine Identity in Shakespeare*. Berkeley: U of California P, 1981.

Kamps, Ivo, and Jyotsna G. Singh, eds. *Travel Knowledge: European "Discoveries" in the Early Modern Period*. New York: Palgrave, 2001.

Kaplan, Paul H. D. "Contraband Guides: Twain and His Contemporaries on the Black Presence in Venice." *Massachusetts Review* 44 (2003): 182–202.

——. "The Earliest Images of *Othello*." *Shakespeare Quarterly* 39 (1988): 171–86.

Kemp, Theresa D. "The Family Is a Little Commonwealth: Teaching *Mariam* and *Othello* in a Special Topics Course on Domestic England." *Shakespeare Quarterly* 47 (1996): 451–60.

Kennedy, Gwynne. *Just Anger: Representing Women's Anger in Early Modern England*. Carbondale: Southern Illinois UP, 2000.

Kolin, Philip C., ed. Othello: *New Critical Essays*. New York: Routledge, 2002.

Korda, Natasha. *Shakespeare's Domestic Economies: Gender and Property in Early Modern England*. Philadelphia: U of Pennsylvania P, 2002.

Kretzmer, Herbert. "I Shall Dream of This Othello for Years." *Daily Express* 22 Apr. 1964: 4.

Kristeva, Julia. *The Kristeva Reader*. Ed. Toril Moi. New York: Columbia UP, 1986.

——. "The True-Real." Kristeva, *Reader* 214–37.

——. "Women's Time." Kristeva, *Reader* 187–213.

Lacan, Jacques. *The Four Fundamental Concepts of Psycho-analysis*. Ed. Jacques-Alain Miller. Trans. Alan Sheridan. New York: Norton, 1981.

Lear, Jonathan. "Katharsis." Rorty, *Essays* 315–40.

Leavis, F. R. "Diabolic Intellect and the Noble Hero." *The Common Pursuit*. Harmondsworth: Penguin, 1962. 136–59.

Lewalski, Barbara Kiefer. *Writing Women in Jacobean England*. Cambridge: Harvard UP, 1993.

Lister, Dave. "Can It Be Wrong to 'Black Up' for Othello?" *Independent* 7 Aug. 1997: 13.

Liston, William T. "Paraphrasing Shakespeare." Salomone and Davis 11–17.

Little, Arthur L., Jr. *Shakespeare Jungle Fever: National-Imperial Re-Visions of Race, Rape, and Sacrifice*. Stanford: Stanford UP, 2000.

Lloyd Evans, Gareth. "Fine Othello." *Manchester Guardian Weekly* 18 Sept. 1971: 22.

Loomba, Ania. " 'Delicious Traffick': Racial and Religious Difference on Early Modern Stages." Alexander and Wells 203–24.

————. *Gender, Race, Renaissance Drama*. Manchester: Manchester UP, 1989.

————. "The Great Indian Vanishing Trick—Colonialism, Property, and the Family in *A Midsummer Night's Dream*." Callaghan, *Feminist Companion* 163–87.

————. " 'Local-Manufacture Made-in-India Othello Fellows': Issues of Race, Hybridity and Location in Post-colonial Shakespeares." Loomba and Orkin 143–63.

————. "Shakespeare and Cultural Difference." Hawkes 164–91.

————. *Shakespeare, Race, and Colonialism*. Oxford: Oxford UP, 2002.

Loomba, Ania, and Martin Orkin, eds. *Post-colonial Shakespeares*. London: Routledge, 1998.

Lott, Eric. *Love and Theft: Blackface Minstrelsy and the American Working Class*. New York: Oxford UP, 1993.

Macaulay, Alastair. "Othello Proves a Mixed Blessing." *Financial Times* 18 Sept. 1997: 25.

MacDonald, Ann-Marie. *Goodnight Desdemona (Good Morning Juliet)*. New York: Grove, 1990.

MacDonald, Joyce Green. "Black Ram, White Ewe: Shakespeare, Race, and Women." Callaghan, *Feminist Companion* 188–207.

————. *Women and Race in Early Modern Texts*. Cambridge: Cambridge UP, 2002.

Madoff, Steven Henry. "How Do You Get to the Biennale? Apply, Apply." *New York Times* 1 June 2003, sec. 2: 35.

Malcolm X. *The Autobiography of Malcolm X*. New York: Grove, 1965.

Manvell, Roger. *Shakespeare and the Film*. New York: Praeger, 1971.

Marks, Elise. " 'Othello/Me': Racial Drag and the Pleasures of Boundary-Crossing with *Othello*." *Comparative Drama* 35 (2001): 101–23.

Marshall, Cynthia. "Psychoanalyzing the Prepsychoanalytic Subject." *PMLA* 117 (2002): 1207–16.

Marshall, Herbert, and Mildred Stock. *Ira Aldridge: The Negro Tragedian*. London: Rockliffe, 1958.

Massing, Jean Michel. "From Greek Proverb to Soap Advert: Washing the Ethiopian." *Journal of the Warburg and Courtauld Institutes* 58 (1995): 180–201.

Matar, Nabil. Introduction. Vitkus, *Piracy* 12–16.

————. *Turks, Moors, and Englishmen in the Age of Discovery*. New York: Columbia UP, 1999.

Matthews, G. M. "*Othello* and the Dignity of Man." *Shakespeare in a Changing World*. Ed. Arnold Kettle. London: Lawrence, 1964. 123–45.

Matz, Robert. "Slander, Renaissance Discourses of Sodomy, and *Othello*." *ELH* 66 (1999): 261–76.

McCandless, David. "A Tale of Two *Tituses*: Julie Taymor's Vision on Stage and Screen." *Shakespeare Quarterly* 53 (2002): 487–511.

McDonald, Russ. *The Bedford Companion to Shakespeare: An Introduction with Documents*. 2nd ed. Boston: Bedford–St. Martin's, 2001.

————. "The Flaw in the Flaw." O'Brien 8–12.

McGuire, Philip. "Whose Work Is This? Loading the Bed in *Othello*." *Civitas: Cultural Studies at MIT* 2.2 (1993): 1–8.

McMillin, Scott. "The Mystery of the Early *Othello* Texts." Kolin 401–24.

McPherson, David C. *Shakespeare, Jonson, and the Myth of Venice*. Newark: U of Delaware P, 1990.

Mendelson, Sara Heller. *The Mental World of Stuart Women: Three Studies*. Amherst: U of Massachusetts P, 1987.

Merleau-Ponty, Maurice. *Phenomenology of Perception*. Trans. Colin Smith. London: Routledge, 1962.

Miller, Naomi. "Domestic Politics in Elizabeth Cary's *Tragedy of Mariam*." *Studies in English Literature: 1500–1900* 37 (1997): 353–69.

Mizejewski, Linda. *Divine Decadence: Fascism, Female Spectacle, and the Makings of Sally Bowles*. Princeton: Princeton UP, 1992.

Morrison, Toni. *Playing in the Dark: Whiteness and the Literary Imagination*. New York: Vintage, 1993.

Muir, Kenneth. *The Sources of Shakespeare's Plays*. New Haven: Yale UP, 1978.

Murray, Timothy. "Dirty Stills: Arcadian Retrospection, Cinematic Hieroglyphs, and Blackness Run Riot in Olivier's *Othello*." *Like a Film: Ideological Fantasy on Screen, Camera and Canvas*. London: Routledge, 1993. 101–23.

Neely, Carol Thomas. *Broken Nuptials in Shakespeare's Plays*. New Haven: Yale UP, 1985.

———. "Circumscription and Unhousedness: *Othello* in the Borderlands." *Shakespeare and Gender: A History*. Ed. Deborah Barker and Ivo Kamps. London: Verso, 1995. 302–15.

———. "Women and Men in *Othello*: 'What Should Such a Fool / Do with So Good a Woman?'" *Shakespeare Studies* 10 (1977): 133–58.

Neill, Michael. "'His Master's Ass': Slavery, Service, and Subordination in *Othello*." Clayton, Brock, and Forés 215–29.

———. "'Mulattos,' 'Blacks,' and 'Indian Moors': *Othello* and Early Modern Constructions of Human Difference." *Shakespeare Quarterly* 49 (1998): 361–74.

———. "Opening the Moor: Death and Discovery in *Othello*." *Issues of Death: Mortality and Identity in English Renaissance Tragedy*. Oxford: Oxford UP, 1997. 141–67.

———. "Post-colonial Shakespeare? Writing away from the Centre." Loomba and Orkin 164–85.

———. *Putting History to the Question: Power, Politics, and Society in English Renaissance Drama*. New York: Columbia UP, 2000.

———. "'Servile Ministers': Othello, King Lear, and the Sacralization of Service." *Words That Count: Essays on Early Modern Authorship in Honor of MacDonald P. Jackson*. Ed. Brian Boyd. Newark: U of Delaware P, 2004. 161–80.

———. "Unproper Beds: Race, Adultery, and the Hideous in *Othello*." *Shakespeare Quarterly* 40 (1989): 383–412. Rpt. in Neill, *Putting History* 237–68; in Young 117–45; in Barthelemy, *Essays* 187–215.

Nelson, Tim Blake. "The Story of O." Interview with Stephen Talty. www.wmagazine.com (Sept. 2001): 256+.

Newman, Karen. "'And Wash the Ethiop White': Femininity and the Monstrous in

Othello." *Shakespeare Reproduced: The Text in History and Ideology.* Ed. Jean E. Howard and Marion F. O'Connor. New York: Methuen, 1987. 141–62. Rpt. in Barthelemy, *Essays* 124–43.

———. *Fashioning Femininity and English Renaissance Drama.* Chicago: U of Chicago P, 1991.

Novy, Marianne, ed. *Cross-Cultural Performances: Differences in Women's Re-Visions in Literature and Performance.* Urbana: U of Illinois P, 1993.

———. *Love's Argument: Gender Relations in Shakespeare.* Chapel Hill: U of North Carolina P, 1984.

———. "Saving Desdemona and/or Ourselves: Plays by Ann-Marie MacDonald and Paula Vogel." Novy, *Transforming Shakespeare* 67–85.

———, ed. *Transforming Shakespeare: Contemporary Women's Re-Visions in Literature and Performance.* New York: St. Martin's, 1999.

———, ed. *Women's Re-Visions of Shakespeare: On the Responses of Dickinson, Woolf, Rich, H. D., George Eliot, and Others.* Urbana: U of Illinois P, 1990.

O'Brien, Peggy, ed. *Shakespeare Set Free: Teaching* Romeo and Juliet, Macbeth, *and* A Midsummer Night's Dream. New York: Washington Square, 1993.

O'Dair, Sharon. "Teaching *Othello* in the Schoolhouse Door: History, Hollywood, Heroes." *Massachusetts Review* 41 (2000): 215–36.

Okri, Ben. "Leaping out of Shakespeare's Terror: Five Meditations on *Othello.*" *A Way of Being Free.* London: Weidenfeld, 1997. 71–87.

Onions, C. T. *A Shakespeare Glossary.* Rev. Robert D. Eagleson. Oxford: Clarendon, 1986.

Orgel, Stephen. "Shakespeare and the Kinds of Drama." *Critical Inquiry* 6 (1979): 107–23.

Orkin, Martin. "*Othello* and the 'Plain Face' of Racism." *Shakespeare Quarterly* 38 (1987): 166–88.

———. *Shakespeare against Apartheid.* Craighill, South Africa: Donker, 1987.

Orlin, Lena Cowen. *Othello.* New Casebooks. London: Palgrave, 2003.

Orr, Bridget. *Empire on the English Stage, 1660–1714.* Cambridge: Cambridge UP, 2001.

Parker, Barry M. *The Folger Shakespeare Filmography: A Directory of Feature Films Based on the Works of Shakespeare.* Washington: Folger, 1979.

Parker, Patricia. "Fantasies of 'Race' and 'Gender': Africa, *Othello*, and Bringing to Light." Hendricks and Parker 84–100.

Paster, Gail Kern. "Leaky Vessels: The Incontinent Woman of City Comedy." *Renaissance Drama* ns 18 (1987): 43–65.

Pearson, Jacqueline. "Gender and Narrative in the Fiction of Aphra Behn." Todd, *Aphra Behn* 111–42.

Pechter, Edward. Othello *and Interpretive Traditions.* Iowa City: U of Iowa P, 1999.

Peele, George. The Battle of Alcazar, *1594.* Ed. W. W. Greg. 1907. Oxford: Malone Soc. Rpts., 1907.

Plasse, Marie A. "An Inquiry-Based Approach." Salomone and Davis 120–26.

Potter, Lois. *Othello*. Shakespeare in Performance. Manchester: Manchester UP, 2002.

———. " 'Unhaply for I Am White': Questions of Identity and Identification When *Othello* Goes to the Movies." *TLS* 5 March 1999: 18–19.

Pressly, William L. *A Catalogue of Paintings in the Folger Shakespeare Library*. New Haven: Yale UP, 1993.

Quarshie, Hugh. Program note for *Othello*. Dir. Sue Dunderdale and Hugh Quarshie. Greenwich Theatre. Greenwich, Eng. 1989. N. pag.

———. *Second Thoughts about* Othello. Intl. Shakespeare Assn. Occasional Paper 7. Chipping Camden, Eng.: Intl. Shakespeare Assn., 1999.

Rakoff, Robert M. "Ideology in Everyday Life: The Meaning of the House." *Politics and Society* 7 (1977): 85–104.

Ramsay, George Daniel. *English Overseas Trade during the Centuries of Emergence*. London: Macmillan, 1957.

Reynolds, Bryan, and Joseph Fitzpatrick. "Venetian Ideology or Transversal Power? Iago's Motives and the Means by Which Othello Falls." Kolin 203–19.

Rich, Adrienne. "When We Dead Awaken: Writing as Re-Vision." 1971. *On Lies, Secrets, and Silence: Selected Prose, 1966–1978*. New York: Norton, 1979. 33–49.

Riggio, Milla Cozart, ed. *Teaching Shakespeare through Performance*. New York: MLA, 1999.

Roberts, Sasha. "Reading Shakespeare's Tragedies of Love: *Romeo and Juliet*, *Othello*, and *Antony and Cleopatra* in Early Modern England." Dutton and Howard 108–33.

Rorty, Amélie Oskenberg, ed. *Essays on Aristotle's* Poetics. Princeton: Princeton UP, 1992.

———. "The Psychology of Aristotelian Tragedy." Rorty, *Essays* 1–22.

Rose, Mary Beth. "Gender and the Heroics of Endurance in *Oroonoko*." Behn [ed. Lipking] 256–64.

Rosenberg, Marvin. *The Masks of Othello: The Search for the Identity of Othello, Iago, and Desdemona by Three Centuries of Actors and Critics*. Berkeley: U of California P, 1961.

Rothwell, Kenneth. *A History of Shakespeare on Screen: A Century of Film and Television*. Cambridge: Cambridge UP, 1999.

Royster, Francesca T. *Becoming Cleopatra: The Shifting Image of an Icon*. New York: Palgrave, 2003.

———. "The 'End of Race' and the Future of Early Modern Cultural Studies." *Shakespeare Studies* 26 (1998): 59–69.

———. "Everyday Shakespeares: Confronting *Othello* at the Mall." *Shakespeare in an Age of Visual Culture*. Ed. Bruce R. Smith. 15 Jul. 2005 <http://www.folger .edu/html/folger_institute/visual/pmabsfr.html>.

———. "Everyday Use; or, How I Stole Othello and What I Did with Him." *Talking Back and Acting Out: Women Negotiating the Media across Cultures*. Ed. Sandra Jackson and Ann Russo. New York: Lang, 2002. 163–77.

———. "White-Limed Walls: Whiteness and Gothic Extremism in Shakespeare's *Titus Andronicus*." *Shakespeare Quarterly* 51 (2000): 432–55.

Rozett, Martha Tuck. Rev. of *The Norton Shakespeare*, ed. Stephen Greenblatt et al., and *The Riverside Shakespeare*, ed. G. Blakemore Evans, and *The Complete Works of Shakespeare*, ed. David Bevington. *Shakespeare Quarterly* 48 (1997): 465–72.

———. *Talking Back to Shakespeare*. Newark: U of Delaware P, 1994.

Rudnytsky, Peter L. "*A Woman Killed with Kindness* as Subtext for *Othello*." *Renaissance Drama* ns 14 (1983): 103–24.

Ruggiero, Guido. *The Boundaries of Eros: Sex Crime and Sexuality in Renaissance Venice*. Oxford: Oxford UP, 1985.

———. *Violence in Early Renaissance Venice*. New Brunswick: Rutgers UP, 1980.

Rutter, Carol Chillington. "Looking at Shakespeare's Women on Film." Jackson 241–60.

Rymer, Thomas. *A Short View of Tragedy*. London, 1693.

———. "A Short View of Tragedy." *The Critical Works of Thomas Rymer*. Ed. Curt A. Zimansky. New Haven: Yale UP, 1956. 132–64.

Salih, Tayeb. *Season of Migration to the North*. Trans. Denys Johnson-Davis. London: Heinemann, 1976.

Salomone, Ronald E., and James E. Davis, eds. *Teaching Shakespeare into the Twenty-First Century*. Athens: Ohio UP, 1997.

Schmidgall, Gary. *Shakespeare and Opera*. New York: Oxford UP, 1990.

Schmidt, Alexander. *Shakespeare Lexicon and Quotation Dictionary*. 3rd. ed. Ed. Gregor Sarrazin. Rev. and enl. 2 vols. New York: Dover, 1971.

Schücking, Levin. *Character Problems in Shakespeare's Plays*. 1922. New York: Smith, 1948.

Scragg, Leah. "Iago—Vice or Devil?" *Shakespeare Survey* 21 (1968): 53–65.

Sears, Djanet. *Afrika Solo*. Toronto: Sister Vision, 1990.

———. *Harlem Duet*. Fischlin and Fortier 285–317.

Sedgwick, Eve Kosofsky. *Between Men: English Literature and Male Homosocial Desire*. New York: Columbia UP, 1985.

Shaffer, Brian W. " 'To Manage Private and Domestic Quarrels': Shakespeare's *Othello* and the Genre of Elizabethan Domestic Tragedy." *Iowa State Journal of Research* 62 (1988): 443–57.

Shakespeare and the Black Experience. Clemson Shakespeare Festival 7, 1998. 22 Mar. 2005 <http://virtual.clemson.edu/caah/Shakespr/2002–03%20CSF%20Site/pastfestivals/1998/CFstVII.htm>.

Shakespeare, William. *Comedies, Histories, and Tragedies: First Folio, London, 1623*. CD-ROM. Oakland: Octavo, 2001.

———. *The Complete Pelican Shakespeare*. Stephen Orgel and A. R. Braunmuller, gen. eds. New York: Viking, 2002.

———. *The Complete Works of Shakespeare*. Ed. David Bevington. 5th ed. New York: Longman, 2004.

———. *The First Folio of Shakespeare: The Norton Facsimile*. Ed. Charlton Hinman. 2nd ed. Introd. Peter W. M. Blayney. New York: Norton, 1996.

——. *The First Quarto of* Othello. Ed. Scott McMillin. New Cambridge Shakespeare. The Early Quartos. Cambridge: Cambridge UP, 2001.

——. *Four Great Tragedies:* Hamlet, Othello, King Lear, Macbeth. Ed. Sylvan Barnet, Alvin Kernan, and Russell Fraser. Signet Classic. Rev. ed. New York: New Amer. Lib., 1998.

——. *New Variorum Edition of Shakespeare:* Othello. Ed. Horace Howard Furness. 1886. New York: Dover, 1963.

——. *The Norton Shakespeare.* Ed. Stephen Greenblatt et al. New York: Norton, 1997.

——. *Othello.* Ed. David Bevington. Fwd. Joseph Papp. Bantam Shakespeare. New York: Bantam, 1988.

——. *Othello.* Ed. Julie Hankey. Plays in Performance. Bristol: Bristol, 1987.

——. *Othello.* Ed. E. A. J. Honigmann. Arden Shakespeare. 3rd ser. London: Thomson Learning, 2001.

——. *Othello.* Ed. Alvin Kernan. Signet Classic. 2nd rev., updated ed. New York: New Amer. Lib., 1998.

——. *Othello.* Ed. Russ McDonald. Pelican Shakespeare. New York: Penguin, 2001.

——. *Othello.* Ed. Michael Neill. Oxford Shakespeare. New York: Oxford UP, 2005.

——. *Othello.* Ed. Edward Pechter. Norton Critical Ed. New York: Norton, 2004.

——. *Othello.* Ed. M. R. Ridley. Arden Shakespeare. 2nd ser. London: Methuen, 1958.

——. *Othello.* Ed. Norman Sanders. New Cambridge Shakespeare. 2nd ed. London: Cambridge UP, 2003.

——. *Othello. Drama: A Pocket Anthology.* Penguin Academics. Ed. R. S. Gwynn. 2nd ed. New York: Longman, 2002. 89–208.

——. *Othello. Literature: The Human Experience.* Ed. Richard Abcarian and Marvin Klotz. 8th ed. Boston: Bedford–St. Martin's, 2002. 1144–235.

——. *Othello. Literature: An Introduction to Fiction, Poetry, and Drama.* Ed. X. J. Kennedy and Dana Gioia. 8th ed. New York: Longman, 2002. 1468–567.

——. *Othello.* Othello *and* The Tragedy of Mariam. Ed. Clare Carroll. Longman Cultural Ed. New York: Longman, 2003. 1–133.

——. *The Riverside Shakespeare.* Ed. G. Blakemore Evans et al. 2nd ed. Boston: Houghton, 1997.

——. *Shakespeare's Plays in Quarto: A Facsimile Edition of Copies Primarily from the Henry E. Huntington Library.* Ed. Michael J. B. Allen and Kenneth Muir. Berkeley: U of California P, 1981.

——. *Titus Andronicus.* Ed. Jonathan Bate. Arden Shakespeare. 3rd ser. London: Routledge, 1995.

——. *The Tragedy of Othello, the Moor of Venice.* Ed. Barbara A. Mowat and Paul Werstine. New Folger Lib. Shakespeare. New York: Washington Square, 1993.

——. *The Tragœdy of Othello, the Moore of Venice.* Ed. Andrew Murphy. Shakespearean Originals: First Editions. New York: Prentice, 1995.

——. *Troilus and Cressida.* Shakespeare, *The Norton Shakespeare* 1823–913.

————. *William Shakespeare: The Complete Works*. Stanley Wells and Gary Taylor, gen. eds. Oxford Shakespeare. Oxford: Clarendon, 1986.

Sharpe, J. A. *Crime in Early Modern England, 1550–1750*. New York: Longman, 1984.

Sherman, Nancy. "Hamartia and Virtue." Rorty, *Essays* 177–96.

Siemon, James R. " 'Nay, That's Not Next': *Othello*, V. ii in Performance, 1760–1900." *Shakespeare Quarterly* 37 (1986): 38–51.

Silverstone, Catherine. "*Othello*'s Travels in New Zealand: Shakespeare, Race and National Identity." *Remaking Shakespeare: Performance across Media, Genres, and Cultures*. Ed. Pascale Aebischer, Edward J. Esche, and Nigel Wheale. Basingstoke, Eng.: Palgrave, 2003. 74–92.

Simpson, Richard. "The Biography of Sir Thomas Stucley." *The School of Shakespeare*. London: Chatto, 1878. 1–156.

Singh, Jyotsna. "Othello's Identity, Postcolonial Theory, and Contemporary African Rewritings of *Othello*." Hendricks and Parker 287–99.

Skulsky, Harold. "Revenge, Honor, and Conscience in *Hamlet*." *PMLA* 85 (1970): 78–87.

Skura, Meredith Anne. *The Literary Use of the Psychoanalytic Process*. New Haven: Yale UP, 1981.

Smith, Anna Marie. *New Right Discourse on Race and Sexuality: Britain 1968–1990*. Cambridge: Cambridge UP, 1994.

Smith, Bruce R. *Shakespeare and Masculinity*. Oxford: Oxford UP, 2000.

Smith, Ian. "Barbarian Errors: Performing Race in Early Modern England." *Shakespeare Quarterly* 49 (1998): 168–86.

Snow, Edward A. "Sexual Anxiety and the Male Order of Things in *Othello*." *English Literary Renaissance* 10 (1980): 384–412.

Snyder, Susan. *The Comic Matrix of Shakespeare's Tragedies*. Princeton: Princeton UP, 1979.

"Sooty." Def. 1. *The Oxford English Dictionary*. 2nd ed. 1989.

Sousa, Geraldo U. de. *Shakespeare's Cross-Cultural Encounters*. New York: St. Martin's, 1999.

Southerne, Thomas. *Oroonoko: A Tragedy*. Behn [ed. Lipking] 125–44.

Spengemann, William C. "The Earliest American Novel: Aphra Behn's *Oroonoko*." *Nineteenth Century Fiction* 38 (1984): 384–414.

Sprengnether, Madelon [Gohlke]. " 'All That Is Spoke Is Marred': Language and Consciousness in *Othello*." *Women's Studies* 9.2 (1982): 157–76.

Stallybrass, Peter. "Patriarchal Territories: The Body Enclosed." *Rewriting the Renaissance: The Discourses of Sexual Difference in Early Modern Europe*. Ed. Margaret W. Ferguson, Maureen Quilligan, and Nancy J. Vickers. Chicago: U of Chicago P, 1986. 123–42.

Starks, Lisa. "The Veiled (Hot) Bed of Race and Desire: Parker's *Othello* and the Stereotype as Screen Fetish." *Post-script: Essays on Film and the Humanities* 17.1 (1997): 64–78.

Stendhal. "From Racine to Shakespeare." 1823. *The Romantics on Shakespeare*. Ed. Jonathan Bate. London: Penguin, 1992. 218–37.

Steiner, George. *The Death of Tragedy*. New York: Knopf, 1961.

Stewart, J. I. M. *Character and Motive in Shakespeare: Some Recent Appraisals Examined*. London: Longmans, 1949.

Straznicky, Marta. " 'Profane Stoical Paradoxes': *The Tragedie of Mariam* and Sidnean Closet Drama." *English Literary Renaissance* 24 (1994): 104–34.

Styan, J. L. *The Shakespeare Revolution: Criticism and Performance in the Twentieth Century*. Cambridge: Cambridge UP, 1977.

———. *Shakespeare's Stagecraft*. Cambridge: Cambridge UP, 1967.

Suchar, Charles S. "The Little University under the El: The Physical Institution of Memory." *DePaul University: Centennial Essays and Images*. Ed. John L. Rury and Suchar. Chicago: DePaul UP, 1998. 117–69.

Sussman, Charlotte. "The Other Problem with Women: Reproduction and Slave Culture in Aphra Behn's *Oroonoko*." Behn [ed. Lipking] 246–56.

Taylor, Gary. *Buying Whiteness: Race, Culture, and Identity from Columbus to Hiphop*. New York: Palgrave, 2005.

Taylor, Neil. "National and Racial Stereotypes in Shakespeare Films." Jackson 261–73.

Teaching Shakespeare. Folger Shakespeare Lib. 22 Mar. 2005 <http://www.folger .edu/template.cfm?cid=618>.

The Thomas Hearings Website. Aug. 1997. 2 May 2005 <http://www.people.virginia .edu/nybf2u/Thomas-Hill>. Path: Transcript; Reopened Hearings; Second Statement of Judge Thomas.

Todd, Janet, ed. *Aphra Behn*. New York: St. Martin's, 1999.

———. *The Critical Fortunes of Aphra Behn*. Columbia: Camden, 1998.

Todd, John, and Kenneth Dewhurst. "The Othello Syndrome: A Study in the Psychopathology of Sexual Jealousy." *Journal of Nervous and Mental Disorder* 122 (1955): 367.

Traub, Valerie. *Desire and Anxiety: Circulations of Sexuality in Shakespearean Drama*. London: Routledge, 1992.

———. *The Renaissance of Lesbianism in Early Modern England*. Cambridge: Cambridge UP, 2002.

Troilus and Cressida. By William Shakespeare. Dir. Richard Monette. Tom Patterson Theatre. Stratford, Ont. 29 July–28 Sept. 2003.

Tyacke, Nicholas. *Anti-Calvinists: The Rise of English Arminianism, c. 1590–1640*. New York: Oxford UP, 1987.

Tynan, Kenneth. Othello, *by William Shakespeare: The National Theatre Production*. New York: Stein, 1967.

"Unhoused." *The Oxford English Dictionary*. 2nd ed. 1989.

Vaughan, Alden T., and Virginia Mason Vaughan. "Before *Othello*: Elizabethan Representations of Sub-Saharan Africans." *William and Mary Quarterly* 54 (1997): 19–44.

Vaughan, Virginia Mason. Othello: *A Contextual History*. Cambridge: Cambridge UP, 1994.

Vaughan, Virginia Mason, and Kent Cartwright, eds. Othello: *New Perspectives*. Rutherford: Fairleigh Dickinson UP, 1991.

Verdi, Giuseppe, and Arrigo Boito. *Otello*. Libretto. Perf. Chicago Symphony Orchestra. Cond. Sir Georg Solti. London Records, 1991.

Vitkus, Daniel. *Piracy, Slavery, and Redemption: Barbary Captivity Narratives from Early Modern England*. New York: Columbia UP, 2001.

———, ed. *Three Turk Plays from Early Modern England*: Selimus, A Christian Turned Turk, *and* The Renegado. New York: Columbia UP, 2000.

———. *Turning Turk: English Theater and the Multicultural Mediterranean, 1570–1630*. New York: Palgrave, 2003.

———. " 'Turning Turk' in *Othello*: The Conversion and Damnation of the Moor." *Shakespeare Quarterly* 48 (1997): 145–76.

Vogel, Paula. *Desdemona: A Play about a Handkerchief*. Fischlin and Fortier 236–54.

Wales, Katie. "An A to Z of Rhetorical Terms." *Reading Shakespeare's Dramatic Language: A Guide*. Ed. Sylvia Adamson, Lynnette Hunter, Lynne Magnusson, Ann Thompson, and Wales. London: Arden, 2001. 271–301.

Warren, Michael. *The Complete* King Lear, *1608–1623*. Berkeley: U of California P, 1989.

Wayne, Valerie. "Historical Differences: Misogyny and *Othello*." *Making a Difference: Materialist Feminist Criticism of Shakespeare*. Ed. Wayne. Ithaca: Cornell UP, 1991. 153–79.

Weller, Barry, and Margaret W. Ferguson. Introduction. Cary [ed. Weller and Ferguson] 1–59.

Wells, Stanley, and Gary Taylor, with John Jowett and William Montgomery. *William Shakespeare: A Textual Companion*. Oxford: Clarendon, 1987.

Wheeler, Richard P. " 'And My Loud Crying Still': The *Sonnets, The Merchant of Venice,* and *Othello*." *Shakespeare's "Rough Magic": Renaissance Essays in Honor of C. L. Barber*. Ed. Peter Erickson and Coppélia Kahn. Newark: U of Delaware P, 1985. 193–209.

Whitney, Lois. "Did Shakespeare Know Leo Africanus?" *PMLA* 37 (1922): 470–83.

Williams, Raymond. "Dominant, Residual, and Emergent." *Marxism and Literature*. Oxford: Oxford UP, 1977. 121–27.

———. *Modern Tragedy*. Stanford: Stanford UP, 1966.

Willis, Deborah. " 'The Gnawing Vulture': Revenge, Trauma Theory, and *Titus Andronicus*." *Shakespeare Quarterly* 53 (2002): 21–52.

———. *Reflections in Black: A History of Black Photographers, 1840 to the Present*. New York: Norton, 2000.

Willis, Deborah, and Carla Williams. *The Black Female Body: A Photographic History*. Philadelphia: Temple UP, 2002.

Wilson, Fred. *Speak of Me as I Am: The United States Pavilion, 50th International Exhibition of Art, the Venice Biennale, Venice, Italy*. Cambridge: MIT List Visual Arts Center, 2003.

Wilson, Richard. Program note for *Othello*. Young Vic Theatre, London. 1984. N. pag.

Wine, Martin. Othello: *Text and Performance*. Basingstoke, Eng.: Macmillan, 1984.

Worthen, W. B. "Shakespearean Performativity." *Shakespeare and Modern Theatre: The*

Performance of Modernity. Ed. Michael Bristol and Kathleen McLuskie, with Christopher Holmes. London: Routledge, 2001. 117–41.

Young, David, ed. *Shakespeare's Middle Tragedies: A Collection of Critical Essays*. Englewood Cliffs: Prentice Hall, 1993.

Zhiri, Oumelbanine. "Leo Africanus' Description of Africa." Kamps and Singh 258–66.

Žižek. Slavoj. *The Sublime Object of Ideology*. New York: Verso, 1989.

Audiovisual Materials

Branagh, Kenneth, dir. *Hamlet*. Film. Music by Patrick Doyle. Castle Rock, 1996.

Buchowetzki, Dimitri, dir. *Othello*. Silent Film. Perf. Emil Jannings, Lya de Putti, and Werner Krauss. 1922. 81 min. English subtitles.

Burge, Stuart, dir. *Othello*. Film. Perf. Laurence Olivier, Frank Finlay, Maggie Smith, and Derek Jacobi. British Home Entertainments / Warner Brothers, 1965. Color. 166 min. A film version of *Othello*. Dir. John Dexter. National Theatre, London. 1964.

Cukor, George, dir. *A Double Life*. Film. Perf. Ronald Coleman, Signe Hasso, Edmund O'Brien, and Shelley Winters. Universal Pictures, 1948. 104 min.

Davies, Anthony, dir. *Othello*. BBC, 2001.

Dearden, Basil, dir. *All Night Long*. Film. Perf. Patrick McGoohan, Marti Stevens, Betsy Blair, and Keith Mitchell. Bob Roberts Prod. / Rank Org. 1962. 91 min.

Eyre, Richard, dir. *Stage Beauty*. Film. Perf. Billy Crudup, Claire Danes, Rupert Everett, and Tom Wilkinson. Lion's Gate, 2004. Color. 110 min.

Mastrocinque, Camillo, dir. *Anna's Sin*. Film. Perf. Anna Vita, Ben E. Johnson, and Paul Muller. Giaguaro Film / Atlantis, 1953. 86 min.

McGoohan, Patrick, dir. *Catch My Soul (AKA Santa Fe Satan)*. Film, Perf. Richie Havens, Lance LeGault, Season Hubley, and Tony Joe White. Cinema/Metromedia, 1974. Color. 97 min.

Miller, Jonathan, dir. *Othello*. Videocassette. Perf. Anthony Hopkins, Bob Hoskins, and Penelope Wilson. BBC Time-Life Films, 1982. Color. 208 min.

Nelson, Tim Blake, dir. *O*. Film. Perf. Mekhi Phifer, Julia Stiles, Josh Hartnett, Martin Sheen, Elden Henson, and John Heard. Miramax, 2001. Color. 94 min.

Nunn, Trevor, dir. *Othello*. Videocassette/DVD. Perf. Willard White, Ian McKellen, and Imogen Stubbs. Primetime, 1990. Color. 210 min.

Parker, Oliver, dir. *Othello*. Film. Perf. Laurence Fishburne, Kenneth Branagh, and Irène Jacob. Dakota Films / Imminent Films; Sony Pictures, 1995. Color. 125 min.

Sax, Geoffrey, dir. *Othello*. Granada, 2001.

Suzman, Janet, dir. *Othello*. Videocassette/DVD. Perf. John Kani, Joanna Weinberg, and Richard Haddon Haines. 1988. Color. 187 min.

Welles, Orson, dir. *Othello*. Film. Perf. Orson Welles, Michael MacLiammoir, and Suzanne Cloutier. Restored and rereleased, 1992. Mercury / United Artists, 1952. 90 min.

White, Liz, dir. *Othello*. Videocassette. Perf. Yaphet Kotto. 1980. 115 min.

Yutkevich, Sergei, dir. *Othello*. Film. Perf. Sergei Bondarchuk, Andrei Popov, and Irina Skobtseva. Mosfilm / Universal Pictures, 1960. Color. 108 min. English dubbed for Russian (no subtitles).

Zeffirelli, Franco, dir. *Otello*. By Giuseppe Verdi. Film. Perf. Placido Domingo, Katia Ricciarelli, and Justino Diaz Libretto by Arrigo Boito. Italian with English subtitles. Cannon Productions, 1986. Color. 123 min.

INDEX

Modern Language Association of America

Approaches to Teaching World Literature

Joseph Gibaldi, series editor

Faulkner's The Sound and the Fury. Ed. Stephen Hahn and Arthur F. Kinney. 1996.

Flaubert's Madame Bovary. Ed. Laurence M. Porter and Eugene F. Gray. 1995.

García Márquez's One Hundred Years of Solitude. Ed. María Elena de Valdés and Mario J. Valdés. 1990.

Gilman's "The Yellow Wall-Paper" and Herland. Ed. Denise D. Knight and Cynthia J. Davis.

Goethe's Faust. Ed. Douglas J. McMillan. 1987.

Gothic Fiction: The British and American Traditions. Ed. Diane Long Hoeveler and Tamar Heller. 2003.

Hebrew Bible as Literature in Translation. Ed. Barry N. Olshen and Yael S. Feldman. 1989.

Homer's Iliad *and* Odyssey. Ed. Kostas Myrsiades. 1987.

Ibsen's A Doll House. Ed. Yvonne Shafer. 1985.

Henry James's Daisy Miller *and* The Turn of the Screw. Ed. Kimberly C. Reed and Peter G. Beidler. 2005.

Works of Samuel Johnson. Ed. David R. Anderson and Gwin J. Kolb. 1993.

Joyce's Ulysses. Ed. Kathleen McCormick and Erwin R. Steinberg. 1993.

Kafka's Short Fiction. Ed. Richard T. Gray. 1995.

Keats's Poetry. Ed. Walter H. Evert and Jack W. Rhodes. 1991.

Kingston's The Woman Warrior. Ed. Shirley Geok-lin Lim. 1991.

Lafayette's The Princess of Clèves. Ed. Faith E. Beasley and Katharine Ann Jensen. 1998.

Works of D. H. Lawrence. Ed. M. Elizabeth Sargent and Garry Watson. 2001.

Lessing's The Golden Notebook. Ed. Carey Kaplan and Ellen Cronan Rose. 1989.

Mann's Death in Venice *and Other Short Fiction.* Ed. Jeffrey B. Berlin. 1992.

Medieval English Drama. Ed. Richard K. Emmerson. 1990.

Melville's Moby-Dick. Ed. Martin Bickman. 1985.

Metaphysical Poets. Ed. Sidney Gottlieb. 1990.

Miller's Death of a Salesman. Ed. Matthew C. Roudané. 1995.

Milton's Paradise Lost. Ed. Galbraith M. Crump. 1986.

Molière's Tartuffe *and Other Plays.* Ed. James F. Gaines and Michael S. Koppisch. 1995.

Momaday's The Way to Rainy Mountain. Ed. Kenneth M. Roemer. 1988.

Montaigne's Essays. Ed. Patrick Henry. 1994.

Novels of Toni Morrison. Ed. Nellie Y. McKay and Kathryn Earle. 1997.

Murasaki Shikibu's The Tale of Genji. Ed. Edward Kamens. 1993.

Pope's Poetry. Ed. Wallace Jackson and R. Paul Yoder. 1993.

Proust's Fiction and Criticism. Ed. Elyane Dezon-Jones and Inge Crosman Wimmers. 2003.

Rousseau's Confessions *and* Reveries of the Solitary Walker. Ed. John C. O'Neal and Ourida Mostefai. 2003.

Shakespeare's Hamlet. Ed. Bernice W. Kliman. 2001.

Shakespeare's King Lear. Ed. Robert H. Ray. 1986.

Shakespeare's Othello. Ed. Peter Erickson and Maurice Hunt. 2005.

Shakespeare's Romeo and Juliet. Ed. Maurice Hunt. 2000.

Shakespeare's The Tempest *and Other Late Romances.* Ed. Maurice Hunt. 1992.

Shelley's Frankenstein. Ed. Stephen C. Behrendt. 1990.

Shelley's Poetry. Ed. Spencer Hall. 1990.

Sir Gawain and the Green Knight. Ed. Miriam Youngerman Miller and
    Jane Chance. 1986.

Spenser's Faerie Queene. Ed. David Lee Miller and Alexander Dunlop. 1994.

Stendhal's The Red and the Black. Ed. Dean de la Motte and Stirling Haig. 1999.

Sterne's Tristram Shandy. Ed. Melvyn New. 1989.

Stowe's Uncle Tom's Cabin. Ed. Elizabeth Ammons and Susan Belasco. 2000.

Swift's Gulliver's Travels. Ed. Edward J. Rielly. 1988.

Thoreau's Walden *and Other Works.* Ed. Richard J. Schneider. 1996.

Tolstoy's Anna Karenina. Ed. Liza Knapp and Amy Mandelker. 2003.

Vergil's Aeneid. Ed. William S. Anderson and Lorina N. Quartarone. 2002.

Voltaire's Candide. Ed. Renée Waldinger. 1987.

Whitman's Leaves of Grass. Ed. Donald D. Kummings. 1990.

Woolf's To the Lighthouse. Ed. Beth Rigel Daugherty and Mary Beth Pringle. 2001.

Wordsworth's Poetry. Ed. Spencer Hall, with Jonathan Ramsey. 1986.

Wright's Native Son. Ed. James A. Miller. 1997.